Please pick up the companion book to this one by the same author, Natalie Clountz Bauman – "Gone With The Water….The Saga of Preston Bend and Glen Eden" to learn more of the history of Preston Bend and its people throughout the years. Thank you for reading!

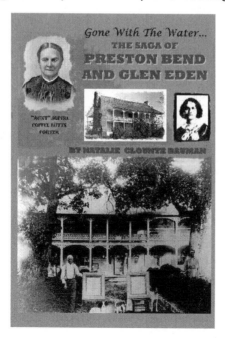

1

WHEN THE WEST WAS WILD – VOLUME 3

CRIME AND CALAMITY
AT
PRESTON BEND

BY NATALIE CLOUNTZ BAUMAN

CONTENTS

The West Was Wild In Preston Bend!

Wild and Wooly Days in Preston

1. Murders at the Old Preston Bend

2. Other Crimes in Preston Bend

3. The Storms of Life...Didn't Pass Preston Bend By – Natural Disasters

4. Calamities & Accidents Plague Preston Bend

5. Just Plain Weird!

6. The Spirit of Crime - Moonshining

This book is dedicated to the memory of all those who tragically lost their lives in the stories to follow.

Picture on back cover painted by George Catlin when visiting the Comanche tribe.

The West Was Wild In Preston Bend!

Visit the Wild Wooly Early Days of Preston Bend

One Half MILLION Buffalo at Preston Bend in 1840

The Sunday Gazetteer. (Denison, Tex.), July 3, 1904 — The newspaper men of the day read a fascinating book published in England that they thought might be of interest. This book gave the hunters' experiences in the Southern States of America, principally in Texas. Captain Flack, the author, they concluded, must have been in this very area on the Washita River. His description of a buffalo hunt placed him roughly in the Preston Bend area, not many miles west of Denison. He saw one herd of buffalo which he estimated at 500,000 individuals. This was in the year 1840. The buffalo took several days to cross the river near Preston Bend. How soon all these buffalos perished!

Flack, while on the old Chisholm Trail in West Texas, went into camp one night on Clear Water, an affluence of the Canadian River. He declared that for many miles there was a wild turkey roost, and compared the noise of all the huge birds flying to their roost like unto thunder. There were thousands of wild turkeys.

All English sportsmen declared Texas was the greatest game country in the world. Flack killed a wild turkey in the Comanche country that was taken to the trading post and weighed in at forty pounds. Happy Thanksgiving to you and your entire neighborhood!

Early Recollections of the Settlement of Grayson County

From the Sunday Gazetteer (Denison, Tex.), on June 6, 1886 — This article in 1886 was penned in an effort to preserve early history that seemed at that time to already be in danger of being obliterated in the name of progress. Fortunately for us today, this record has been left for those of us today, so much further removed from those early days. The author claimed it to be an imperfect sketch due to the lapse of so many intervening years, but it gives us a fairly accurate flavor of what it was like in the early days at Preston Bend.

The population of the first settlement was on average, not very refined, but were generally of steady habits. "It is true that contention and scalping matches, caused by 'tanglefoot' whiskey, happened occasionally, and in some cases resulted in the death of one or the other parties; but generally, difficulties were easily adjusted, and the parties were greater friends than before their sparring matches."

"I believe the first store or trading post established in (the eastern part of) the county was in 1838 by Abel Warren, called Fort Warren at the time, and goes by the same name yet; it is about eight or nine miles below (east of) Denison on Red River. I knew Mr. Warren well; he was a square and honest man. I think he remained there several years and then removed his trading post to the Washita." However, "**the principal town and settlement when I arrived in this section was Preston Bend**, about ten miles from Denison on Red River. It was a lively little one-horse town from 1844 to the time I left the country in 1848. Colonel Holland Coffee was the first settler I knew of from about 1840. At the time when I first made his acquaintance, he had one of the finest plantations in the country, and the place has lost none of its prestige under the management of its present owner, Judge Porter and Mrs. Porter, formerly Mrs. Coffee, who is one of the oldest settlers now alive in this county. Time has dealt kindly with her. I saw her a few days ago riding in a buggy with her husband, and the indications are she will survive many a year.

I believe Mrs. Thompson, wife of the late Judge Thompson, of Preston Bend, moved here somewhere in the 1840s. The majority of the old settlers have gone to their long homes, though a great many of their descendants are living in the county still. I recollect their names when I hear them, such as Mr. Shannon, Snell, etc.

The principal trading houses at the time, in the town of Preston Bend, were Tom Murphy's and Gooking & Hall. I believe Cunningham also had a little store. Gooking & Hall went to California in 1849 in the same company with myself; Murphy and Cunningham went there also in 1850 (for the "Gold Rush"). Preston Bend was a lively town, settled mostly by people from Arkansas. They were on average, a jolly, whole-souled set of men, honest and hospitable as the day was long; would take their sprees and jollifications occasionally, very peacefully on average, then attended to their business again." Buck Young also had a store there. "Hardly a vestige of the former town remains. Time, the leveler of everything, has leveled it completely. The county of Grayson was not organized at that time, and if anybody had any law business to attend to, which was not often, he had to go to Bonham, in Fannin County. Texas when I came here, was still the Lone Star Republic. I believe, Grayson County was organized in 1846. There were some farms and settlements on Red River, below the bend, and towards Bonham, but south and west even farms were scarce, in general, 20 to 30 miles apart. Sherman, Gainesville, or any other town south or west was not in existence. The nearest town south from here was Dallas, and Collin McKinney, by the by, an old friend of mine and after whom Collin County and the town of McKinney were named, lived within a few miles where the present town of McKinney now stands. I visited him occasionally; he was hospitality itself. Let me here mention that the greatest hospitality prevailed over the whole of Texas. To make a man displeased and almost insult him was to ask him your bill after remaining all night with him. Distances in miles were seldom thought of; it was generally measured by day's ride. There were but few farms to the west from here. Capt. Fitzhugh's

Company of Rangers was stationed about six miles from where Gainesville is located now. I cannot omit telling a little accident that happened there on Christmas night 1846. I had been sutler for the company for several months and a few days before Christmas concluded to spend the holidays at Preston Bend. Fort Washita or Hatsboro were still my headquarters. The rangers at the station also wanted to spend the holidays as pleasant as possible and invited what married or single female friends they could find within a radius of 20 miles, say, a dozen more or less. The houses or cabins where the men were stationed, were on one side of the road and the stables and horses on the other side. The space between them was hardly as wide as Gandy street. During the height of the dance Christmas night, the Comanches slipped in and stole every one of the Rangers' horses, and they were left afoot, my horse accidentally escaping by not being there. I did not return to the station."

"I do not exaggerate when I say that I could have purchased thousands of acres of good land in this county at the time for a good horse, saddle and bridle, and what a change has come over the vision of my dreams. Grayson County with its few hundred inhabitants at that time is now the most popular and one of the richest counties in the State of Texas. It has more prosperous towns within its limits than any other county in the state, an enlightened industrious population, school houses and institutions of learning that cannot be excelled by any other part of the state, churches to supply the wants of her numerous population and sufficient railroad facilities with a good prospect of soon increasing the supply for all her commercial, manufacturing and agricultural wants. Can any county in the state boast of more with Red River to wash her boundary and the trade of the Indian Nation at her doors?" 'Steinthal.

It was wild…. but beautiful.

Landmark Map of Preston Bend and surrounding area from the Frontier Village Museum.

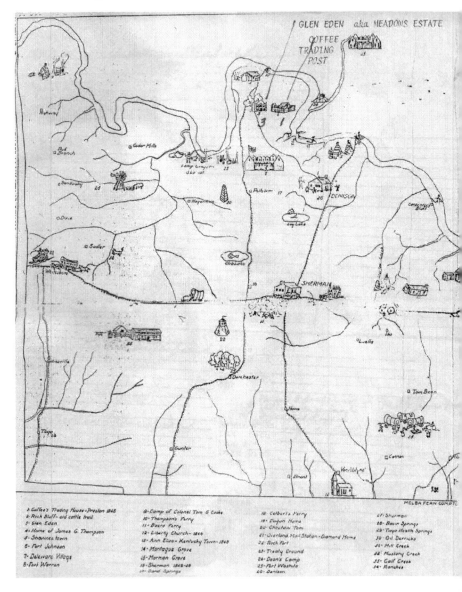

CRIME AND CALAMITY AT PRESTON BEND

1. MURDERS AT THE OLD PRESTON BEND

It once was said by local resident J. W. Fawcett that Preston Bend resembled the Garden of Eden. In the Garden of Eden, it wasn't very long before murder entered the beautiful garden – committed by one brother against another. Just like that beautiful Garden, it wasn't long before the ugly sin of murder and other crimes and calamities marred the wonderful country found there at the old Washita Bend of the Red River.

Murder between the native people and the white men began as soon as early white explorers had entered the country around five hundred years ago. It continued once white settlers began to arrive here in the early 1820s and 1830s, like the following story:

MURDER AND KIDNAPPING OF JUDGE'S FAMILY BY COMANCHES

The most historic section in Grayson County is Preston Bend. Some of the most startling episodes of frontier history have happened at Preston. The first visit of the American dragoons to the Comanche Indians was the result of a horrible murder committed there. A prominent, wealthy planter, and Judge named Martin was in the habit of going into camp every summer with his family. Either the Pawnee Picts, or the Comanches, descended on the camp, killed several members of the Martin family including the Judge himself, and a servant. The Judge's son, a youth, was carried into captivity. General Leavenworth and his command of several hundred troops were ordered to visit the Comanches and rescue the boy. He crossed with his command near Preston Bend. This was in 1834. General Leavenworth and his command of several hundred troops eventually encountered the band of Comanches and rescued the boy. He crossed the River with his soldiers near **Preston Bend**. It is said this was the first time that a white trooper had ever been seen in the Comanche Nation, and but very few of the Indians had ever seen a white person at all. General Leavenworth estimates the number of the Comanche Nation at 40,000. He must have first met the Comanches about where old Harneyville was, some miles north of Red River and Preston, about twenty miles from Denison. The great village of the Comanches was then on the Washita River. A war party had just started out for Mexico. They encountered Leavenworth's command and returned with them to the great village. The boy was rescued after a great deal of diplomacy. He was concealed in a field of maize, was stark naked, armed with a bow and arrow, and in company with several Indian boys. - The Democrat (McKinney, Tex.), on August 11, 1904 declared that an interesting book might be written of border reminiscences of our neighbor, Preston Bend. Hopefully, you are about to read such a book!

The story to follow also concerns General Leavenworth and his troops around Preston Bend.

PAINTER GEORGE CATLIN VISITS PRESTON BEND IN 1834

The Sunday Gazetteer of Denison, Tex., on April 26, 1903, recalled about 70 years earlier, George Catlin, the Indian historian, crossed the Red River where Preston Bend was established. George Catlin was an American painter, and author, who specialized in portraits of Native Americans in the Old West. Traveling to the American West five times during the 1830s, Catlin was the first white man to depict Plains Indians in their native lands.

He traveled with a group of dragoons from Fort Gibson, Arkansas Territory, in 1834 on their expedition to consult with the Comanche and Pawnee tribes. (The Comanche called themselves the Numinu, The People). This expedition, on which more than 200 men died from disease, was the source for several paintings depicting Texas, as well as the basis for Catlin's later descriptions of his experiences in Texas. There is disagreement as to whether Catlin crossed the Red River between Indian Territory and Texas. It is certain if Catlin was not in Preston Bend itself, then he was within "shouting distance" of it, based on the descriptions made concerning the Comanches and their great village. The Comanches, he wrote, lived in a place where "buffalos were plentiful" and described them as "one of the most powerful and hostile tribes in North America, inhabiting the western parts of Texas and the Mexican provinces, and the south-western part of the territory of the United States, near the Rocky Mountains; entirely wild and predatory in their habits; the most expert and effective lancers and horsemen on the continent. Numbering some 25 or 30,000, living in skin lodges or wigwams; well mounted on wild horses, continually at war with the Mexicans, Texians, and Indian tribes of the north-west. Their horsemanship and their training for war were inseparable, and they could throw

11

themselves on the side of their horses, while at full speed, to evade their enemies' arrows - a most wonderful feat." On his trip in 1834, Catlin saw a mock battle staged by the chief of a small village "to show to the author the mode of combat by his warriors." Below: Painting by George Catlin of the Comanches.

They first encountered a party of Comanches who were headed toward Mexico and the border settlement of Texas. The war party turned back and conducted General Leavenworth to their grand village. They rode for three days through countless herds of buffalo. The Comanche village numbered at least 10,000 souls, and the estimated strength of the nation as a whole was 40,000. By 1903, it was estimated that only 3,000 of them remained. Leavenworth stayed with the Comanches for several weeks. Half of his command perished from fever. Catlin narrowly escaped death from illness himself. Leavenworth himself died, but both himself and Catlin believed it was due to complications from a fall he took while chasing a buffalo calf on horseback.

The Comanches informed the soldiers that the Pawnee Picts to the west had murdered the Martin family and had captured the boy and they would find him there at their village. When the company became sick, they were about to head west from the Comanche village to the Pawnee Pict village to search for the son of Judge Martin who was taken captive. This account is in Catlin's book: "We were four days traveling over a beautiful country, most of the way prairie, and generally along the base of mountains of reddish granite, in many places piled up without trees or shrubbery on them. Such we found the mountains enclosing the Pawnee village, on the bank of Red River, about ninety miles from the Comanche town. To our surprise, we found these people cultivating quite extensive fields of corn (maize), pumpkins, melons, beans, and squashes; so with these aids, and an abundant supply of buffalo meat, they may be said to be living very well. The next day after our arrival there, Colonel Dodge opened a council with the chiefs, in the chief's lodge, where he had the most of his officers around him. He first explained to them the friendly views with which he came to see them; and of the wish of our Government to establish peace which they seemed to appreciate. Col. Dodge told them he wished to receive some account of the foul murder of Judge Martin and his family on the False Washita, which had been perpetrated a few weeks before, and which the Comanches told them was done by the Pawnee Picts. He also said the son of the murdered gentleman, was in their possession and that he expected them to deliver him up as an indispensable condition of the friendly arrangement that he was now making. They positively denied the fact, and all knowledge of it; firmly assuring us repeatedly that they knew nothing of the murder or of the boy until at length a negro man was discovered in the village, who was living with the Pawnee, who spoke English; and coming into the council-house, gave information that such a boy had recently been brought into their village, and was now a prisoner amongst them. This excited great surprise and indignation in the council, and Colonel Dodge then informed the chiefs that the council would rest here; and certainly nothing further of a peaceable nature would transpire until the boy was brought in. They remained in gloomy silence for a while, when Colonel Dodge informed the chiefs, that as evidence of his friendly intentions towards them, he had purchased at a great price from their enemies the Osages, one Kiowa and two Pawnee girls; which had been held by the Osage for some years as prisoners, and which he had brought the whole way home, and had here ready to be delivered to their friends and relatives; but who he certainly would never show, until the little boy was produced. He made another demand, for the restoration of a United States Ranger by the name of Abbe, who had been captured by them during the summer before. They acknowledged the seizure of this man, and all solemnly declared that he had been taken by a party of the Comanches, over whom they had no control and carried beyond the Red River into the Mexican provinces where he was put to death. They held a long consultation about the boy, and had the boy brought in from the middle of a cornfield, where he had been secreted. He is a smart, very intelligent boy of nine years of age, and when he came in, he was entirely naked as they keep their own boys of that age. The boy said 'What! Are there white men here?' to which Colonel Dodge replied, and asked his name; and he answered, 'my name is Matthew Wright Martin.' He was then received in Col. Dodge's arms and the Indian girls were returned to their relatives. The heart of the venerable old chief melted at this evidence of white man's friendship and rose to his feet, taking Col. Dodge in his arms, placing his left cheek against the left cheek of the Colonel, held him for some minutes without saying a word while tears streamed from his eyes." He embraced each officer in this way.

Catlin wrote in his book that the little boy Matthew Martin who was rescued from the Pawnees was brought the whole distance back to Fort Gibson in the arms of the dragoons, who took turns in carrying him. After the command arrived there, he was transmitted to the Red River, by an officer, who had the enviable satisfaction of delivering him into the arms of his disconsolate mother.

Pioneer History in the Days of the Indians and the Buffalo

The Sunday Gazetteer (Denison, Tex.), May 6, 1900 – One of the most fertile and picturesque communities in Grayson County is Preston Bend in the northwest. This is the oldest settled part of the county. More history clings to this neighborhood than to any other part of the county.

In days long gone, when Texas was indeed a wilderness and the wild Indian and the buffalo had possession of the country and the habitation of the white man lay far away, this settlement was started. It was settled by Holland Coffee in about 1835. His remains were buried in the yard of the home he built there. He provided fortifications and men for the protection of the community from the Indians. Holland Coffee was an Alcaide of the Mexican government before the Texas revolution. With him in the early settlement of the county were those sturdy pioneers at Preston like Judge Thompson, Brogdon, Quillan, and Davis. Preston is about 15 miles to the northwest of Denison. The route there is over beautiful country, most of it rolling prairie where formerly the wild rose and prairie blossoms and grouse held unlimited sway, but now they have given way to the man with the plow, who as he makes his furrow does not labor under the difficulties which attended the first settlers of that community way back in the 1830s.

"Then," said Col. Wm. J. Moseley who now owns and lives upon the old Holland place, better known to recent comers as the Foster place, "it took two men to run one plow. One man would do the plowing while another walked beside him with his trusty rifle to guard against the attack of Indians." Continuing, Col. Moseley said that when Navasota was raided by the Indians and several white people – women and children – were captured by

them and taken away, Col. Coffee interested himself in the rescue of the captured ones. He had a friendly Indian with him whose name was "Jim Nod," whom he sent to locate them. The Indian was successful in his mission and after some negotiations, a Mrs. Plummer and her little son were ransomed, Col. Coffee paying quite a sum in merchandise for their deliverance.

The Coffee homestead was built of lumber hauled on a wagon from below Clarksville, Texas. (It stood for 99 years until Lake Texoma inundated Preston Bend.) It is an ideal country home. A broad avenue leading from the house to the gate is bordered on either side by ancient and time-scarred Catalpa trees and rose bushes which bend gently to the breeze, beckoning the traveler to a hospitable resting place.

Many artifacts are around this old place, bringing to mind the splendidly tragic events in the nation's life. Among a pile of rocks in the yard, (of Glen Eden at Preston Bend), are cannon balls used at the battle of New Orleans where "Old Hickory" (Andrew Jackson) taught the British a lesson at arms. About the time Old Hickory was using these bullets with such fine effect, the great Napoleon held the world in terror at his deeds, but he fell and left to mankind a lesson of the vain-gloriousness of man's ambition when it is not predicated upon right and justice.

An earthen pot made by the hand of man when time was yet young is another curiosity there. It was taken from the earth a hundred feet below the surface. The brain that planned it and the hand that executed the workmanship of the pot and the race of people who made it are passed from the face of the earth now, leaving only such records of their former existence as will engage the fancy of the antiquarian in his attempt to trace the footsteps of man through the ages.

Col. Moseley is an interesting character. He married a niece of Holland Coffee who with him lives on the old homestead of Glen Eden. He caught the mining fever early and has hunted for the wealth which lies concealed beneath the earth in all of the mountain ranges of America. He was admitted to practice law in this county 45 years ago and was prosecuting attorney for Midland county for eleven years. He is a typical Southerner in hospitality and once within his lovely home, one feels entirely welcome.

The Preston of older days when the wild Indian was the terror of the citizen has gone. There remains no trace of the fortifications once there. The Thompson homestead (in 1904) still stands, now owned by J. P. Meadows - a delightful place on the high bluffs of Red River surrounded by stately trees, where singing birds make merry the forest and meadow, mingling their voices with the murmur of the river as it winds its muddy course to the sea.

ON THE WASHITA BEFORE THE CIVIL WAR - ONE WOMAN'S STORY

Mrs. Jane Jussie Remembers the Early Days on the Washita & Preston & Events Leading up to the War

The Oklahoma State Capital. (Guthrie, Okla.), April 24, 1904 - Great changes in the land, the cities, and the government are at hand. The grey-haired men and women speak of the old days with an edge of sadness for what is lost and gone forever.

The first home on the Washita was built near the site of the old Fort Washita. Mrs. Jane Jussie, whose father built the house, is a citizen of this place. Mrs. Jussie is a citizen of this place. She has Chickasaw blood in her veins, but her Irish ancestry stamped itself so firmly upon her that her Celtic features, her wit and even in her slight accent, it is unmistakable. Mrs. Jussie lives alone in her

17

widowhood and with means sufficient to maintain her in comfort. She was born in Mississippi about 71 years ago. She enjoys telling of her early experiences in the Indian country.

"My father, James McLaughlin, was interpreter for the Chickasaws when the tribe lived in Mississippi," said Mrs. Jussie. "His father came to America from Ireland at the age of 14 and settled among the Chickasaws. I was about 4 years old when I came to the Indian Territory with my parents. That must have been about 1837. We had no sawmill and my father hewed logs for his house which he built on land now farmed by "Doc" Thompson near the town of Bee. My father owned twenty slaves and cultivated a big farm. He died about 8 years before the war."

"The land was a wilderness, and we were often in fear of hostile Indians, especially the war-like Kiowas and Comanches who lived west of us. The buffalo had moved from our locality to the Wichita mountains, but everywhere were heaps of fresh buffalo bones. Bears, panthers, cougars, wolves and wild cats were plentiful. The cliffs along the Washita gave them almost inaccessible dens. Deer went in droves. Turkeys, partridges and prairie chickens could be killed anywhere."

"The settlement suffered considerably from raids by Kiowas and Comanches. My father, who traded among them, induced these tribes to attend the council at Boiling Springs, where a treaty was made, and the peace pipe smoked. They came once and stole practically all our livestock. On our corral, they painted red pictures of the horses, with their brands marked, and then the picture of an Indian leading the horses away with his bow drawn, as if shooting at somebody behind him. We knew only too well what it meant, which was if anybody pursued the thieves, he would be killed.

The Tonkawas would come out and camp near us for months at a time and were a great nuisance. The Kickapoos and Delawares brought deer hides, and bear oil to the traders after Fort Washita was established. The children at home were often badly frightened by the Indians. The latter were always in paint and feathers and when they came to our house they would come yelling and riding as fast as their horses could run. The first time we saw the Kickapoos the children ran under the bed. My mother gave away all my father's tobacco to get rid of the Kickapoos."

"All the devilment in the country was not due to Indians, as this incident will show: The Billookchees lived at Burneyville. At Preston's Bend, across Red River in Texas, was a white settlement. The white men told these Indians that if they would come to Preston's Bend, they would be given a lot of corn. About ten Indians went and camped on the north side of the river in the Chickasaw country. The whites crossed the river from Preston, surprised the Indians and killed all of them except an old woman and two boys, one of whom was her grandson. The massacre took place about twenty miles from Fort Washita.

I was about ten years old and remember hearing the old woman crying as she came to our house. Her feet were badly swollen. The two boys were on a half-starved pony which she led with a hickory rope fastened around its lower jaw. The old woman's grandson told my father that he intended to kill white men as long as he lived, and he did it. He was known afterward as "Biloxi John."

"My father sold the federal government the four-square miles of land on which Fort Washita was established. I was about 9 years old when the soldiers came. The fort was occupied until the civil war began when it was abandoned, and the Cherokees burned most of the buildings. The soldiers were cavalrymen and the first came from Fort Leavenworth. At the beginning, there were three or four troops but finally only troops C and I of the First Cavalry. My father sold his log house to the government. It was moved to the fort and occupied as quarters by Col. Henry. He was a tall, slender, fine-looking man of fair complexion. He was fond of children and asked them to call him 'Uncle Henry.' I sat on his knee many a time. He was at Fort Washita several years and then went away to the Mexican war. He never came back. I remember a Lieutenant Hancock and a General Belknap. The latter died at the fort when I was about 15 years old. An inscribed marble slab which lay over his grave is still at the old fort. About two miles from the fort on the prairie was a hill used as a signal station by whiskey peddlers. At night they would build a fire and the soldiers would sneak out and buy whiskey."

"When the war broke out, the troops marched away to Fort Arbuckle and thence to Leavenworth. They were joined at Fort Washita by troops moving northward from Texas. I stood on a hill and watched them come. The whole prairie was covered with men, horses, tents, and wagons. When the flag was hauled down, the soldiers threw lots of plunder into the Washita at the ford crossing where the livestock were usually taken for water. Plugs of lead, old guns, and cannon balls, are still found in the river bed. A small cannon was left behind, but I never knew what became of it. Saddles, harness, guns and other surplus stores were piled in rows and burned to prevent their falling into the hands of the Confederates. I got an old Minié rifle as a relic."

"Captain Carr wanted me to go with the army to the northern states, saying, "You'll be sorry, Jane, if you stay in this rebel country,' I laughed and said, 'They'll be after you pretty quick,' to which he replied boastfully: 'We want just three weeks to play with them.' Little did he think of the dreadful war which was to follow. The Confederate troops came in the next day, followed the Union troops to Fort Arbuckle and then went back to Texas."

Indian Troubles from Preston Bend to Warren

By Natalie Bauman

In the early days of Grayson County in 1841, then known as Fannin County, there were few real settlements in the area, Preston Bend, Georgetown, and Warren. The early pioneers who did live here were often in fear of hostile Indians like the Comanches and Kiowas. There were other local tribes which were not so hostile, like the Caddoan tribes, the Delawares and some Shawnees. But there were plenty of hostilities between the two cultures.

About this time, some relief was gained by the installation of a few local forts and the residence of the Texas Rangers, though they were few and widely scattered. Local men also volunteered their services in "posses" and impromptu militias to restore order when trouble arose. People didn't have 911. It took a long time to call for help, so they had to rely upon themselves. But the bountiful nature of the land and the adventuresome pioneer spirit encouraged people to settle here, regardless of the privations they experienced, in exchange for freedom and a chance for a prosperous future, which may not have been available to them in the area from which they came.

In the spring of 1841, a large group of families and single men, stopped for a short time at the Daniel Dugan farm near Warren until they could "look around" for good locations to settle. Among these were John Kitchens and family, Rev. Mr. Spring, a Methodist preacher and family, with the Green and Long families. Mr. Kitchens' family consisted of his wife, two sons, William and Daniel, and three daughters, Elizabeth, Melinda, and Melissa, with one daughter and one son being grown. Kitchens rented a farm about one mile south of the Dugans. He moved his family there and put in a crop. The farm was owned by a Mr. Abred but had been abandoned because of Indians.

21

In July, after the crops had been "laid by," Daniel W. Dugan, second son of Daniel Dugan Sr., engaged William Kitchens to help him cut some logs for a new house for his land which lay near Choctaw, about two miles northwest of his father's place and where he hoped to bring a young bride.

The young men prepared to camp on the ground, taking provisions, with what game they would kill, to last them about a week. **Two days after they left for their camp, John Kitchens went up above Choctaw on business and while there, heard that a party of eleven Indians had been seen crossing Red River above Preston Bend and were making their way down towards the settlements. Preston Bend, even before the white occupation, had been a popular river crossing for the Indian people. At this time, it was even more popular given the existence of Holland Coffee's trading post. Pictures of John and Nancy Kitchens below from Frontier Village Museum.**

Hearing that Indians were heading from Preston toward Warren, Kitchens then turned back towards home to warn the settlers so that they would be on their guard. He hurried to the camp of his son and young Dugan to warn them of their danger and have them abandon their work for a while and go home. The sun was down as he rode up to the young men's camp, and as he could not see them, he thought they had already been warned and had gone home, so he also headed home.

Unknown to Mr. Kitchens, the two unfortunate young men at this time were lying nearby, quite dead, having been killed that evening by the Indians. Kitchens stopped at the home of young

Dugan to inquire if the boys had returned, but to his horror was told that they had not returned. Runners were sent to Warren for the Rangers and for more help to search for the missing men. The Rangers were off scouting, but friends and neighbors soon gathered together and at the first dawn of day, a group of them set out for the camp. A few were left to guard the families at the Dugan home where they had gathered in case the Indians came.

About 9 o'clock, Mr. Henderson, one of the search party, was seen coming at full speed towards the house and before he could dismount, he was surrounded by anxious relatives and friends. He reported they had found the body of William Kitchens lying where he and Dan Dugan had been cutting logs. William had been shot and scalped. The body of Dan Dugan was found about three hundred yards from where Kitchens fell.

Evidence of a long and bloody fight were found all around the body of young Dan Dugan and it was plain he had killed and badly hurt some of the Indians. He had no chance to get his gun, so sudden and unexpected was the attack, and being there alone, his companion being dead, he fought them with no weapon but his axe. They closed in on him, hacking and stabbing him until he could fight no more, whereupon they shot and scalped him and stole all the valuables.

The bodies were brought to the Dugan house and on the following day, funeral services were held by the Rev. Mr. Spring. The young pioneers were buried side by side in a beautiful spot on the Dugan farm. After the Kitchens family returned home from the men's funeral, and attended to the night work, Mr. Kitchens and his son Daniel, and a young man named Stephens, were sitting out in the yard with their chairs tilted against the house when a horse, which was tied to a wagon, began to snort and look towards a cornfield nearby. At almost the same moment, three shots, one for each man, were fired from the field fence. Their guns were leaning against the wall near their chairs, but in the excitement of the moment, they all ran into the house without them.   Mr. Kitchens and his son Dan were both wounded in the foot. The old man, however, returned to the yard and handed the guns in and was not hit again, although several shots were fired at him, one bullet striking a log near his head.

The Indians advanced and now the fight began in earnest, even Mrs. Kitchens joined in with an old hostler pistol, and the girls molded bullets. The men aimed and fired between the logs of the house, the cracks of which had never been stopped up, always changing their position at each shot. Once while Mr. Kitchens was looking for a chance to shoot, he saw a runaway slave who had joined the Indians raising a gun and aim towards the crack where he stood. Kitchens fired first, and the former slave fell but arose to his feet and ran some distance before he fell again and gave up the ghost. About this time, young Stephens saw an Indian trying to untie the horse from the wagon and making a quick and lucky shot, killed him in his tracks. One bullet came through the door shutter and buried itself in a table leg on the opposite side of the room, while many hit the logs and even the roof of the house on the outside. The Indians finally quit the fight and left, carrying their own dead away, but leaving the body of the black man.

As soon as it was safe to do so, Mr. Kitchens sent Dan, wounded as he was, to carry the news to the Dugans. They had heard the firing and were preparing to come to the rescue or resist an attack as the case might be. Dan was taken from his horse and his wounded foot tied up, which was still bleeding. Guards were stationed at both houses during the balance of the night, but no more Indians came – THAT NIGHT.   There WOULD be more.

- Adapted from a story from A.J. Sowell in the San Antonio Daily Express
- November 2, 1902.

One of the prominent men called to help defend the settlers from attacks was the following man, who also had a close connection with Holland Coffee.

Captain Joseph Sowell - His historical marker states he came to Texas in September of 1836 and settled on his 1,280-acre Land Grant, located just west of where Texas State highway 78 crosses the Red River. His home overlooked the Red River and the site was called Sowell's Bluff. The designation is still used on the highway markers and the Texas Highway maps. In 1837, he served as Postmaster at Warren. He and his brother, Richard were on the committee requesting the formation of Fannin County. When the county was established and organized, he served as the first County Treasurer in 1841.

During this period, there were many raids from Indians residing north of the Red River. Hoping to discourage such often fatal attacks, there were several organized retaliatory attacks.

At least four times, Captain Sowell was called to be the leader of his company of the Militia (Minute Men) to protect the communities and settlers from hostile Indian activity.

These dates are the times he was on active duty: August 1-31, 1839; July 6-9, 1841; July 17-25, 1841, and August 15-25, 1841.

One account of this activity is recorded as follows:

"Incensed at the repeated depredations upon the frontier, Capt. Joseph Sowell with a company of rangers crossed the river in the Summer of 1841, stole upon a band of Coushatta, burned their huts, killed 10 or 12 Indians and captured the spoils they had stolen on Texas soil. A retaliatory expedition of the Coushatta resulted in the death of Captain Sowell."

25

Death of Sowell, Fannin County, Texas By Judge J. P. Simpson

After the battle with the Coushatta (or Koasati) Indians by the Dugan family, the Indians left Dr. Rowlett's and fled to the Indian Territory north of the Red River. The Texans, being greatly angered at the course practiced by them while living in Texas, they determined they should not remain so near us. Captain Joseph Sowell, with ten or twelve men, crossed the river at night, ascertained where they were camped, charged on them and fired into their wigwams, killing ten or twelve. This matter was kept secret for some time, since the act was a violation of International law with the U. S. Government.

The district court for Fannin County was to commence in 1841 at Warren, on Monday morning. Owing to the long distance those summoned as witness and jury-men had to travel to court, many went on Sunday evening, who would be put up at the tavern kept by Capt. Sowell and J. S. Scott. After securing lodging for themselves, and their horses cared for, they would indulge in drinking, and engage in a recital of their narrow escapes, and combats with the Indians.

Capt. Sowell had a fine and favorite charger which he kept to himself securely locked in the stable, his guests' horses in a substantial enclosure close by. That night the Indians had cut the door facing in two with their knives and removed the chains and lock from the door shutter, bridled the fine stallion and mounted him to drive out the horses in the lot. The Indians had laid down in the fence corners and stationed themselves at the bars armed with bows and arrows, with their horseman on the fine charger in the lot driving the horses out. The neighing and stamping of the horses gave the alarm to those at the tavern, not-withstanding by this time they were in high glee and uproar at the house; for they had decided at that point, that every man was a hero, a general, a statesman, or some great man, in his own estimation; hearing the mighty crash and tramp of horses their amusement ended in short order; all hands ran for their horses in a panic, most of them without their guns or pistols.

Sowell and Scott ran to the gap laid down by the Indians; Sowell armed with a pistol, Scott with a double-barrel shotgun; Sowell discharged his pistol at them without effect, then they sent a volley of arrows at him, one passing through his stomach and out at his back. He fell at the Indian's feet, and called to Scott to shoot the Indian, and expired without a groan. Scott discharged his gun and one Coushatta fell dead with Capt. Sowell. The other Indians left the horses and fled in every direction, and collected on the road near Brushy creek beyond where Col. Bradford now lives, filled the road with brush and other obstructions, and hid themselves on each side of the road, so if any man had gone that way that night, either with dispatches to Fort Inglish (near modern Bonham) for help, or to protect his wife and children at home, he could not possibly have escaped the Indians.

Looking Back 100 Years

—News Staff Photo.

Special to The News.
BONHAM, Texas, Dec. 25.—Moving along into its second 100 years, Bonham is one of the pioneer cities of the Lone Star State. It was established in 1836 and Bailey Inglish who was its founder, has left monuments to his prowess as a city builder. In the picture is shown a replica of the fort which Inglish erected to protect his family and the early settlers from the Indians. At the door of the fort is C. R. Inglish, Bonham newspaperman and grandson of the pioneer.

From the moccasin tracks next day at the place, we supposed there were twelve Indians. Had I as sheriff went to Warren that evening, which was my usual custom, instead of next morning, I should have tried to return that night to my family at Fort Inglish with the dispatch to the people here, and certainly would have fallen a victim to savage cruelty.

Capt. Sowell when I came to the county, was living on a bluff at Red River, below the mouth of Sandy Creek in this county and yet known and called Sowell's Bluff."

JOHN SOWELL CAPTURED BY INDIANS IN 1835

"Sowell's oldest son John was captured by Indians about 1835 and held as a prisoner for twenty-two months, after which he was ransomed in 1837 by Sam Houston and returned to his father." There is a family tradition telling of a meeting between the Indian tribe and Captain Sowell where several young men were lined up for inspection. Captain Sowell was to receive his son if he recognized him. He nearly gave up, but at the last minute, some flicker of recognition occurred, and the boy was reunited with his father.

One of Sowell's services was as a land commissioner to inspect grants at the Land Office. At one session, several applications were denied. Among them was that of Holland Coffee who had established the trading post and the plantation that became Glen Eden on Preston Point in today's Grayson County. Sowell's will requested **Mr. Holland Coffee of Preston Bend** to serve as guardian of the son of Joseph Sowell if the need ever arose. When Sowell's will was probated, the request was presented to Mr. Coffee to serve as his son's guardian. Holland Coffee declined to do so.

Taken from the Rogue River Courier Thursday, June 8, 1899, **Thrilling experiences of Indian Captive John H. Sowell, son of Capt. John Sowell.** When a boy, he was held captive for nearly two years. The following is a narration of the **capture of John H. Sowell**, in his own words, at age nine in 1835, by Comanche Indians in Texas copied by Francis J. "Frank" Barker, nephew-in-law of Sowell. His aunt, Temperance M. Barker, was Sowell's wife. The article was copied from the Rogue River [Oregon] Courier and the Dallas Texas Morning News:

"On July 12, 1835, I was captured in Franklin County [TX] near the Red River by Comanches. The Indians were hiding in the high grass about a quarter of a mile from the house in the edge of a prairie, I tried hard to escape, but they were so close when they rose from the high grass, they soon caught me. There were two of them and they both had horses hidden in the brush.'"

"They soon got mounted, putting me on behind one of them. They traveled up the river, keeping in the timber as much as possible, to not be seen until they reached a creek called Caney about six miles from home. At this place, we were joined by some others all on horseback, and some of the same tribe I think. They stopped and talked for a few minutes and then stripped off my clothing. They then all mounted but one, he grabbed me by the shoulder or arm and one leg and threw me up behind a big Buck Indian for comfort and you can imagine how much comfort there was in it, slung up behind a big Indian, naked, on a poor horse with a sharp backbone and no protection from the hot sun. We traveled up Red River until we reached Choctaw and then crossed into the Indian Territory and camped for the night. The Indians now thought they were safe. After taking care of their horses, they broiled some meat and wanted me to eat, but I declined as I was not hungry. After supper, they tied me hand and foot and laid me out on the grass to sleep, naked and without cover. The Indians watched all night, taking turns about until daylight. I slept but little, but Oh, what thoughts passed thru my mind that night of home, Father and Mother and my unfortunate situation. Next morning, we were off as early as we could see. For breakfast, I managed to eat a little. When they started, they put me up behind another Indian, but being sore from the previous ride,

29

I could not see that the change was in any way beneficial for me, but I had to bear it as best I could under the circumstances. We traveled up Red River until we came to the mouth of the Washita, and here we met about forty warriors, all painted and well-armed, with bows and arrows. All were mounted on good horses. Here they talked a few minutes, and all retired to a secure place and camped for the night. After taking care of the horses and eating supper, all commenced talking, telling their adventure I suppose, to each other. The party I was with, however, seemed to do the most talking and looking at me occasionally, hitting me on the back with such force as to break the blisters made by the sun in traveling. It seemed to be sport to them, but I did not see where the fun came in. They enjoyed this sport for some time but saw that I did not flinch, looking them steadily in the eye. They quit and looked at me. One old buck which seemed to have a little heart and some brains, came to me and took me up in his arms and made signs that he was my friend. I had no objections to this, although I was not on very good terms with them. When the time for sleeping came, I was tied as usual and slept beside the old Indian who had befriended me. The Indian that tied me was the same one who slapped me on the back and he tied me so tight the strings buried themselves in my wrist. Next morning the old Indian seeing the condition of my wrist began talking very loud and fast and taking his knife, cut the strings."

"'All being now ready to start, the old Indian who took such a liking to me called the two bands together and formed them into line. He then sent a young Indian to the band I was with and took the one who hit me on the back in his party and ordered my shirt to be put on which was done. When we were ready to start, the old Indian gave me a friendly hug and we parted. I afterward found that the old Indian was a big chief and was called **Buffalo Hump**. They put me up behind the young Indian that the old man had detailed out of his party. When we separated, our party went up the river and the old chief with his party went down the river. We traveled up the river until noon, and then crossed over to the Texas side and then left the river, and traveled along in the edge of the prairie, until night and camped on a little creek running in the direction of the Red River. I was not tied this time for the first time since my capture.

30

The young Indian who was detailed to go with us appeared to take some interest in me. I slept with him and had a buffalo hide to cover me. Next morning, we traveled in a southwest direction, aiming for the headwaters of the Trinity River. We traveled over a rolling prairie all day and camped on a little stream running east. Here one of the Indians killed a small deer. They had a good time roasting and eating it. Being very sore and tired, I lay down on the grass and was soon asleep.

"Next morning, I was up in time for some of the venison and some penola which the young Indian gave me, for we had no bread. ("Penola" is parched corn ground fine and eaten with milk or honey.) After eating, we made a start over the rolling prairie almost west. We traveled all day without stopping. In the evening we came in sight of some timber and were not long in coming to it. It was a branch of the Trinity and here was the Indian Village in the bend of the creek. The creek was afterward called **Denton Creek**. It was here that Captain Denton was killed about six years afterward in an attack on the village. We all dismounted, and I think every eye in the village was looking at me. I was then delivered over to an old squaw by the young man that had charge of me. I attracted but little attention after the first day, except among the young class, who had a great deal of sport at my expense. They would stick me with sharp sticks through the day and at night when all who were around the fire, would set sticks on fire and burn me. With them, this sport lasted more than a week and the old Squaw in whom I was in charge seemed to get tired of the fun and it was stopped for a time. I got tired of it before the Old Squaw did.

The squaw had a little girl about my age who seemed to take a liking to me and would stay with me nearly all the time. That appeared to make the boys hate me worse than ever and they renewed their punishment, by kicking, fighting and pulling my hair. One day one of the boys about my age came up and gave me a kick in the presence of the old squaw. She made a sign for me to hit him, but I thought best not to. That seemed to make him a little braver, and he came up and gave me a very severe kick on the shin which hurt considerably. The old squaw made a motion to me to hit him, and I did it as hard as I could, knocking him down. There was a boy standing by with a bow and arrow and he drew

31

it to shoot me, but the old squaw knocked him down before he could do so. That gave me a license to fight, and I would hit them every opportunity. This appeared to make the old woman take a greater liking to me and she made me some knuckles out of wood to fight with. That gave me courage and I felt as brave as a warrior.

We remained in this village for about six weeks. During this time the Old Chief and his party returned. They were gone about a month and brought back several scalps and quite a lot of horses. A few days after their return the scalp dance commenced, and I thought it was the most miserable sight I ever witnessed. Every one of them would make a noise and wriggle a foot, up and around the scalp pole, which stood in the center of the ring.

When the old chief rode up, he got down and came to where I and the little girl were standing and putting his arms around us said something in his own language. The old squaw I was with was his wife, and the little girl was his daughter. They had no other children. I was treated well after I got with them and did my own fighting. The knuckles which the old squaw made for me caused the boys to be very cautious when and where they hit me, for I could make the blood come every lick I hit."

"'After a few days' jubilee, we started for the Wichita Mountains where the village was. They traveled at their leisure and killed many buffalo along the way. We traveled several days and came to a large spring of water on the edge of the desert. It was an old camping ground. Here we stayed for about a week, with the Indians horse racing and gambling. They seemed to be trying the speed of their stolen horses.

I began to get over my sulky ways and get a little friendly, but not so much so but what I would take a little knock with the boys occasionally. They wanted to be the best in everything, but I was on the lookout and wanted to be the best myself, for I could see it pleased the chief's wife and daughter to see me come out first and best. We camped here about a week and the little boys would try me every day while we remained here. After leaving this place we traveled every day until we reached the Big Village in the Wichita Mountains."

"'We traveled up a little creek some distance and came in sight of the village in a large valley in the mountains. When we got near enough I thought all the Indians in the world had come here to yell and make a noise, for they seemed to be all yelling at once, to the utmost capacity of their throats. Our party went on to the upper end of the village and stopped. They appeared to be at home. After packs were taken off and supper over, the whole village assembled, and a general council was held. I, as usual, attracted the attention of the young ones of the tribe, all coming up and looking at me. They said something, but I could not understand what it was, but I thought it was about fighting as that was about all I had done since I had been among them. I made up my mind that I had a new tribe to conquer, and I felt that I could do it as I had done the others with my wooden knuckles. I stood the trip very well, as I had rested up at the other village."

"'Being tired from the long trip I tumbled down on the ground and went to sleep. Next morning, I was up early and after eating a little was thinking of home, Father, and Mother, sisters, and brothers and what might happen to those I had left behind, not knowing but what some of those scalps they were dancing around might be my poor Father's or Mother's. As this was running thru my mind, someone touched me on the shoulder and looking up, I saw the chief standing beside me. He put his arm around me and pulled me up to him and patted himself on the breast and said something, but I knew not what it was. By this time the little girl got up and came to where we were. The chief and his daughter talked a while and then he left me and the little girl alone. We could not understand one another, but she was company for me in my lonely and almost broken-hearted condition. We had not been there long before the Wigwam was crowded with visitors. I paid no attention to them as I was not feeling well and did not want to fight. I think every little Indian in the village came to see me before night. They behaved well the first day, but the next day they began to flock in, I think for a regular combat. I was at the Chiefs Wigwam when here came about 20. They came up to me and felt my arms and legs. The old woman motioned for me to hit them, but I was not on the warpath that day as I thought there were too many for me to tackle. One little fellow came up about my size and hit me hard enough to raise the old Sowell stock that was in me and without thinking I made a lick at him. He dodged, and I hit him on top of the head which made the blood come freely and he at once left for his Wigwam. Presently a big Indian and the boy came back, the man looking as mad as a rattlesnake. He and the Chief's wife commenced talking very loud and fast and motioning to me and then to the Indian. The old woman then sent the girl after the Chief, who soon came. The men talked awhile and then looked at the boy's head and then came to me and looked at the wooden knuckles. They talked a while, and both seemed to be angry. They finally sent off and had two horses brought and tied together, and the Chief made signs to me to take off the wooden knuckles which I did. He then made signs that I must fight the boy. They had bet the two horses on which boy could whip the other – and we went at it in earnest. We fought something like half an hour. I had no idea of giving up, I had no idea of ever giving up. I had almost rather died, situated as I was. He was a tough and wiry little rascal and held out as long as he could but had to give up at last. The Chief took me up in his arms and carried me to the Wigwam, and he and the old woman and the daughter and others who followed had a general jollification."

"'After this, I gained favor with the tribe for I had whipped the boss of the Indian boys. This settled my troubles in that direction for some time. After this, the old Chief gave me a little pony to ride, and the squaw made me a bow and some arrows and a buckskin jumper, waist moccasin leggings, and a hunting shirt. I was then rigged up in Indian style. My plain clothes, which my poor Mother had made were by this time badly worn and very dirty. We stayed in this village the balance of the time I was with them which was 22 months. While here, the old woman and the girl occupied a good deal of their time trying to teach me their language but succeeded poorly. I was treated very well while here. After father came home and found out that I was captured, he went down to the settlement and got a few men, and went in search for me, but could get no trace of the Indians. They were out about two weeks trying to find the trail, but having failed, they returned. After remaining home for a few days, he fitted himself out with blankets and provisions suitable for the trip and set out alone to hunt for me."

"'This he kept up all summer, most of the time alone. In the spring he conceived the idea that he might recover me by making a treaty with the Indians. Being an intimate friend of General Sam Houston, he went to see him and succeeded in getting them to treat and liberate captives. This was in the summer of 1836. The Indians, however, put themselves off a long time, telling them that I was dead and that they had no captives. Thinking this might be true, they gave up in despair. During the fall, the Kiowa's came and camped at the village and had with them a boy whom they had captured below where we lived. They were taking him to Bent's Fort to sell. They would not allow us to talk to each other. They started the next morning and went to Bent's and sold him. He cost his Father $500. Father hearing of his arrival, went to see the boy to find out if he knew anything of me. He told Father he had stayed with me in the village as he went to Bent's Fort and that his lost boy was there. Father had done all he could to find me and could do nothing more until spring."

"'By this time, I was getting to be quite an Indian. I had gained the goodwill of all of them and seemed to be a pet among them. In the spring, Father set out to get me and another treaty was held, but as usual they left me at the village when the Chiefs went to the treaty, and again and told that they had no prisoners, but Father would not listen to this and would insist that they should send after me, but they would again return without me. The news would come to the village, but the old squaw and the girl would not consent for me to go. So quickly had I imbibed the wildlife and the nature of the savage and having learned the language, that I was almost contented to stay. They sent for me the third time before the squaw and the girl would consent for me to go. They, seeing that I was almost reluctant to go, and thinking that Father would not know me, as I was so sunburned, and my hair had grown so long and that I looked so much like an Indian, that he would not claim me, and I could come back. It was as they had predicted, for when I rode up, Father looked at me - shaking his head and burying his face in his hands. As soon as I recognized father a new feeling came over me, and the thought of the folks at home ran through my mind like wildfire. I dismounted and walked up to where father had sat down with his face still covered. I put my arms around his neck and said: "Father, don't

35

you know me?" He looked quickly at the sound of my voice and said: "Good God is this my lost child?" He grabbed me in his arms and wept. Gen. Houston got up and put his arm around both of us and kissed my sunburned face. The council broke up and General Houston had Father and me go home with him and spend the night. This was at Austin, about this time it was made the Capitol of the young Texas Republic. Not being accustomed to a soft bed, I did not sleep very well, but when I did, I was dreaming of home and Mother.'

"'Next morning Father and I prepared to start home. I still had the pony the Chief gave me. We bade the General and family goodbye and came out to get our horses and found Chief Buffalo Hump, his wife, and daughter waiting for us, such was the attachment which the squaw and the little girl had formed for me. They had mounted their ponies and followed our trail many miles across the prairie to the big village of the pale faces on the banks of the Colorado River. They, the Chief, and some others followed us as far out as Brushy Creek, and here we were to separate from the Indians. They camped on the creek and Father and I stayed with a settler named Bryant. Next morning, we prepared to start on our journey. The Chief came up to us and Father and he talked for nearly an hour. I did the interpreting the best I could. The Chief wanted Father to part friendly and he would pledge himself never to molest him or allow any of his tribe to do so. After all this was agreed to, the Chief's wife came and presented me with a new suit of buckskin and a breechclout [or breechcloth] decorated with beads and porcupine quills. Father bought me a suit the night before we left Austin, but General Houston prevailed on him not to let me wear them until I got home, so people could see how I looked when recaptured. We bade the Chief and family goodbye and started on our journey home, leaving the Indians looking after us. We could hear the little Indian girl crying until distance drowned her voice.

We traveled all day over rolling prairie toward our home on the Red River. About sundown, we came to a settler house and stopped for the night and were well treated. I had a great many questions to answer the children and the old folks as well. I think Father called them Guthrey. The next day we traveled among a great deal of timber,

36

creeks, etc. These creeks were called three forks of the Trinity. After crossing the creeks, we came to the sulfur forks of the Brazos at sunset. Here we stayed with another settler. Father called the family his Tennessee friends. Their names were Hamlin. They were nice people and treated us well. Next morning, we again started for home. Mr. Hamlin went with us to the crossing of the **Bois d'Arc creek** and then went back. We crossed the creek about two miles below where the town of **Bonham [TX]** now stands. **We now had about twelve miles to go before we reached home.** When we came in sight and were discovered here came the whole family hollering and crying as loud as they could. Mother was the first one to get hold of me and held on to me like I was going to get away. By the time the negroes had got there, each of them was trying to see which could make the most noise. I stayed at home but a short time. Father fearing the Indians might capture me again, took me to Fort Smith Ark[ansas] and sent me to school. I was there going to school for about 18 months. It was about 200 miles from where we lived. I boarded with Mr. Burney, a merchant, and his splendid family."

"By the time I came back home, people had begun to settle on Red River about five miles below where we lived. Of this number was Captain Mark R. Roberts. Dr. Rowlett, Fitzgerald and Woodrow. These were our nearest neighbors."

I will state in connection with this incident that the Indians [Coushatta Tribe] again raided the settlement and, Capt. Joseph Sowell, the father of the captive boy, pursued them with a squad of settlers, and in the fight which ensued, the Indians were defeated, losing about 12 of their number. They again raided the same settlement, and in a fight with them, Capt. Sowell lost his life. The reason John H. Sowell did not mention his father's death in his narrative was because he knew I [the newspaper reporter] was familiar with the facts. John H. Sowell, the captive, served as a Ranger under Jack Hayes and was with Taylor's Army in Mexico. He later lived in Oregon. The old Comanche Chief Buffalo Hump in 1858 suffered a total and crushing defeat at the hands of Major Earl Van Dorn at the same village where the boy was held captive so long. It was called the Wichita village.

Killed by Indians Near Preston in Spring 1845

The Standard (Clarksville, Texas) - Spring, 1845 - An old man named Underwood, and his son, a small boy, living at a new settlement in the Cross Timbers, were upon Little Mineral, some six miles from the residence of James Shannon, gathering cattle to drive to their new place, and were killed by Indians - what tribe, is not known, but probably this new settlement was Preston.

MURDER AT PRESTON BEND FROM ACROSS THE RIVER?

The Clarksville Standard in Jan 22, 1853 reported: There is on the opposite side of Red River, in the Choctaw Nation, a man who two years earlier, atrociously murdered another man in Preston Bend, Grayson Co., in a most brutal manner, and without provocation. Why the Governor has not been notified of the act and requested to demand him, we do not know; but we do know that it is a wrong to God and Man – a crying sin, that such atrocious villainy should go unpunished, and especially when the offender is within reach. Where is the District Attorney? The house of the offender is in full view of the victim's own plantation on the Red River.

SHOT IN THE HEAD

At Preston, Grayson County, Mark Mitchell shot George D. James, of the Chickasaw Nation, in the head. They were separated before further injury was done. - Sep 2, 1854, Texas State Gazette. (FURTHER injury?? What else does he need to do to him?)

Indian Ravishes White Women at Preston Bend

A drunken Indian ravished two white women at Preston Bend on Christmas Eve 1873. He was pursued by infuriated neighbors, caught on the Red River bottoms and filled with buckshot. He then had to be buried. - Houston Daily Mercury Jan 6, 1874, & Galveston Daily News Jan 8, 1874.

The Most Famous Killings in Preston Bend -

Two Owners of Glen Eden Who Were the Husbands of Sophia

1846 - HOLLAND COFFEE IS KILLED, the second husband of Sophia Suttenfield Aughinbaugh Coffee –

Stories vary about how Coffee died in 1846. Some say it began when Sam Houston was scheduled to dedicate the new county courthouse in nearby Sherman and planned to stay with the Coffee's at Glen Eden. Coffee's niece had married Charles Ashton Galloway, a trader from Fort Washita, who offended Sophia by commenting about her former relationship with Sam Houston.

It is said she demanded that Coffee horsewhip his nephew. When Coffee refused, Sophia was alleged to have said she had rather be the widow of a brave man than the wife of a coward. Coffee started an "Indian duel," a fight to the death, with Galloway who killed Coffee with a Bowie knife. Another story says that Galloway accused Sophia of having a current affair with a local judge.

More of the story: Charles Ashton Galloway, 28 years old, was an Indian agent at Fort Washita and had recently married Holland Coffee's niece, fourteen-year-old Eugenia. Some believe he had accused Sophia Coffee of having an affair with Justice of the Peace Thomas Murphy. Stories vary about who wanted revenge for this insult, Holland Coffee or Sophia herself. But Holland threatened to horsewhip Galloway on sight, either because of that or because of an insult the same man had issued about Sophia having a past relationship with Sam Houston.

In October 1846, Colonel Holland Coffee was killed by Galloway, reportedly after an "Indian duel" to the death, at the old combination grocery store and saloon in Preston Bend.

Here is a letter about the fight: Letter of Major William Armstrong - Chickasaw Agency - Oct. 6th, 1846 - "My dear sir, Are you at home or not? If you are, do write to me. On the first day of this month about breakfast time, Col. Holland Coffee went to the store of Mr. James Galloway at Preston in Texas, where Mr. C.A. Galloway was and called

CRIME AND CALAMITY AT PRESTON BEND BY NATALIE CLOUNTZ BAUMAN

him out. Coffee had a double barrel shotgun loaded with buckshot, a six-shooting revolver, a large single barrel pistol, a Bowie knife and a Bois d'Arc stick. Galloway came to the door and Coffee knocked him down and then got under him by the head and commenced operations to kill. Galloway got out his knife in this situation and struck upwards; he made three licks in that situation and each lick was a mortal one. Coffee fell off Galloway dead, and so strong was his (death) grip (on Galloway) that he carried Galloway with him. Galloway is not much hurt.

Coffee nor Galloway never spoke after they got together. When Coffee called out, Galloway said, "Yes Sir". Those were all the words that were spoken. Coffee had said that he would kill Galloway whenever he could find him off the reservation.

Very respectfully - Your friend and etc. A. M. Upshaw - Maj. Wm. Armstrong" (Letter courtesy of Grayson County GenWeb and Elaine Bay.)

Galloway Not Indicted in Holland Coffee's Death

From the Clarksville Standard November 28, 1846:

"Grayson District Court - Mr. Charles A. Galloway, who was charged with the murder of Col. Coffee, has, we are informed, been acquitted by public sentiment. It seems there were several witnesses of the act, and it was so clearly a case of self-defense in the last extremity, that the grand jury could not find a bill (indictment).

We are told that Mr. Galloway is universally considered blameless for his conduct throughout the difficulty, and in the final act, which terminated so fatally and unfortunately. We are gratified that the case bears this character."

The presiding judge over the case, Thomas Murphy, (who was the man that Sophia was accused of having the affair with, which had sparked the feud between Coffee and Galloway) was soon indicted for misconduct because he knew that Holland Coffee had plans to attack Galloway, but did nothing to stop the fight. He was acquitted of all charges against him. (Can anyone say "conflict of interest"?)

In 1939, a shaft of marble stood on the site of the old Coffee stockade, and few feet from the old trading post. The shaft was erected in his honor by the state during the 1936 Texas State Centennial celebration. This marble memorial was moved and now stands near the present site of the Preston Cemetery where Holland Coffee, Sophia and her last husband are now buried.

Sophia Coffee Butts' 3rd Husband George Butt/Butts Murdered

Sophia's third husband also came to a tragic end at the time of the Civil War. Butts had many enemies because he had been instrumental in forcing men to join the army. Some stories say he was killed for the money which he had obtained from the sale of a large quantity of cotton in town. Highway robbers were a constant threat. Another story is that there had been unpleasantness between he, Sophia and one of Quantrill's men, who were in winter quarters here. At any rate, one evening, Butts failed to return home from Sherman where he had gone to sell cotton. At length, Sophia and several of Quantrill's men who were staying at Glen Eden at the time, went out in search of him. Butts' body was not found until about 2 weeks after his death. His horse, almost starved, was still tied to a nearby tree. Not long afterward, one of the men who had gone with Sophia to hunt for Butts was seen wearing Butts' watch and it was naturally thought that he had something to do with the murder.

The murder of Butts was one of the events which led to the final break-up of Quantrill's band. His men had been causing such disturbance in the territory around Sherman that the residents finally complained to Henry McCulloch, the commander in Bonham. On Christmas Eve, some of the men came to town to celebrate and got drunk. Mrs. Sophia Butts was visiting at Ben Christians' hotel when the celebrants rode into the hotel, tore up the place and in a final burst of cheer, shot the tassels and other ornaments from Sophia's hat. Quantrill finally placed one of his men under arrest for killing Butts. The man escaped and rode to McCulloch to confess he had killed Butts, but under orders of Quantrill, who was called to headquarters, and also arrested. Quantrill escaped with his remaining loyal men, and after a running fight, got across Red River, out of the jurisdiction of McCulloch.

Killing in the Indian Territory

Galveston Daily News July 2, 1898 - Rev. A. G. Noble of Preston Bend was in the city reporting the killing of E. D. Whitehurst, eight miles north of the Red River on the Douglass Lamb farm, in the Wichita Valley, on the previous Tuesday evening. E. Whitehurst, about 21 years of age, son of E. D. Whitehurst, was arrested and charged with the killing.

A special from Gainesville early in the week states that Mrs. Ed Moore and Mr. W. M. Shannon, both of Grayson county, were in that city in attendance on a meeting of those who lost property by Indian despredations. Their father, Col. T. J. Shannon, is an old citizen of Grayson county, and in years gone by engaged extensively in raising horses, and suffered many losses from predatory bands of Comanches The Shannon homestead is one and one-half miles west of Denison. Before the day of railroads it was a stage stand for the mail route from Sherman to Preston Bend and a number of Forts in the Indian Territory.

May 17, 1891

ROCK BLUFF FERRY BODY DUMP GROUND AT PRESTON

The young men spoken of, who so mysteriously disappeared a short time ago near the Red river ferry crossing, have not up to the present time been heard of, notwithstanding that every effort has been put forth by their friends to discover some clue to their whereabouts. The general opinion now is, that they were shot and their bodies thrown into the river. This impression is somewhat confirmed by the discovery of a body in the river, Sunday morning, about fifteen miles below the point where the tragedy is supposed

Denison Daily Cresset to have been enacted.

May 28, 1877

Murderer Surrounded at Rock Bluff Ferry

Denison Daily Herald - April 29, 1878 - J. J. Chadwick, special deputy sheriff of Red River County, that a man named Frank Graves, alias Jackson, who committed a murder in Mississippi last December, after burning two large cotton gins, was tracked to, and come up with, on the prairie near Rock Bluff Ferry at Preston Bend, where he resisted arrest by shooting at his followers when ordered to give up his arms. The posse then fired upon him, wounding him in the right shoulder. But Graves succeeded in remounting his horse and escaping in the brush.   His horse and hat were found, he had abandoned them as soon as he was undercover. Constable Spence and others continued on the hunt for him. Mr. Chadwick believed that Graves would not be taken alive.   May 1 – The posse found Graves lying dead and brought his body to Denison for examination.   The testimony at the coroner's jury explained that Graves died from a self-inflicted gunshot to the head, just as the lawmen had predicted. At the inquest, a man who was not identified by the newspaper articles, confirmed that the body was indeed that of Frank Graves, whom he had known as a teenager in New York; that the boy's family went to Ohio; later Frank went to Mississippi where he saw him two or three years ago. He believed the deceased to be a very bad man. Frank Graves, alias Jackson was about 41 years old, 5 feet 6 inches high, weighing about 120 pounds, with a brown complexion, dark hair, and a light brown mustache.

Assault to Murder

Fort Worth Daily Gazette - Dec 13, 1888 - The jury in the case of Captain J. T. Strother, charged with **assault to murder** a man by the name Daniel, at Preston Bend, in Grayson County, in 1885, returned a verdict finding him guilty, and assessing his penalty at a fine of $1,000, which amount he paid promptly.

SHOOTING AFFRAY AT PRESTON BEND

Fort Worth Daily Gazette - February 23, 1888 - Parties who arrived in the city from Preston Bend on the Red River, brought news of a desperate shooting melee which occurred in that neighborhood on the 21st between Ed Stein, a notorious character, and several other men whose names could not be learned. The reports about the case are conflicting. One version is that a party of several men attacked Stein at his house, firing a volley at him as he came to the door and killed him instantly. Another statement is that Stein and a friend, who was with him in his house, were both seriously wounded, but succeeded in driving away the attacking parties, two of whom were also wounded. Ed Stein has been in prison several times on various charges and was held for some time in the county jail during the last year, together with several others on a charge of theft of cattle, but he was tried and acquitted at the last term of the District Court.   He is considered a daring, desperate character and probably has enemies who, in this last case, had attempted to overpower him and take his life.

Another Preston Bend Shooting Affray

Fort Worth Daily Gazette - July 14-15, 1889 - Monroe Merryman and Davis Reeves met L. D. Driver of Preston Bend in a field of battle. They attempted to shoot, but Driver escaped and ran to his house for a gun. He got his artillery and went out after his assailants. Meeting them, they opened fire on Driver, who replied with his shotgun. None of the parties engaged in the fight were hurt, but Pink Merryman, an onlooker, got a load of shot through the arm, almost tearing it from the body, from which he was expected to die. Officers went after the shooters. The three men, Reeves by name, who assaulted L. D. Driver in Preston Bend, were arrested on the 13th at their residence three miles southeast of Denison. One of the men tried to escape and was promptly overhauled by one of the officers by thrusting a Winchester under his nose.

Merryman and Reeves Arrested for Death of Driver

Sunday Gazetteer July 21, 1889

Monroe Merryman and David Reeves, two farmers living three miles south of the city, were in town Sunday in custody of Constable Creed Porter, on their way to Pottsboro, to have a preliminary hearing on a charge of assult to kill. The two men had come upon L. D. Driver on his farm, near Preston Bend, on the Saturday previous and had then and there made an attempt to shoot him. A difficulty had taken place between the men prior to the meeting, and Reeves and Merryman had come around with shot guns. Driver was plowing cotton in a field, and was unarmed, but when one of the men snapped his gun at him, it failing to go off, he ran to the house and fixed himself. Then he went back and exchanged a couple of vollies with his assailants, but it being at long range no one was hurt, save Pink Merryman, an onlooker, who got a shot in the arm. Merryman and Reeves left the scene at once, and Constable Porter being notified went in pursuit, arresting the men at their homes near this city. At the preliminary hearing in Pottsboro they were bound over and were taken Monday to jail in Sherman.

Mystery Skeleton on Red River Speaks

On April 7, 1889 the decomposed remains of a man were found on a sandbar in the Red River by Indian Policeman Bob Murray. The flesh had fallen away from the bones and the body was so decayed that it was impossible to identify the person. Being dead and decayed, the person couldn't say much, but the skull DID reveal one fact. A small hole over left eye in the skull indicated that the person had died from a gun shot to the head. This was no drowning – it was murder. No more was learned from the body, such as the identity, where the person was killed, or who may have committed the murder. The remains were buried in a lonely unmarked grave by the Red River, his death un-mourned and his murder unavenged.

Over the years, the River had proved to be a convenient dumping ground for murder victims, carrying the incriminating evidence of bodies far east down the River where their identity or those of their killers might never be known, if they were ever found.

DEPUTY SHERIFF KILLS MAN NEAR PRESTON BEND

Arthur O'Mary, a deputy under Sheriff Lee Simmons, shot and instantly killed a black man by the name of Will Devro near Preston Bend shortly after 6 p.m. In so doing, he probably saved the life of Deputy Sheriff Lloyd Etchison, whom Devro was attempting to shoot. The shooting occurred about two miles northwest of the town of Preston Bend, at Devro's home. Devro lived on the farm of John Jackson, a well-known farmer, and landowner at Preston. Don't be too alarmed though, this crime occurred over 100 years ago, according to the Denison Daily Herald of February 12, 1914. The details leading up to the shooting are as follows: About 4 p.m., John Jackson and his son Bob Jackson and a Mr. Kelly, all residents of the Preston Bend community, came to Sherman and appealed to Sheriff Simmons for help. They stated that Will Devro, who lived on the John Jackson farm, was engaged in bootlegging illegal liquor and had been drunk a day or two and had created a great deal of disturbance in the community. On Tuesday night, he had gone to the home of Mr. Kelly in a drunken condition and frightened the women until one of them fainted. They told the sheriff that he was a bad man, dangerous, and carried a gun and that the young man who was a deputy there had refused to go and arrest him without help. A complaint was filed in Justice T. W. Dudson's court charging him with violating the "local option law" and Sheriff Simmons sent Lloyd Etchison and Arthur O'Mary, both deputies, with a warrant to arrest Devro. They went in an automobile, and Bob Jackson accompanied them to show the officers where he lived. As they neared the house, they saw Devro sitting in the door, and as they approached, he got up and went into the house. Mr. Jackson called his name, and Devro poked his head out the door and the officers asked him about some parties in the neighborhood and he replied gruffly that he knew nothing about them. Then they asked permission to come into the house and read some names on a subpoena by the light, as he had a light burning in the house. Devro let them in but kept his hand on his gun all the time, which he had in a belt and holster. Mr. Etchison got over close to the light in front of him, and Mr. O'Mary went over to his left. As Devro took his eyes off Mr. O'Mary and looked at Mr. Etchison, O'Mary drew his gun and said; "We have a warrant for you, put your hands up." Mr. Jackson, who was present, stated that this did not even make Devro flinch, but he replied: "I put nothing up." Four times, Mr. O'Mary repeated the command. The last time, Devro said "I put nothing up" again and then quickly drew his gun, pointing it up at Deputy Etchison. As he did this, Deputy O'Mary fired. The shot entered the left side of Devro and he stepped forward two or three steps and lurched out of the door. The gun, a 45 Colt's double action was held tightly in his hand and the muzzle was buried deep in the mud. Devro was killed instantly. Devro came to Preston Bend from Woodville, Okla., which is just to the north of the river from Preston and had been on the Jackson farm since June of 1913. He was reported to have given that community a great deal of trouble since locating there. Mr. Jackson stated that Devro had often said that no officer could ever arrest him. It seems Devro was correct, they failed in arresting him. However, he paid a high price for "winning" that contest.   Below: Mr. & Mrs. James Jackson of Preston - Brother of John

Above: Mr. and Mrs. Edgel P. Jackson – Just married and 50 year anniversary picture from the newspaper.

Edgel P. Jackson and Bertha Kennedy at Preston Bend

A descendant of Mr. and Mrs. E. P. Jackson, who worked at the Touch of Class Antique Mall in Sherman told me a few stories passed down through her family about their lives at Preston Bend.

Motel 6 at the Kennedy's – "We Left the Fire Lit For You"

E. P. Jackson's wife, Bertha Kennedy, had these parents: James W. Kennedy and Elizabeth Jackson of Preston Bend. When Bertha Kennedy was a little girl at Preston Bend (she was born in 1884) she was told not to bother the Indians if they came at night to sleep in front of their fireplace at night. There was an understanding between the family and the Indians for years. They would come to the Kennedy home to sleep by the fire in their house, no one would bother each other, and they would leave on their travels in the morning. Preston Bend was on a major north-south Indian road. Though no hostilities ever took place in this case, the family still spent many uneasy nights, especially the children.

A Really BAD Kisser

Another recollection of those days Bertha Kennedy Jackson had was of an unfortunate grown man at Preston that had been bitten by a small dog which turned out to be rabid. It soon became obvious that the man also had become ill with rabies. They had no vaccine for the disease and no cure. The man became irrational, yelling for people to come to him so he could kiss them. If they came near, he would try to bite them. To protect people from him, they had to chain him to a tree until his death.

A Rotten Deal for Preston Landowners

Mr. E. P. Jackson owned good, fertile bottom land south of the Red River before the installation of the Denison Dam. His land was farm land that was full of big pecan trees. He told his descendants that the government paid him the same low rate for his premium improved farm land that they paid for unimproved, unusable scrub acreage. There were very few land owners who were happy about having to move or with the reimbursement they received for their life's work.

E. P. Jackson - Politician   Whitewright Sun Apr 13, 1944

E. P. Jackson of near Denison was in Whitewright Tuesday feeling out the voters with reference to entering the race for county commissioner from this precinct. Mr. Jackson stated he met with much encouragement, and that he would make an announcement within the next few days as to whether or not he would be a candidate. Mr. Jackson is a well known farmer and for many years resided in the Preston Bend community. He purchased a farm southeast of Denison several years ago and moved to it. His former home was in the Denison Dam area and was purchased by the government.

Teenage Minnie Hollenbeck Killed by Brother in Law

Galveston Daily News - Aug 16, 1910; and Beaumont Enterprise August 21, 1910 - County Attorney Cal T. Freeman, Sheriff Sam Rich, and Physician J. F. Jones went to Preston Bend late Monday afternoon, where the body of Minnie Hollenbeck, the 16-year-old girl who was shot and killed by her brother in law, prominent young upper Preston Bend farmer, Bud Jackson.

On Aug. 15, the family had all retired for the night except Mr. Jackson, who had remained up to watch for someone or something that had been prowling around the premises for several nights. He was sitting on the front porch, or in the front part of the house, with his shotgun, when he heard a disturbance at the back part of the house. On going to investigate it, he found that someone had entered the kitchen, and he called to them to speak and tell who was there, but there was no answer. After commanding the person to speak several times, and the party refusing to answer, he fired in the direction where he thought the party was, and immediately knew that he had shot someone, and on investigating was horrified to find that it was a member of his own household. (The old maxim "never shoot until you see the whites of their eyes" might have prevented this girls' death had it been followed.) The supposition of some is that the girl was walking in her sleep and did not hear him when he called her or was unable to respond. Others thought she had stepped outside to the well to get a cool drink of water.

Justice W. H. McAden went out to hold an inquest. On Aug. 16, the justice of the peace/coroner's inquest had ruled the shooting was accidental and exonerated Bud Jackson from any guilt. After the inquest, the girl was buried.

A week later, her body was disinterred and given an examination by Dr. Jones and Frank A. Sporer, an undertaker. None of the parties named made any statement except that although the body had been buried for eight days, it was in good condition and the examination was successful.

The cause leading to the disinterment of the body was the fact that Saturday night, A. W. Hollenbeck, brother of the dead girl, came into Sherman and swore out a complaint against Bud Jackson. At the time the girl was killed, W. H. McAden, justice of the peace of the Pottsboro precinct, held an inquest and found that the killing was accidental, exonerating Mr. Jackson. The charge was filed before Justice J. B. Campbell and Mr. Jackson's bond was set at $2,000. He came into the city with his bondsmen and gave the bond.

Again, according to the statement of Mr. Bud Jackson, it was a completely accidental shooting. It is a tragedy that has played out many times before and since.

Later, Bud Jackson himself became a Deputy Sheriff in Grayson County. However, his relative Herb Jackson had been in trouble with the law and by the time Bud Jackson was a Deputy, Herb Jackson was on parole from prison and was involved in some sort of difficulty with resulted in his own death, which was then investigated by Deputy Bud Jackson. This story will be explored later in the book.

Visit to "Beer Joint" Precedes Fatal Shooting of Preston Man By Widow

Denison Press June 14, 1937, & Howe Messenger 18, 1937

Mrs. Betty Higgins, 50, the widow of Charles Higgins was charged with murder, and later released on a $2,500 bond following a habeas corpus hearing before Judge R. M. Carter in the 15th District Court in connection with the shooting of Robert Jackson, age 49 or 50, of Preston Bend, at her home on a farm three miles west of Sherman. According to Mrs. Higgins, who signed a statement, the shooting was preceded (as so many shootings have been) by a visit to the "beer joint," after which Mr. Jackson became quarrelsome and abusive to her.

Mrs. Higgins herself reported the shooting and gave herself up after county officers rushed to the homestead only to find Jackson near death with two bullets in his body, one in the heart and one on the right side below the heart.   Mrs. Higgins and Robert Jackson were well-known already to officers throughout the county.

Robert Jackson was born Dec. 16, 1887, at Preston Bend, where he has lived all his life, the son of Mr. and Mrs. John Jackson. He was married Dec. 3, 1910, to Miss Rennie Thomas, who survives. He was a member of the Masonic lodge.

Mr. Jackson was a successful fruit and pecan grower and was well known to Denison. Surviving is one son, Durwood of Preston; three daughters, Mrs. Odie Barnhill of Denison, Mrs. Grady Layton and Mrs. Charles Burrage of Preston; two brothers, Rueben D. of Lorenzo, Texas and Amos of Lindsey, Ok., and one sister, Mrs. Bud Shipp of Lorenzo. Funeral services at the Preston Bend Methodist Church, Rev. Ray Short of Pottsboro officiating. Burial at Preston Bend cemetery.

Accused Murderer Dies in Wife's Arms

In the prison hospital, Daniel Hemby died with his head resting on the arm of his wife, who stood vigil at his bedside since his serious illness.   He was charged with the murder of an old man named **J. R. Lambert in the Preston Bend country in the spring of 1892**. He was about 45 years old and was childless. He was formerly in the railroad service in Denison, where his body was taken for burial. - Dallas Morning News Dec 8, 1893

THE KILLING OF ALMARINE WATKINS

Denison's Sunday Gazetteer, August 3, 1884 - The following graphic account of the killing of Almarine Watkins in the Indian Territory is taken from the Evening Journal. It goes over the whole ground and is pronounced substantially correct by those best acquainted with all the particulars. The editor, Mr. Burhans, devoted much time and work to gathering the facts for which his paper deserves credit.

"The Indian Territory which may in truth be called the 'dark and bloody ground,' was the scene of another terrible tragedy. Deeds of violence are so frequent, they elicit only a passing notice. Tuesday afternoon about five o'clock, a telegram was received from Colbert Station, directed to Mr. Welsh, the undertaker, requesting him to have a coffin ready, as some parties would arrive on the first train for it. Below: 1886 Ad for Welsh Bros.

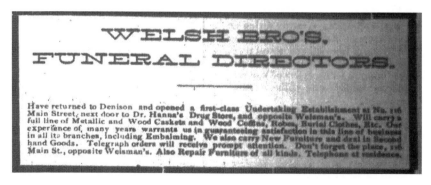

The telegram further stated that Mr. Almarine Watkins had been shot and killed. The death of Watkins was soon circulated over town and caused a profound sensation, as the deceased was well known here.

In the evening a posse of four heavily armed men arrived in the city, having in custody two young men by the name of W. A. Riddle and W. G. Tucker. They were also accompanied by a wagon which came here for the purpose of getting a coffin for young

Watkins. The killing of Watkins comes under the jurisdiction of the U.S. Court, the participants being white men. The posse assisted Marshal Hall, wanting to turn the two prisoners over to U.S. Deputy Marshal Tom Wright. Being in the city, he was sought out, but released the custody of the prisoners, as we understand he is not at present performing the duties of U.S. Marshal. Marshal Hall then took the prisoners in charge, locking them up in the city jail.

A reporter of the Journal visited the jail and in a conversation with the prisoners, Tucker and Riddle, elicited the following facts of the tragic killing:

For some time, there has been a bad feeling existing between the prisoner Riddle and two brothers named Henry and Lewis Weaver. The trouble was renewed the previous Thursday, Riddle having trouble with the brothers near Woodville in regard to a horse. On that occasion, the Weaver brothers insulted Riddle and challenged him to fight. The brothers were armed, and discretion being the better part of valor, Riddle declined the challenge, as he knew that the Weavers would kill him on the slightest provocation. Riddle went his way, and the brothers theirs, but there was a deep-seated feeling of revenge agitating the bosom of Riddle, and he determined to have it out with them at the first opportunity. The occasion was presented the next Saturday. Tucker and Riddle and a companion named Hartinger, saw the Weavers on horseback riding on the prairie near a small skirt of woods. Riddle and his companions awaited their approach in the woods, Tucker telling Riddle that if he did not revenge the insult of Thursday, that he would whip him. Riddle alighted from his wagon and taking out his knife, cut a stout hickory sapling. By that time, the Weaver brothers had entered the woods and rode to the spot where Riddle and his companions had halted. Riddle made the Weavers dismount and administered a severe whipping to Lewis Weaver with the stick. Tucker held his pistol on Henry Weaver, telling him if he attempted to interfere that he would be shot. The Weavers and Riddle and his party then rode off, Lewis Weaver remarking that he would have Riddle in Fort Smith before the judge before many more days, for beating him.

Riddle and Tucker then held a consultation and determined to leave the country until the affair with the Weaver brothers had blown over. That night they went to the Weaver place and stole a mule and horse and rode them to the Washita bottom. In the morning when it was discovered that the horses were missing, the brothers rode from house to house giving the alarm. In a short time, some twenty men armed to the teeth were scouring the country in search of the thieves; among the number was **Almarine Watkins**. After a hard ride of several hours, Tucker and Riddle were discovered lurking in a thicket. They were taken into custody and conducted to the residence of Mr. and Mrs. Watkins **at Harney (just across the river from Preston Bend)** where they were put in a room and placed under a guard. When arrested, Riddle and Tucker denied strenuously having stolen the horses. Sometime during the night, Riddle was taken from his place of confinement, a rope put around his neck and then passed over the limb of a tree and he was jerked vigorously into the air several times, the party demanding where he had hidden the stolen animals. Riddle told them that if they would promise not to hang him, he would conduct them in the morning to where the animals were hidden. The crowd then returned him to his place of confinement and brought Tucker out into the yard to give him a taste of hemp, but desisted, the young man pleading hard for mercy. (Who needed water-boarding to get information, rope-jerking will work!) At daybreak, Riddle and Tucker were taken from their room, placed on horseback, and the crowd to the number of nearly thirty men started with the prisoners for the Washita bottom. Just before starting, one of the Weaver brothers produced a two-gallon jug of whiskey and passed it around to the crowd. Every man in the party was armed with pistols and many also had the inevitable Winchester rifle, which has filled more unmarked graves than the plague and eternally settled more disputes than all other methods.

On reaching the River bottom, many of the party were drunk. A halt was ordered and Riddle showed them where the horses were tied to a post oak tree in the thickest and darkest part of the river bottom. Among the party was a man named **Wasson**, who has long been looked upon as one of the most desperate characters in the Indian Territory. The marshal had several writs out for his arrest. Wasson, who was particularly drunk, demanded that Riddle and Tucker be shot on the spot, and he was seconded by a brother-in-law named **Jerry Lewis**. Wasson was equipped for war at all times, two pistols were belted at his waist and in his right hand, he carried the deadly Winchester '78 rifle. The party all dismounted from their horses and were standing in groups around the prisoners.

Alec Juzan, brother to the deceased man's wife, rode a short distance in the direction of the Washita and was not present at the killing of Almarine Watkins. He returned afterward. Watkins stepped forward and insisted that the law take its course and that the prisoners be turned over to the custody of a U.S. Marshal. Wasson was beside himself with rage and demanded the life of the prisoners. Watkins replied that they should not be harmed and that he would defend them to the death. Then Wasson, Jerry Lewis, and Watkins drew their pistols and the firing commenced almost simultaneously. Watkins' aim was bad, while Wasson and Lewis fired with deadly precision. Almarine Watkins was shot in the left arm, the ball passing entirely through the body. He was also shot through the hip. He fell to the ground and expired without a groan.

Wasson then attempted to kill Tucker but was prevented. Tucker seeing him coming, attempted to take a pistol from his guard named Meeks, to defend himself. During the struggle between Tucker and his guard, Dr. Berg drew his Winchester down on Wasson and ordered him to desist at the peril of his life. Wasson then quieted down, and in a few moments, accompanied by his brother-in-law Lewis, rode off and was seen no more. No attempt was made to detain either of them.

A brother of Watkins, who was at Colbert Station, telegraphed for a coffin, stated that he was present at the shooting and that his brother Almarine was given no chance for his life, but was grasped from behind when he was drawing his pistol. This must be a mistake, as Watkins fired three shots. The dead man was carried to his home and his wife went frantic with grief, sorrowing and crying most piteously. A physician was called to attend her.

A DOUBLE HANGING.

James Wasson and Joseph Jackson Executed at Fort Smith, Arkansas.

FORT SMITH, Arkansas, April 23.

James Wasson and Joseph Jackson were executed here to-day for murders committed in the Indian Territory. Anticipating a respite, United States Marshal Carroll postponed the hour of execution until afternoon. At two o'clock the prisoners were dressed and the death warrants read. They were then ironed and, after bidding their fellow-prisoners good-bye were taken to the scaffold at three o'clock. Before being handcuffed Jackson attempted to cut his throat with a bottle that some of the prisoners used as a flower vase, but was prevented by the guards, after he had cut an ugly gash in his neck. Some delay occurred at the gallows awaiting Wasson's minister and after the minister's prayer the doomed men bade each other good-bye and as the ropes were adjusted bade their last farewell to the guards, reporters and others present. The drop was sprung at 3.46 P. M. and both men died without a struggle. The execution was witnessed by about one hundred persons, mostly Deputy Marshals, guards and reporters. Both men protested their innocence and Jackson said the witnesses swore lies against him. This makes seventy-one men hanged on this gallows within the past twelve years, all for murders committed in the Indian Territory.

James Wasson was convicted of the murder of Henry Martin in the Chickasaw Nation in November, 1881. Wasson and a young Indian named John McLoughlin, nephew of the Governor of the Chickasaw Nation, were together on the day of the killing and were tried jointly for the crime, but the jury disagreed as to McLoughlin and convicted Wasson. The men were somewhat under the influence of liquor, and having an old grudge against Martin went from place to place seeking him. Finally they met him near the road in the woods and shot him down. After riding away some distance Wasson, fearing that his victim might not be dead, returned and fired another bullet through his head. Wasson is also charged with the murder of Almarine Watkins, a Texas cattle king, whose widow offered $1,000 reward for his arrest.

Joseph Jackson, negro, is charged with a most horrible and atrocious wife murder. Simply because he thought his wife was too much trouble to him he emptied the contents of a double-barreled shot-gun into her breast while she was washing dishes one morning after breakfast. This killing occurred March 9, 1885, at Sculleyville, Choctaw Nation, and was a case of circumstantial evidence alone, there being no eye witness. Jackson is very desperate and had to be chained up like a wild beast while being taken to the United States jail.

(James Wasson born in 1853, was wanted for the 1881 murder of a man named Henry Martin but escaped capture until 1884. After he killed Almarine Watkins, he was finally captured because the widow offered a $1,000 reward for his arrest. Wasson was tried before "Hanging Judge" Isaac C. Parker in Fort Smith, Ark. Wasson was convicted and hanged on April 23, 1886. John Duke McLaughlin was also indicted with Wasson, for the murder of Henry Martin, killed in 1872. McLaughlin was acquitted.)

The Misfortunes of Almarine Watkins' Widow -

The killing of Almarine Watkins was not the only tragedy that had befallen Lucy Juzan Harney Watkins, his widow.

About four years earlier, **Eastman Harney,** who was the previous husband of Mrs. Lucy Watkins, while crossing the Washita River was drowned. At that time **Almarine Watkins** was employed as a farm hand on Mrs. Lucy C. Harney's place. He was born and brought up in the neighborhood of **Preston Bend** where his parents continued to reside. This is no doubt how he became acquainted so closely to the **Widow Lucy Harney,** marrying her thereafter.

A short time after Eastman Harney's death, his widow Lucy showed a great fondness for young Watkins, and it was reported that they were to be married when she put off her mourning weeds. Mrs. Harney in company with young Watkins visited Denison frequently. He conducted her business and assumed control of her large cattle interests in the Indian Territory, which amounted to many thousands of dollars.

The winter before this tragic shooting, Mrs. Harney and Watkins were married. The newspaper reported the bride was at least forty, (According to Ancestry.com, she was 34) while the groom was not much over twenty. The marriage was the subject of considerable gossip, even in Denison, where they are both well known. The marriage was distasteful to the relations of Mrs. Harney and her deceased husband, and dark threats hinted of the assassination of Watkins. Mr. Watkins was regarded with disfavor as an intruder who had married for gain.

Was Almarine Watkins, formerly of Preston Bend, who married a wealthy widow across the Red River, murdered by jealous relatives of the widow's former husband? Stranger things have happened. Such things continue to happen.

Case in point: in February before the killing of Watkins, Mr. Alec Juzan, brother to Mrs. Harney-Watkins, had a serious difficulty at Preston Bend with Watkins. Pistols were drawn, and Mr. Juzan was attacked by Watkins and beat over the head with the butt end of a pistol until he bled like a slaughtered cow. Watkin's life was threatened, and he crossed the river to Denison, remaining there for ten days. However, the trouble was said to be amicably resolved and Watkins returned home.

At the time, Mrs. Watkins made an effort to dispose of her cattle, for which she was offered forty thousand dollars cash, but the sale was interrupted, her brother and others declaring that the cattle should not leave the Indian Territory. It is assumed they felt the cattle should remain in the Juzan family or be sold to a member of the same tribe of which her former husband Eastman Harney was a member – the Chickasaws. It was her intention to use the money from the the sale to come to Denison with her new husband and live.

With all the hard feelings and hatred toward Mr. Watkins and all the money involved in the estate, it is not surprising in hindsight that he was the only one out of that large group of men who rode out to the river bottom that day to end up dead. Watkins was seemingly killed in a very unexpected manner, from a source not looked for, at least by him.

However, he had a premonition that he would be assassinated and told the people in Denison about it, but he looked for the danger to come from another quarter. He was heavily hated by both whites and Indians in the Territory. He was also hated by all sides of his wife's family.

Once again, Almarine Watkins WAS the only person who was actually killed in the shooting. Coincidental?

Marshall Merchon and an Indian policeman named Charley LeFlore, arrived in the city and took Tucker and Riddle into custody and conveyed them to Fort Smith, Arkansas. Riddle and Tucker were both professional horse thieves, and Marshal Merchon had a requisition for them for the prior two years. It was a lucky find for the Marshal.

Tucker and Riddle are both Texas boys and were brought up in the neighborhood of Preston Bend, just as Almarine Watkins was. Riddle was a farm hand for Judge Porter of Glen Eden at Preston for one or two seasons.

HARNEY

Eastman Harney and his wife Lucy lived on a huge ranch in the Chickasaw Nation. There is an excellent description of the **Harney Ranch** just across the river from Preston Bend in the 1886 Handbook of Northern Texas to be found on the Portal to Texas History: "Harney" is the 7,000-acre plantation of Mrs. Lucy C. Watkins, a cultivated and wealthy Chickasaw Indian lady, whose lands and herds and home are worth a week's journey of inspection. "Harney," like "Glen Eden," is a wondrously rich and attractive estate. It is the same productive, sandy loam, or reddish alluvial that has given this great valley world-wide fame as a corn and cotton country. Mrs. Watkins has 800 acres of this farm in cultivation to cotton, corn, oats, and millet, all of which yield heavy crops. Her pretty home is finely furnished, stands against a charming background of heavy forest, which improvement has made a beautiful park, and is flanked on the sides and front with tastefully platted lawns, whose walks, ven-clad arbors and a profusion of rare flowers and plants make them a veritable paradise of beauty and bloom. Over the front doorway is a pair of mammoth elk antlers, a souvenir of Mrs. Watkins' own skill in the woods.

"HARNEY."—HOME AND STOCK FARM OF MRS. L. C. WATKINS, IN THE INDIAN NATION, FIFTEEN MILES NORTHWEST OF DENISON.

Picture of the **Harney Ranch** from the Hand Book of Northern Texas 1886 on the Portal to Texas History website.

MRS. L. C. WATKIN'S "HARNEY," INDIAN TERRITORY, 15 MILES NORTHWEST OF DENISON.

1887 Indian Territory map showing Harney north of Preston Bend

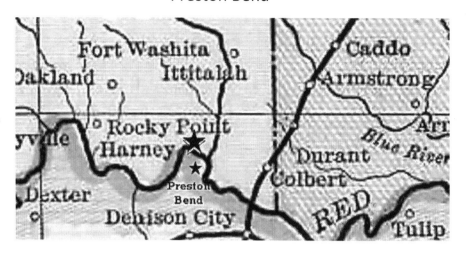

1898 Railroad Map showing Harney just across the river from Preston Bend.

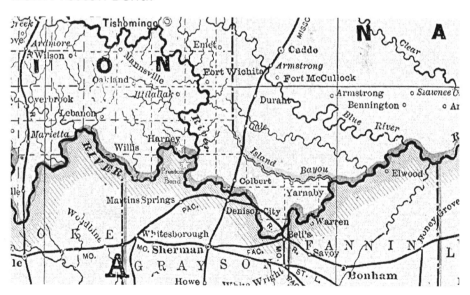

1902 Rand McNally Industrial Atlas Map shows the name of Harney was changed to Woodville.

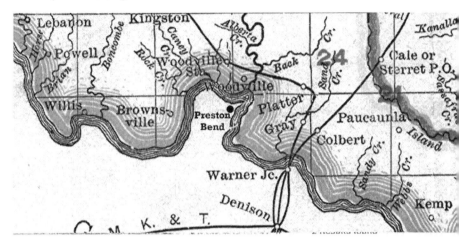

The Towns of Harney and Woodville

The Harney Ranch was just north of Preston Bend on the Indian Territory side of the Red River. Woodville, or New Woodville, as it is also known today, is situated east of State Highway 70A on McDuffie Road, approximately five miles southeast of Kingston in Marshall County, just north of the Red River across from Preston Bend. Woodville was originally named Harney and was also called **Harneyville**. The actual town of Woodville in 1887 was described in a murder trial then as being **"about a half mile south-east of Harneyville."** A post office was established on November 8, 1881, with James H. Darland as postmaster. According to historian George H. Shirk, the town was renamed Woodville on July 9, 1888, in honor of a local settler named L. L. Wood, whose full identity is not known. The early Woodville public well, a pavilion type, boarded up and covered with a peaked roof, was the pride of the community. Dug in a Main Street intersection, the well was deemed so important that road construction was rerouted to the edge of town to protect it. Farmers often came to the well for barrels of water to take home. In 1900 the St.

Louis, Oklahoma and Southern Railway built tracks just north of town. In later years there was a school two blocks south of the well, and nine brick buildings and the railroad depot were constructed nearby. West of the depot was a grain elevator and stock pens with loading ramps for cattle shipments. Several cotton gins were clustered near the railroad tracks. The town was vacated upon the completion of the Denison Dam on the Red River in 1944. Lake Texoma soon covered the site. Some homes and the cemetery were moved to New Woodville, where 69 individuals lived in 2000. Between 1997 and 1998 and between 2001 and 2002 the community was disincorporated. Information from Marshall County Genealogy and Historical Society. The photo below from Sherman Democrat Aug 13, 1939.

Woodville One of Two Towns in Reservoir Area

—Democrat Photos

One of the two postoffice towns within the area tobe covered by the reservoir which will be created by the proposed dam on Red river is Woodville, Okla.,with a population in 1930 of 353. Above are shown some scenes taken recently. In the top photo is themain street crossing which joins the business section with the Frisco railroad station (right center) andwith the two school buildings (lower photograph) and the churches. There are four or five brick business buildings, all on the street shown above, and the two brick schoolbuildings. Note the famous "See Wiley" shed over the public well in the center of the main streetcrossing. "Wiley" being one of Woodville's enterprising merchants Woodville residents were not overlyexcited over prospects for construction of the Red river dam, being apparently more interested in theMurray lake near Ardmore.

Lucy C. Juzan Harney Watkins Thompson Dies

The Sunday Gazetteer. (Denison, Tex.), April 10, 1898 – On April 3rd, Mrs. Lucy Thompson occurred at her home at Harneyville, just across the Red River from Preston Bend. No resident of the Indian Territory was better known to the people of Denison than Mrs. Thompson. She was a constant visitor there for the previous twenty-five years.

Mrs. Thompson was first married to a Chickasaw named Eastman Harney, who was drowned while crossing the Washita River with a drove of cattle. Her second husband was a young white man named Watkins, who was killed in the Washita woods during a "round-up." **Several years before her death, she was married to James Thompson, resident of Preston Bend.** Mrs. Thompson's strongest characteristic was fealty to her friends. In the 1870s she was considered the richest woman in the Chickasaw Nation. It is estimated that in one way or another she spent $50,000 in defense of relatives and friends on trial in Fort Smith for murder and other offenses. Her first husband, Eastman Harney, left her vast herds of cattle which were converted into ready cash very soon. The patronage of Mrs. Thompson was eagerly coveted by our merchants and she spent thousands of dollars with them. She was greatly attached to Mrs. Grey Collins, of R. D. Beirne's; they were intimate friends for many years.

Denison TX

The old Eastman Harney place where Mrs. Thompson was laid to rest was a beautiful and romantic spot, of prairie and woodland scenery. In the front yard, a magnificent monument marked the grave of Eastman Harney. There was a large attendance at the funeral, which was conducted by her request in the old Chickasaw Indian custom. She was buried in a beautiful spot in the lawn at her homestead where she had arranged for her remains to sleep eternally. (Unfortunately for that wish, her body would have to later be moved to prevent it from being inundated by the new Lake Texoma.) All her trinkets and personal effects were buried with her in accordance with the old Indian custom, and the Indian rites of burial – something rarely seen even in those days – were used for the ceremony.

Lucy Juzan Thompson was the daughter of Jackson Juzan and Mississippi Allen. BIRTH on 03 FEB 1849 - Chickasaw, Pontotoc, Indian Territory / Oklahoma, DEATH 03 APR 1898 - Chickasaw, Pontotoc, Indian Territory / Oklahoma, First Marriage - 24 Jun 1868 to Eastman HARNEY - (1847–1882), they had one son - Overton HARNEY - 1870–1891. Second Marriage in 1883 - Chickasaw Nation, to Almarine A. WATKINS - (1855–1884). Third Marriage in 1886 - Chickasaw Nation to James Petty THOMPSON -(1850–1923) - they had a son - Harry Massey "H. M." THOMPSON - 1882–1940 - Her Burial at McBride, Marshall, Oklahoma, USA.

Her last husband, James P. Thompson, applied as an intermarried white on the Chickasaw rolls.

Lucy Thompson was originally buried in the Howard Cemetery located east of Woodville, Marshall County, Oklahoma. During the construction of Lake Texoma in 1942-43, her grave was moved to the New Woodville Cemetery. Source: Madeline S. Mills and Helen R. Mullenax (Relocated Cemeteries in Oklahoma) (1974)

Wanted Men Brought in by Marshal

Fort Worth Daily Gazette - October 13, 1886 - **Deputy US Marshal Henry Hackney**, who has been on the trail of wrong-doers for the last two weeks in the Territory, arrived in the city today with three United States prisoners, **Charles Luttrell**, captured thirty miles north of Paris, in the Choctaw Nation, wanted for murder in Hunt County. Marshal Hackney turned him over to Officer McKay, who took him on to Hunt County. **The next two are Hardy Henry and Bud Jordan, captured at Tuscahoma, Indian Nation, wanted for robbing the store of Joseph Meadows in Preston Bend, several years ago.** One of these last two is said to be wanted in Missouri for murder; which one it is cannot be told at present. This is a good haul for Marshal Hackney and speaks well for his perseverance and vigilance.

ALEC (ALEX) JUZAN, BROTHER OF LUCY HARNEY WATKINS

MORE BLOOD. POTTSBORO POSSE IN THE TERRITORY MAKES EFFORT TO ARREST SLAYER OF CHRISTIAN AND LUTTRELL

Fort Worth Daily Gazette, April 14, 1887 - Dave Hardwick, H. Hackney, John Christian, and two other gentlemen came in tonight from the Chickasaw Nation, and an interview was had with Mr. Hackney, Deputy US Marshal who stated that he did not go to the Nation as an official, but at the earnest request of Mrs. Jim Christian, the wife of the murdered man. He was summoned by Officer Hardwick into the posse, and they went to the home of Alex Juzan and sent him word that if he would surrender, they would protect him from the mob, but he would not do it, so yesterday evening they went in pursuit, stopping near Harney until night, when they were surprised by Juzan and Bussell coming up behind on horses. When ordered to halt, they began firing. When the posse returned fire, with Juzan and Bussell advancing until over 100 shots were fired, they started to run, but got only a short distance when Juzan fell from his horse, but Bussell made good his escape. Whose bullet killed Juzan, is not known, and John Christian did say he would kill him but wanted him caught and tried. The whole Nation is aroused over the death of Christian, and Bussell will undoubtedly be run down within a few days. A posse is in hot pursuit.

Indianapolis (IN) News   April 16, 1887, Pottsboro Tex., -- John Christian, a brother of James Christian, who was killed a few days ago, organized a posse of twelve or thirteen to hunt the murderers down and ran on them Tuesday night, and as they would not surrender, the ball was opened, and **Alex Juzan was killed**, and Steve Bussell mortally wounded. They were the two men who killed Christian and Luttrell, making four lives lost, and the end is not yet.

OFFICERS IN CHARGE OF A PRISONER

Encounter Armed Men and Two Are Slain; The Pursuit Leads to Another Death - A Second Account

April 14, 1887--Dallas Morning News--Sherman, Texas--From Officer Fink, of the northwestern part of the county. The News Reporter gleaned the following facts in regard to the killing of Jim Christian and Ben Luttrell in the Indian Territory, about twenty-five miles north of Sherman, on last Sunday afternoon between 5 and 6 o'clock and as he (Fink) received them from Billie Hamilton, who was under arrest in the hands of Christian at the time of the affair, which has thrown the entire Chickasaw Nation and the northwestern part of Grayson County into a state of feverish excitement.

Hamilton had been arrested just across the river from **Preston, in Texas** and was being taken to Tishomingo. He and Officer Jim Christian were in a light vehicle in front, while James Bounds and Dave Hardwick, two other officers, followed some distance behind on horseback. When about two miles from the river, Christian and Hamilton overtook and took into the vehicle Ben Luttrell, a farmer who lives some distance from the river. Nothing unusual occurred, although trouble was expected until the vehicle drove into Rooster Creek bottom. A sudden rustling noise was heard behind a jagged pile of stone on the left of the old ford and just as Christian turned to pick up his Winchester, which was leaning on the seat behind him, two forms appeared from behind the stone and opened fire upon the occupants of the vehicle. Jim Christian fell dead, with a Winchester ball crashing through his brain and tearing the skull almost into fragments. With the blood and brains of his companion in his face, Hamilton was unable to move, but Luttrell jumped out and ran around the horses. The relentless two, however, did not cease firing, but kept up their fusillade until at last Luttrell, too, fell mortally wounded with an ounce ball hole opening a gaping wound in his neck and a terrible wound from another shot in the left side, which after tearing the muscle out of the left arm, had gone clear through the body, lodging against the right shoulder blade. Officers Bounds and Hardwick at the first shot put spurs to their horses and galloped into the scene at full speed, but just arrived in time to see two men disappear in the forest, which is dense up and down the creek bottom. They halted to see if they could be of any assistance to the men who lay weltering in their gore in the middle of the road, but it was of no use, Luttrell giving his last expiring gasp as they dismounted. Hamilton, the prisoner, made no endeavor to escape and is still in custody. The two men were buried yesterday afternoon in the quiet churchyard near Christian's home.

Later intelligence just received in this city is to the effect that Alec Juzan and Jim Bussell, the two men said by Hamilton to be the men who shot Christian and Luttrell near the river, were overtaken by officers at a late hour last night at a point about forty miles northwest of Sherman and ordered to surrender, which they refused to do. A desperate fight ensued, in which Alec Juzan was literally riddled with bullets and buckshot and Bussell is known to be wounded and it is thought mortally, although in the terrible battle in the dark he managed to escape. Officers from Grayson County and the Indian Territory are in hot pursuit and half of the trouble expected has not yet taken place. Several the parties to the sad and tragic affair were formerly from Sherman and are highly related in this city. Many them left this afternoon for the scene of the tragedy and burial material has been forwarded to **Preston** for the dead body of Juzan. The affair is the current street talk as both sides have friends. The excitement here continues to grow with each additional piece of news.

FATAL FEUD.

Three Prominent Men Bite the Dust in the Chickasaw Nation.

More Details

Fort Worth Daily Gazette - April 21, 1887 - Buck Young, a leading merchant of Preston Bend, arrived in the city bringing the news of the killing of **Dave Hardwick**, sheriff of Pickens County, Chickasaw Nation, which occurred near what is known as the E ranch, situated fifteen miles from Red River, in the Indian Territory. The particulars of the killing of Sheriff Hardwick had not been learned, though he is supposed to have been killed by the friends of **Bussell and Juzan,** who were killed by the officers a few days since while trying to arrest them.

The Denison Gazetteer on April 24, 1887, reported that another of those reckless, off-hand murders, for which the Indian Territory has become famous, occurred that Sunday afternoon in the Rooster Creek river bottom, between Woodville, I. T., and Tishomingo. The cause which led to it being as follows: Some time ago, **Alec Juzan** and Dick Sacra shipped some cattle among which were several head claimed by Jim Christian and Jim Bounds, For this, Christian and Bounds swore out warrants for the arrest of Sacra, Juzan and a man named Hamilton who had helped drive the cattle to the train and who was wanted as a witness. Sacra was arrested and jailed at Tishomingo, and Sheriff Hardwick and Jim Christian came to Pottsboro to effect the arrest of the man Hamilton who was working on a farm near that town. This was Saturday week, and having got their man with the aid of Constable Porter of Pottsboro, they set out for Tishomingo with him. They were accompanied by Jim Bounds and Bud Luttrell. Christian, Luttrell, and Hamilton were in a buggy in advance, while Hardwick and Bounds followed on horseback.

They were passing through Rooster Creek bottom, and the latter was some distance in the rear when they heard the quick discharge of firearms in advance, and spurring up to the buggy, they found both Christian and Luttrell dead, having been shot in their seats as they drove along. **Hamilton stated that the shooting had been done by Alec Juzan and his nephew, Steve Bussell,** who had appeared suddenly before them in the road mounting on horses, and fired the fatal shots and rode rapidly away. The officers and Bounds returned at once to Christian's ranch, where the two victims were buried Tuesday when the officer went on to Tishomingo with his prisoner.

Meanwhile, Marshal Hackney of Denison had been sent for, and together with several others, joined Sheriff Hardwick in the work of capturing Juzan and Bussell. Marshal Hackney states that he not there as an officer, but was summoned as a law and order citizen to help in taking two desperate men.

Monday night Sheriff Hardwick and half a dozen men called at the residence of Juzan and enquired if Mr. Juzan was at home. They were informed by the ladies of the house that Juzan and his nephew, fearing that they would be lynched, had left the country. Tuesday evening the same party rode up to the "E" ranch where Bussell had been stopping, and tying their horses about a quarter of a mile from the house, began to approach on foot. They had only gone a few hundred yards when they heard someone following, and looking back, they spied Juzan and Bussell on horseback about 600 yards distant and coming directly towards them. When within a hundred and fifty yards of the party, they were summoned to halt and throw up their hands. Each of them carried a Winchester, and when they heard the command to raise their hands, they raised their hands with their rifles in them and commenced firing. The fire was returned by the officers and no sooner was the first volley fired than **Juzan fell from his horse dead**. Bussell was evidently severely wounded, for he was seen to reel in his saddle, but he spurred his horse into a thicket and made good his escape. We learn that the officers are still in search of him, and will take him dead or alive. Juzan was buried at the homestead near Woodville, Wednesday. Both Juzan and Christian are wealthy and influential citizens of the Territory, and both have a host of warm friends among the business men of Denison.

Another Account from Pottsboro About Juzan

Pottsboro, Texas-- W. C. Porter, Constable of this precinct, arrested one William Hamilton near here Saturday night. He was wanted as a witness against parties in jail at Tishomingo and another party who has not been arrested yet and was turned over to Dave Hardwick and James Christian in the Nation Sunday morning. As they were conducting the prisoner to Tishomingo, the advance party, consisting of Christian, Luttrell, and Hamilton, were met in the road by two men.

James Christian was killed dead in the buggy. Bud Luttrell was shot at the same time but jumped out and fell dead beside the mules. As James Bounds and Hardwick rode up, the men who did the killing rode off. The prisoner did not attempt to get away. They all returned to Christian's home, where the bodies were buried, after which Hardwick proceeded to Tishomingo with his prisoner.

The charge against the parties arrested is theft of cattle. The News reporter learned the above facts from two men just from the Nation today, but the reports are very conflicting, and the full details are hard to learn.

[from Fort Worth Regional Branch, National Archives]

Juzan – Christian - Steve Bussell Murder Case

Below are documents from the court of Judge Isaac Parker (also known as the "Hanging Judge" of Fort Smith, Arkansas), Western District of Arkansas, where cases from Indian Territory were heard. This case regards the killing of deputies Bud Luttrell and Jim Christian by Steve Bussell and Alex Juzan. Juzan was later shot and killed by deputies. Bussell escaped but was eventually captured and tried for murder. Juzan was Bussell's uncle (both are members of the Chickasaw nation). Called as witnesses for the defense are brothers Flem, Robert and William Birdsong. Also called is Polk Evans brother in lieu of Mattie Birdsong. Other persons named in testimony include Tom Juzan, John McLaughlin, and William Finch.

From the evidence below it seems there was a **pre-existing feud** between Christian & Luttrell and Bussell & Juzan. The only eyewitness to the event, a prisoner named Hamilton, was intimidated by the families of Christian & Luttrell and never testified at the trial.

Bussell was convicted and sentenced to hang, but the evidence was weak. There was no court of appeals for the Indian Territory, the only recourse was the US President, and **Bussell received a Presidential commutation and was eventually paroled.**

United States vs. Steve Bussell, 1887-1888 UNITED STATES OF AMERICA, WESTERN DIST. OF ARKANSAS - On this, the 8th day of June 1887, came the United States of America, the Plaintiff in this cause, by U. S. Attorney, and the defendant in his own proper person, in the custody of the Marshal and by his Attorney John F. Lyons when the following testimony was heard and proceedings had to-wit: **David Hardwick,** being duly sworn, deposes and says: I reside near **Harney**, I. Ty. and know the defendant in this cause. Some time, about, the 10th of May last I was on my way to Tishomingo with a prisoner named Hamilton. About 6 miles from Red River, Harney, I. T., we were traveling and Mr. Luttrell and Mr. Christian were ahead of us with the prisoner Hamilton. I stopped a while with Mr. Bounds to speak to a man and the rest of the party rode some distance ahead. When we started ahead we come upon their buggy in the bed of the Creek and we saw a man lying on the ground by the buggy, whom, upon closer examination we saw was Luttrell, dead. Hamilton said "not to blame him as he had nothing to do with it", that parties from the bank had done the shooting. We went to the bank and saw places behind the bank where two men had been kneeling. We followed the tracks and met a boy who said there were some men running across the prairie. Mr. Bounds and I chased these men about a mile and a half across the prairie and then turned back as we saw they would reach the timber. I recognized the two men we chased, as the defendant and Alex Juzan. I have known the defendant about 20 years. The next day we raised a party to arrest the defendant and Juzan and came upon them, and in trying to arrest them, Juzan was killed, and Bussell escaped. About a week before the murder occurred Bussell told me that he had bought a 38 caliber gun. At the place where Hamilton said the parties who killed Luttrell fired from, Mr. Bounds and I found one 38 calibers empty shell. The man Hamilton told me that he saw Juzan and Bussell both shoot and that there were three shots fired; that Juzan and Bussell, the defendant, both shot together at first and that when Luttrell went to get out of the buggy, Bussell fired again. There was no understanding that if Hamilton would testify to certain things concerning the killing that I would turn him loose. Hamilton was turned loose by me on the advice of Dep. US Marshal Hackney of Texas. That the charge upon which Hamilton was held could not be sustained. -**David Hardwick**

James Bounds being duly sworn on his oath deposes and says: I live in Chickasaw Nation and I know the defendant in this cause. Sometime about the tenth of April last, Luttrell, Christian and Hamilton started north from **Harneyville I.T.** and me and Dave Hardwick rode horseback behind. They drove ahead and were probably 1/4 of a mile in advance of us when they reached Rooster Creek. When we were about 60 yards from the creek we saw

CRIME AND CALAMITY AT PRESTON BEND BY NATALIE CLOUNTZ BAUMAN

somebody lying on the ground in front of the buggy. We approached and found it was Luttrell lying dead in the road. The body of Christian was lying in the buggy. Hamilton was standing by the buggy and said: "It was not me boys" and said finally it was Steve Bussell and Alex Juzan. A boy called our attention to two men running on horseback across the prairie away from us, and we followed them about a mile and I believed they were Alex Juzan and Steve Bussell, but I could not recognize them; we turned back to the place where the bodies were. When we first came up to the buggy, Hamilton showed us where the parties who did the shooting stood behind a bank in the creek. We examined this place and found footprints against the bank and marks where they had kneeled down. I picked up a 38 caliber cartridge shell at this place. - **James Bounds**

The Defendant – Bussell - was sworn & testified that he was with Juzan riding when Christian, Hamilton & Luttrell came up in a buggy & that Christian raised his gun & called on them to throw up hands. That Juzan shot Christian & then Luttrell, who grabbed Christian's gun & got out of the buggy, & Juzan shot him again. That Juzan had a 44 Winchester, & that he (Deft.) had a 38 Winchester. That he did not shoot at all. That Juzan did all shooting with a 44 Winchester.

Material witnesses: By John Prynes, Kit Morton, Mary Taylor, Wm Luttrell he can show that they were out fishing on the little branch when the killing of Luttrell & Christian took place and shortly after coming to the place of the killing and that Dave Hardwick and Bounds were intoxicated and that Dave Hardwick threatened to kill Wm Hamilton if he did not lay the killing on this defendant, and would have done so if he had not been prevented by the parties there present taking his gun away from him.   **By Albert Brogden, Mrs. Oney Brogden and Mrs. John Wilson** he can show that defendant was not at Daniel Jones the day that said Jones and his daughter testify that defendant made a statement to him to the effect that he did some shooting at the time Luttrell and Christian were killed.   **By John Yarborough, James Yarborough & Robert Watkins** he can show that two or three days before the alleged conversation with Daniel Jones and his daughter, this defendant was with them and started to go to Texas and they rode several miles with him and parted, they returned to their house and the defendant going on down Red River and that they parted some twelve miles from the place where said Jones lived.   **By Roe Mays** who lives near the ferry over Red River near the mouth of Blue River, that on the following night, the defendant stayed with him going on towards Texas and by **Wm B Trout** who lives near Honey Grove in the State of Texas and that he stayed with him the following night.   **By Wm Birdsong, Robert Birdsong and Flem Birdsong** he can show that the next day he arrived at their house in the State of Texas about one hundred miles from the place where said statement is alleged to have been made to said Jones and daughter and remained and was there at the time of the said supposed conversation. **By Rev Mr. Cisk** that Christian on the morning of the day he was killed, threatened to kill Alec Juzan on sight.   **By Lem Mitchell & Polk Evans Robert Watkins** he can show that Wm Mann told them Hardwick would have killed Wm Hamilton if he had not prevented him and that the said Hardwick and Bounds were drunk, which is now denied by said Mann.   **By James Vaughn,** he can show that he himself cut the iron ring off of the defendant's gun which Jones swears he took off for the defendant.   **By Charles Wasson,** defendant states he can show that the morning Christian was killed, he borrowed a [belt?] from him and said he was going to arrest some cow thieves. Alex Juzan and Steve Bussell and Wasson said it would be pretty hard or bad for Alex and Steve to get the lash from the belt. When Christian replied there would be no lash, only they would be lashed by the muzzle of his gun the first time he could meet up with them.   These Statements are true and these Witnesses reside in and can be found in this District. Steven Bussell Sworn & Subscribed Before me this 28th Day of September 1887 Stephen Wheeler Clerk

William A. J. Finch. - Q. Where do you live? A. On the Washita river about 4 miles from the mouth. Q. How far is that from Rooster creek where Christian and Luttrell were killed? A. Not over 5 or 6 miles I reckon. Q. You remember the day they were killed? A. Yes, sir. Q. On that day did you see Aleck Juzan and Steve Bussell? A. Yes, sir; I saw them both at my house. Q. What time in the day did they come to your house? A. Sometime in the evening. It might have been 3 or 4 o'clock. Q. Did you have a conversation with Aleck in regard to the killing of Christian and Luttrell? A. Yes, sir; I went out and shook hands with Steve and Aleck and invited them in, but they didn't get off of their horses. They were on the hunt of John McLaughlin and John was at my house, and John McLaughlin came out and Steve and him went off to the lot to catch John's horse and after they had gone I saw there was something the matter with Aleck, and I says to Aleck, what is the matter, "well" he says, Uncle Billy I will tell you the truth, I met Jim Christian a while ago, and he commenced cussing me, he called me a d--n cow thief, and I never stole anything, and he started to draw his gun on me, and I shot his brains out, and there were two other men in the buggy, one of them was Bill Hamilton, and says the other man, I didn't know, he grabbed the gun and I shot him, I killed them both." I asked him, says I, what was Steve doing, well says he, he didn't do anything. Says I, didn't he shoot, says he, "no, he didn't, I did it myself." He said Christian jerked up his gun and I shot his brains out. I asked him who was that other man you shot Aleck, says he, "I don't know." Q. Did he say why he shot him? A. He said

77

because he grabbed the gun. Q. Did he tell you where it was done at? A. Yes, sir; he said on Rooster creek. He said they just happened to meet right in the creek. He was going one way and then the other.   Q. Did he tell you which way they were going? A. No, sir.   Q. Did you ever see Aleck alive after that? A. No, sir.

Joseph H Godfrey Being duly sworn on his oath deposes and says: I live at Colbert Station, Chickasaw nation. I am practicing law in the Indian nation and after the conviction of Steve Bussell, I was employed by his friends to hunt up the testimony in support of a motion for a new trial. I came to Fort Smith with an eyewitness, Mr. Dauson, to the killing.   On the 6th day of Dec. 88, I went to **Harneyville** and remained in that neighborhood until Sunday evening the 9th inst searching for testimony to show that William Hamilton had been either bribed by the Christian family or through fear of them, to run off and not appear in the Bussell case. On Saturday the 8th, I saw several parties who I am satisfied are in possession of information of the fact that William Hamilton was bribed by the Christians to leave the country or was driven off by their threats. I was unable to get the witnesses before any Notary Public except Dudley Luttrell and John Merriman who went as they said at the peril of their lives before a Notary Public and made their statements on last Monday the 10th inst. I remained at Harneyville over Sunday until four o'clock PM and on Sunday morning about seven or eight o'clock two men came riding up to the **store at Harneyville,** they were whooping and discharging firearms and acting in a very boisterous manner and I was told it was Billy Luttrell and Sealy Moyer by parties who knew. They remained there I suppose probably three-quarters of an hour and rode off as they rode up, discharging their firearms and whooping in a very boisterous manner. About half an hour after that, one of the party, Billy Luttrell came back whooping and discharging his pistol and came up within forty yards of Jim Thompson's house where I was stopping, he was apparently very drunk and reeling on his horse and I was told by a brother of Billy Luttrell's, Dudley Luttrell, that the pistol, horse, saddle, and bridle all belonged to Jim Moyer. Dudley Luttrell went out to where he was and told him he didn't want him to come there shooting his pistol and he wanted him to go away, that Thompson and I were in the house and he was liable to get hurt. Billy Luttrell then turned and rode up to the store at Harneyville and then rode off and then I suppose in about half an hour after that, ten or twelve men rode up. Two of them were in a buggy, they were apparently all drunk, whooping and shooting and discharging their firearms. They rode around on the east side of the house and a part of them went still to the north side of the house, that is, Jim Thompson's house. They appeared to be drunk and it seemed as if they were trying to provoke a difficulty with Mr. Thompson and those in the house, their purpose being very evidently to insult and defy the inmates of Mr. Thompson's house. Mr. Thompson and I remained in the house, he at one door and I at the other, and we watched the whole proceedings. They remained around the house about three-quarters of an hour at a distance of about one hundred and fifty or two hundred yards from the house and they went away as they had come - discharging their firearms in front of Thomas Juzan's house, a blind brother of Alec Juzan, now deceased. It seems as if every time they passed Tom Juzan's house they would shoot off their firearms. Bill Luttrell, I think he discharged his pistol five or six times; he was about one hundred yards from the house going back when he discharged his pistol. After the crowd had whooped and shot around Harneyville for some time, they rode off discharging their guns and **went towards Woodville which is about a half mile south-east of Harneyville.** After I started home about four o'clock on Sunday evening I got out probably a quarter of a mile from Harneyville going north, I saw a man standing off about one hundred and fifty yards from the road to the left against Mrs. Thompson's home pasture on a horse. I wasn't near enough to recognize who he was; and still half a mile or not so far was another man right on the road that I had started on, on his horse who discharged his gun about the time I got even with this first man, and being alone, I then changed my course and remained all night with **Mrs. Alec Juzan.** On Monday morning I rode to Colbert Station to my home and went on to Denison and met by appointment Dudley Luttrell and John Merriman who gave their affidavits which are hereto annexed. The reason I stayed at Mrs. Alec Juzan's is my seeing these men on the road and not knowing them, I believed my life to be in danger if I continued my journey on Sunday evening. The following persons have been pointed out to me as persons who have knowledge as to why and how Hamilton came to leave the country without coming to court to give his testimony in the Bussell case: Thorton Prevo was commonly known as Mayberry, he is a brother in law of Bill Hamilton and J A Counts, a friend and neighbor of Bill Hamilton and a lady by the name of Mrs. Patent, and William Pevito. Some of these I have called upon personally and from their manner, I was satisfied they were afraid to tell what they knew on account of the feeling on the part of the Christians and that they had told parties what they did know. I had information from parties whom they had told confidentially what they knew about the case. Affiant is satisfied owing to the circumstances by which those parties are surrounded down there that they will never give their testimony in the case unless they are summoned before this court. J. H. Godfrey.

In 1889 Bussell was found guilty and sentenced to hang. Later his sentence was commuted to life in prison, and later he was paroled.

THE FATE OF DUDLEY LUTTRELL

A few years ago, Alec Juzan, Bud Luttrell and Jim Christian were killed near Woodville, I.T. and Preston Bend. Dudley Luttrell, Bud's brother made his Texas after the fight. He rode away with a horse belonging to Mr. Jim Thompson, of Harneyville, I. T. — without the owner's permission! The saddle and bridle were the property of a nephew of Mr. Thompson's, who was living with him.

Nothing was known of Luttrell's whereabouts and was supposed by parties who claimed to be cognizant of the facts that he was in south Texas.

On February 19, two men, supposed to be horse thieves, were shot and killed by a posse of officers of Burnett County. The fight occurred on Dry Devil's Creek in Crocket County, and after the officers had slain the thieves, an examination of the personal effects developed the fact that one of the men was Dud Luttrell.

Dud had a cousin named Joe Brown at Buckner, in Parker County, Texas, and a letter was found on the body addressed to Joe Brown. Another letter was found in the wagon addressed to **J. P. Thompson, Preston Bend, Texas.** The description of the man upon whom was found the letter tallies exactly with the description of Luttrell.

It is now known that the man killed was Dudley Luttrell, the brother of Bud Luttrell who was killed a few years ago. A further investigation will be made, as it is probable that the deputies killed a man who was wanted badly in the Indian Territory. - Wichita eagle. (Wichita, Kan.) March 27, 1889.

80

LOVE AND MORPHINE - Preston Bend Native, J.M. Massey, Takes Narcotic Route into the Afterlife

The dead body of J.M. Massey was taken from Gainesville last night in a hack to Pottsboro and will be interred in the Preston Bend graveyard near that town. - The Gainesville Daily Hesperian - January 4, 1888.

Geo. Massey of Colbert, I.T., brother of J.M. Massey who committed suicide at the Lindsay House Monday night, arrived in the city Tuesday evening and took charge of the remains and conveyed them to Pottsboro where they will be interred.

The Sunday Gazetteer January 8, 1888 - Shock and surprise were occasioned among the friends and acquaintances of Mr. J.M. Massey by the news that he had suicided at the Lindsay House in Gainesville, on Monday night, by taking an overdose of morphine. He had arrived in Gainesville on Monday morning, registered at the Lindsay House, and after taking breakfast had gone out into the city, remaining out till some time in the afternoon. At what time he returned to the hotel is not known, his room having been assigned him upon his arrival. Tuesday morning at about 8 o'clock the discovery was made that Mr. Massey had not been attending his meals, and the hotel porter was sent to see if anything was the matter with him. The porter rapped, but receiving no response tried the door and finding it locked, climbed upon a chair and looked through the transom window into the room. To his horror, he discovered the form of its occupant stretched out upon the bed, cold and lifeless.

The alarm was given, and the door forced open when the true nature of the tragedy became apparent. On the table, they found a bottle of morphine with about half the contents gone, the photograph of Miss Jessie Manning, who resides at Anadarko, Indian Territory, and a letter addressed to the same young lady.

This letter explains the suicide's reason for the rash act, the contents of which are reproduced in full: "Gainesville Jan 2, 1888 - Dear Jessie - You have wrecked my life, now I care not to live. When I placed the engagement ring on your hand, you told me that if there was any backing out, I would have it to do, but I find that it is you instead of myself. The reason I came to this place was, so I could lock myself in a room and then no one could find me until I am dead, which I prefer rather than live without you. May God bless you and may you find a husband that will love you as I do. I take my life tonight. Goodbye. J.M. Massey"

He was a member of the old Massey family which flourished on Red River before the war and was raised in Preston Bend, this county, where large numbers of his family connection still reside. He was a brother to Mr. George Massey, the Chickasaw cattle king, who, with his mother, resides at Colbert, Indian Territory. He was 37 years of age at the time of his death. The deceased was well known in Denison, having resided here for several years in the early days of the city. He was a member of the police force on the memorable 4th of July when so much blood was shed in Denison and was one of the parties credited with the killing of the desperado, **Charley Russell,** on that occasion. On July 4, 1879, Constable Nelms was killed by a half breed Negro-Indian named Charley Russell, in what was known as the Bank Exchange Saloon. A big picnic was being celebrated in Denison." - Charley Russell Shoots Constable Nelms in Saloon - Brenham Weekly Banner Jul 11, 1879

— Denison was the scene of a fearful tragedy on the 4th. A negro desperado, Charley Russell, resisting arrest shot and killed constable Nelms in a saloon, he then fled upstairs where he was pursued by several officers. He again resisted arrest and shot an officer in the arm. The officers fired and Russell fell dead.

82

More Murder!

July 2 – from Fort Worth Gazette July 3, 1887 - The soul of Tom Sprandling joined many others that have suddenly left the Indian Territory via the Winchester rifle route. R. D. McDougal came to Denison to acquire a coffin and told the story of the murder.

Tom and Neiser Sprandling and Joe and Will Burse were returning home about dark, and near the southwest corner of Charles Gorden's field someone fired a shot in the brush near them, and never dreaming of danger, Tom Sprandling, drew his revolver and gave an answering shot, shooting into the air, and immediately a fusillade of shots were fired from the brush, and Tom Sprandling fell from his horse a dead man, with two bullet holes in his side and two in each leg. His brother Neiser fell also, not from a wound, but to protect and stay by his brother, but the murderers never let themselves be seen and their identification is unknown. If the living brother has an idea who the guilty parties are, he keeps it to himself.

The remains of the murdered man are to be buried in Texas soil at **Preston Bend** on the farm of **Uncle Billy Watkins**. He was a single man, twenty-one years of age, with a good reputation.

Rumor of Political Succession by Murder by Chickasaw Governor Candidate

in Fort Worth Daily Gazette, August 31, 1890 - from the Pottsboro Gazette on Aug 29 - A rumor was circulating at Preston Bend and Willis, Indian Territory for some days to the effect that Sam Paul, recent candidate for governor of the Chickasaws, had killed his successful competitor, Governor Byrd, but no authoritative confirmation or denial were obtained and no details were given (and no confession was made!).

ENDS HIS LIFE
WITH A BULLET

FARMER NEAR PRESTON SHOOTS HIMSELF THROUGH HEART, DYING SOON AFTER.

SAD AFFAIR IS A MYSTERY

Denison Daily Herald Nov 19, 1904

The wife of a Preston Bend farmer heard a gunshot and ran to the spot, finding her husband in a death struggle. W. E. Popejoy, a farmer living three miles west of Preston, shot himself in the region of the heart at noon on Nov. 18th with a forty-four caliber revolver, dying soon afterward.

The shooting is something of a mystery, and there seems to be no satisfactory clue as to how it occurred. No one knew if the man accidentally shot himself or if the shooting was deliberate suicide.

Popejoy was out behind the corn crib, and his wife heard a pistol shot. She called her husband and he did not answer. She went to the point from whence the sound of the shot proceeded, and found her husband in a dying condition, with the pistol by his side and a ghastly wound in the chest. She called for help immediately. Her husband died without speaking to or recognizing her, very soon after she found him.

Popejoy was about thirty-five years of age and had lived in Preston community since the previous spring, moving to Preston from Woodville, I.T. He was a straightforward, good man, and lived happily with his wife and two little children and was respected by all his neighbors. If the shooting was otherwise than accidental, it was assumed it must have been attributable to ill health.

Widow Popejoy of Preston Bend Re-marries

Denison Daily Herald Oct 3, 1906

> Woodville, I. T., Oct. 2.—Married, at the residence of Capt. Williams, in Preston Bend, J. J. Johnson and Mrs. Harriet Popejoy, on Thursday afternoon, Sept. 27. Rev. A. G. Noble officiating. Mr. an Mrs. Johnson have many friends here, all of whom wish them much happiness and prosperity through their married life.

Black Man Almost Lynched by Black Community – Saved by a White Man

The Galveston Daily News March 31, 1894 - To follow is a much different story about the attempted lynching of a black man who was born in Preston Bend. He was almost hanged by a lynch mob of his own people.

James Upkins was a black man born at Preston Bend in Grayson County, Texas in 1867, two years after the end of the Civil War. He was raised in Denison and was a bootblack when a boy. When he grew up, he worked at the yards of the Missouri, Kansas and Texas railway. He married in about 1890 and moved to Ardmore, I.T. in 1891. He was employed there carrying brick and mortar. When a boy, he had a good many fights, but only paid one fine in his life. Upkins was a member of the Baptist church and was baptized by the preacher Sin-Killer Griffin in 1891.

The crime for which Upkins was accused was almost as revolting as that of Henry Smith, who a short time earlier, was burned at the stake for his crimes.

On September 6, 1893, during the absence of his wife from home, Upkins sent his 9-year-old step-son from home on some pretext and during the boy's absence, Mary Wood, his 6-year-old step-daughter, was criminally assaulted by Upkins. Others in the black community there at Ardmore were so greatly incensed over the outrage, they made a determined effort to lynch him. T

hey would doubtless have succeeded, but for the prompt and vigorous action of the United States commissioner, who made a speech to those wishing to lynch him, warning them of the consequences in case they took Upkins out of the hands of the officers of the law and carried out their vigilante justice. They themselves would have been guilty of an even greater crime than the man they killed. (Lynching without trial and burning another man at the stake are indeed horrific.)

Fred Combs Pardoned For Killing Preston Man

Sherman Daily Democrat, June 5, 1915 - **Fred Combs,** one of the young men convicted in the Fifty-ninth district court here fourteen months ago in connection with the killing of a man at Preston Bend, and was given two years for manslaughter, has been pardoned by Texas Governor Ferguson and arrived in Sherman. He returned to Preston, where he has relatives. The pardon provides for the restoration of his citizenship and states that his prison record has been excellent.

Young Combs states that he is going to work and make a good record as a citizen from now on.

It seems, however, that Fred Combs did not remain out of trouble for long….

Fort Worth Star-Telegram   Sep 24, 1917 & The Daily Herald
(Weatherford, Tex.), September 24, 1917

FARMER KILLED

Bob Edwards, prominent farmer and plantation owner in Preston Bend on Red River, was shot and killed between 12 and 1 o'clock Sunday morning.

Officers stated Edwards was said to have gone home in an intoxicated condition in the Preston Bend community on Saturday night and proceeded to abuse his wife when the shooting followed. Fred Combs, Edward's stepson, 23 years of age, shot Edwards in the head with a shotgun, perhaps in an attempt to defend his mother and stop the domestic abuse in progress. It succeeded.

Fred Combs, who telephoned to the sheriff's office himself, was brought to Sherman under arrest. His bond was fixed at $5,000 at a preliminary hearing by Justice Henry Wilson. Combs refused to make a statement.

MAN WITH 100 HOLES SHOT INTO HIS BODY

Frank Boyd, a Preston Bend farmer, who was brought to Sherman weeks earlier and taken to St. Vincent's sanitarium with more than one hundred shot (birdshot, buckshot?) in the upper portion of the body, is reported to be getting along as well as could be expected. One wouldn't expect him to be doing very well after all that. - Sherman Daily Democrat - January 31, 1911

DEATH BY HER OWN HAND

MRS. ETHEL BRUNER FOUND HANGING TO A RAFTER.

Body Discovered by Husband When
He Returned from Field—Home
Is Near Preston Bend.

Newlywed Hangs Herself

Denison Daily Herald, June 15, 1906 -Mrs. Ethel Bruner, aged 19 years and a bride of only seven months, was found hanging from a rafter in her home by her husband George Bruner. An inquest was held by Justice McAden of Pottsboro, who returned a verdict that the woman met death by her own hand.

The Bruners resided on the Jackson farm near Preston Bend. When Mr. Bruner left for work in the fields, his wife seemed in good health and in a normal frame of mind. About 10 o'clock he returned to the house to obtain some money to pay off a hired hand and when he entered, he was met by the ghastly spectacle of his wife hanging dead from the rafters with a large cat sitting on her shoulder. Mr. Bruner at once cut down the body, but life was then extinct.

The cat had to find a new perch.

The woman made a rope in tearing a sheet into strips. She then tied the improvised rope about her own neck, stood up on a chair and kicked the chair away. Mrs. Bruner left a note to her husband in which she said she was afraid she was losing her mind and her health and did not want to be a burden to him. The note was dated June 21, 1906, which is the only irrational thing that can be credited to her, since it was the incorrect date.

The funeral was held at Preston Bend, and interment was made in Helvey Cemetery.

WOMAN KILLS SELF

Miss Leona Holland of Preston Bend shot herself through the head, dying instantly. She was survived by her father, M. M. Holland and six sisters and four brothers. - Ft Worth Star-Telegram Apr 26, 1919.

Below: Helen Dawson Holland & Millard Holland of Preston Bend

Slaughter of Tot Slaughter at Preston Bend - 1921

A fight took place between two black men at Preston Bend resulting in the fatal shooting of Tot Slaughter and the wounding of Charles Rice. Slaughter and Rice met at a farmhouse and after a short argument began firing at each other, it is alleged. Slaughter was killed instantly.

The wife of Rice came from a house and fired twice at her husband, part of a load of small shot taking effect on his left hand, resulting in the amputation of three fingers. Rice and his wife were both put in jail. It is said the fight resulted from a family quarrel. - Ft Worth Star-Telegram Jan 29, 1921

Charley Rice - Bored at His Own Murder Trial

Charley Rice, charged with the murder of Tot Slaughter, sat calmly in his chair and showed no interest, much less emotion, as the state opened its arguments in the morning of the trial. In February 1921, Rice secured a shotgun, went to Slaughter's home and killed him after Rice had seen his wife enter Slaughter's home. On the stand, Rice said that he had told both his wife and Slaughter repeatedly that they must stay away from one another. Persistent attention to his wife that forewarned the wrecking of his home prompted him to shoot Slaughter, he said. After Slaughter had been fatally wounded, Rice's wife secured a shotgun and opened fire on her husband, wounding his left hand to an extent that several fingers had to be removed.

A special venire of 100 men was present when the trial opened, but the jury was easily selected, only about thirty of the men being examined before the jury was completed.

During the trial, amazingly, Rice looked bored, tilted his chair back against the wall and gazed out of the window as the prosecuting attorney began his plea for conviction of the defendant. He seemed especially unconcerned when the jury was close to rendering a verdict. Perhaps he had a premonition..... The Denison Herald August 9, 1921

Aug 10, 1921 – **Unwritten Law Frees Rice of Murder Charge** "Not Guilty" was the verdict in the case against Charley Rice charged with the murder of Tot Slaughter. The case took two days and the jury deliberation took only five minutes. One of the jurors stated that there was only one ballot taken and each one of the twelve was for acquittal.

Rice's defense was based on the "Unwritten law" (of a man's right to defend his wife against another man's attention) and according to the jurors, Rice won his freedom by the straight-forward manner in which he told his story while on the witness stand.

The case attracted a great deal of interest and throughout the two days, the courtroom was filled to capacity. Large crowds from Preston Bend community were gathered around the courthouse continually during the trial and after Rice was freed he received the congratulations of many people, both black and white. (Mr. Rice probably didn't have to worry about any men bothering his wife after that, either.)

Government Trapper Slain; Man Is Charged

Dallas Morning News Dec 14, 1930 - R. L. Anderson, 49, a government trapper, was shot and killed near Preston Bend. Allen Bailey, age 25, who had been working with Anderson, was placed in the Grayson County jail on a charge of murder. Anderson was found lying in a pool of blood **in the bedroom** of a small house about two miles west of the Preston Bend store. Two bullets had gone through his head.

Corsicana Daily Sun - April 10, 1931 - Allen Bailey was acquitted of a murder charge in connection with the killing of R. L. Anderson the government trapper, who was his employer, at Preston Bend. Witnesses testified in the trial that Anderson had made advances to Bailey's wife and Bailey reacted accordingly.

Apparently, the jury was sympathetic. Once again, don't impose on other men's wives at Preston Bend!

Above: Clountz family picking cotton to earn extra money in the 1920s.

COTTON PICKIN' MURDER AT PRESTON

Denison Herald, Dec. 13, 1913 - John Thornton, an aged black man, accompanied by his daughter Jessie Thornton Howard, came up to Preston from Plano to look into the murder of Essie Thornton, who was killed at Preston Bend two weeks prior and his body thrown in the Red River.

Thornton has been on the Harrington farm near Plano for the past twenty-five years. Essie Thornton was his son. He said that he had not seen Essie since the previous May. The son lived in Dallas but had been going to Preston Bend for several years to pick cotton since it was a good cotton country and farmers hire good workers to pick their crops yearly.

Farmer Murdered   Bryan Daily Eagle Sep 24, 1917
Bob Edwards, 45 years old, a well to do farmer of the Preston Bend community, was shot and instantly killed shortly after midnight. A man who was thought to be the assailant telephoned the sheriff's office and the next morning was brought to Sherman for a preliminary hearing where his bond was set at $5,000.

Frank Miller Killed
Near Preston Bend

Whitewright Sun, April 8, 1926 - Frank Miller, about 20 years old, was killed at a filling station just across the Red River from Preston Bend. It was reported he was shot by an aged man and died instantly. Miller was said to have owned an interest in the filling station where the killing occurred.

Albert Collins Has Head Split Open at Preston Bend

Brownwood Daily Bulletin & Ft Worth Star-Telegram Sep 10, 1909

Albert Collins was found in a cabin at Preston Bend with his head split open, his skull fractured and was taken to the sanitarium for treatment. His injuries were so dire, he soon succumbed to them and died. Charges of murder were filed against his attackers, brothers Jeff and Jack Daniels, and Duke Stanley, who worked for the Daniels.

Unruly Preston Bend Boy Tries to Shoot Family

Denison Press, June 2, 1939 - There was a juvenile court action against a 16-year-old Preston Bend youth after his mother told District Attorney R. C. Slagle Jr. that he was becoming unruly.

The boy was arrested on the road near Preston Bend Wednesday by Sheriff Pleasant M. Porter, and Deputy M. G. Dicken, after he had allegedly attempted to shoot his mother and sister.

County Judge Jake J. Loy sentenced the youth to the Gatesville reformatory until he is 21, or until his conduct wins a parole.

R. H. McLean, Owner of Hi-Land Lodge Murdered

Dallas Morning News May 6, 1947

12-POUNDER—R. H. McLean, an ardent Oak Cliff angler, usually doesn't go in for fish trophies but he's going to have the 12-pound bass he's holding here mounted. He made the catch Sunday on a deep-running white lure fishing from a boat at Preston Bend at the head of Little Mineral Bay, Lake Texoma. In the party were Mrs. McLean, Mr. and Mrs. Bert Crandall and Major A. M. Andrus. The record Texas catch for a fresh-water bass weighed slightly more than fourteen pounds and was taken by an angler from San Antonio.

R. H. McLean loved the Preston Peninsula area so much when he came here to fish, he eventually bought the Hi-Land Lodge at Preston. It became very successful. It would not end well though.

R. H. McLEAN   WILLIAM MORRIS JONES

Death Trap at Preston

By Natalie Bauman

One seemingly ordinary February day, business had probably been slow at the Hi-Land Lodge on the Preston Peninsula since it was winter. That day in 1950, R. H. McLean, 43, was the owner and operator of the resort which boasted nice air-conditioned rooms (when air-conditioning was uncommon) with kitchenettes for Lake Texoma visitors, a café and recreation room, a pool and the Highlander Club - with nightly dancing and a live orchestra on weekends. At the time, this was one of the most expensive pleasure resorts on the Lake.

When Mr. McLean was innocently driving back to the Resort that day, there was nothing to warn him of the deadly trap that had been set for him there on the lonely road at Preston.

William Morris "Frosty" Jones, a 26-year-old Pottsboro farmer had bitter feelings against McLean for implicating him in pilfering at the Hi-Land Lodge and some burglaries of several Lake Texoma homes. Jones set a trap on the road to the Lodge by placing a log across the road where McLean was expected to pass. Another party came first and removed the log, going on his way, forcing Jones to place the log in the road again while he lurked behind a tree on the roadside. On Feb. 21, at 5:30 pm, the intended target arrived at the trap. Getting out of his car, he began to remove the barricade when Jones opened fire on him with a .22 caliber semi-automatic rifle, while McLean was pleading for him not to shoot.

All this detail is known because following immediately behind McLean on the road and witnessing the shooting, was a Sherman man named E.H. "Red" Perrin, driving in his family car with his wife and three children. Mr. Perrin said he also pleaded with Jones not to shoot McLean, but he told him to get going quick and

95

tell no one what he saw, or he would "let him have it too." Perrin, being worried for the safety of his family, was forced to drive on, though he "hated it more than one could imagine leaving that man shooting down another man, but there was nothing I could do about it. The man with the gun approached the death car and kept shooting until the victim dropped on the road."

McLean was rushed to a hospital in Denison but died on the way in his wife's arms. She had been summoned to his side in time to say goodbye. Jones was soon arrested in a nearby barn close to his home by Sheriff Merkle Dicken and Deputy Bruce Barton and was charged with murder with malice aforethought.

There have since been many deaths on that lonely road on the Preston Peninsula, mostly tragic traffic accidents. However, Frosty Jones' cold-blooded death trap murder of Mr. McLean will continue to stand out as one of the most diabolical, for which he received a life sentence in prison.

2. OTHER CRIMES IN PRESTON BEND

HORSE THIEVES

Preston Bend seemed to be a magnet for horse thieves. This is perhaps due to its central location as a hub between the Indian Territory and Texas, the East and the West and its location on a river and a major North/South road. Horse thieves based at Preston Bend in the old days could be close to many farms in the surrounding countryside and three substantial towns, Pottsboro, Denison, and Sherman full of horses to steal. Once stolen, they could be taken a very short distance across the Red River to the Indian Territory where law enforcement from Texas had no jurisdiction and where the U. S. Marshals were kept busy by "more serious" crimes, like the frequent murders which occurred there.

HORSE THIEVES HEADED FOR PRESTON BEND, THE GATEWAY TO THE INDIAN TERRITORY

Denison Daily News, September 11, 1878 - A valuable horse, the property of Mr. J. B. Lalonde of Denison, was stolen right out of his lot. Mr. Lalonde and several others, armed with shotguns and other implements of war, started in pursuit the next morning. They knew it was probably up to them to go after them, considering where the criminals were heading. The thief or thieves went in the direction of Preston Bend. No surprise there.

Galveston Flakes Daily Bulletin, Jun 30, 1870, from McKinney Enquirer

HORSE STEALING.—We learn that a band of horse thieves were surprised in Elm Fork bottom a few days since and six horses recaptured. The thieves, it appears, were resting, and had not time to put on their shoes or mount their horses, but took to the brush. Parties were in our place on Thursday night in pursuit.—[McKinney Enquirer, June 18.

HORSETHIEF HUNG.—We learn that on Tuesday night of last week, an Irishman, name unknown, who had stolen a horse at Pilot Point, was caught near Mr. Fares, on the Dallas and Preston road, and carried over to 'Elm bottom and hung.—[McKinney Enquirer, June 18.

MORE HORSE THIEVES AT PRESTON

Denison Daily News March 22, 1874 - **Preston**, Texas, March 10, 1874, To the Editor of Denison Daily News – On Saturday, the 8th, a full-blood Indian, a half breed and a black man from the Nation passed here, all riding and leading one horse, and as was afterward learned, on their way to Rock Bluff at Preston Bend. Later in the day, three white men from the same side passed in pursuit of them; the latter reporting that the pursued had stolen a horse belonging to one of them. At Rock Bluff the parties met, where most of the day was spent, neither party knowing fully the designs of the other; all leaving in the evening together for the Nation. About sunset on the same day, a tremendous cannonading was heard directly across the river from Preston. Apparently, twenty or thirty firearms of different kinds were discharged in rapid succession, loud talking could be heard, but not distinctly. People at Preston concluded that the Chickasaws had come to take the nation and thereby deprive us of one of the best governments that Grant ever ruled over.

I have just learned that the first party that passed here had stolen a horse from one of the white men and concealed him on the Nation side (on which side the horse as well as both the parties, belong) intending, no doubt, to get him on their return. That was just what the white men had anticipated, accordingly, all went together until they arrived in the vicinity of the stolen horse. Here the fight commenced resulting in the death of the full-blood Indian, wounding of the black man, the escape of the half breed, and in the recovery of the stolen horse. I learn further that the half-breed went to Mr. Finches, reported the whole affair, and was then and there taken into custody. Allow me in conclusion, Mr. Editor to say, it is my earnest belief that if ever any nation has been or ever will be totally damned for a wrong Indian policy, that nation will be the United States of North America. Un Amigo.

Constable Cummins Keeps the Peace at Preston

Denison Daily News   December 30, 1874 - Some horses were stolen from parties residing in Dr. Holder's and T. J. Cashion's neighborhood, and Wm. Holder Jr., Jacob Copp, Thomas, and Jeptha Barbee started in pursuit of the thief, supposed to be Bill Strait, who had the reputation already of being a horse thief. While hunting Strait, they came up with his step-father, Crabtree, with whom Strait had been living, and told him they didn't want his kind in the country and that he had better pack up his traps and leave. This coming to the ears of Constable Cummins, he had warrants issued and arrested the above parties, on the charge of unlawful assemblage (called a Ku-Kluk or Ku Klux). They were held to bail in the sum of $500 each for their appearance before Esquire Kirk on January 6th. So it seems that in this free country, law-abiding citizens cannot tell a man they believe to be a horse thief, to leave the neighborhood without being arrested as desperadoes. (However, the TRUTH may be that they did more than ASK him to leave, but threatened him to leave, OR ELSE. The arrest may have been a protective measure for not only Strait, but to help keep the "law-abiding" citizens from committing a vigilante act.)   Strait is now in jail in Sherman for stealing the above horses and has been bound over by Esquire Kirk several times, on different charges. He is evidently a bad man.

Fire at the Holder Residence

Sunday Gazetteer, Apr 5, 1896 – Early Preston Bend doctor, Dr. Issac Newton Holder, died in February 1893. More tragedy darkened the door of this family when the residence of Mrs. I.N. Holder, on the Preston Bend road, NW of Denison, burned on Friday night. The contents were destroyed, and Mrs. Holder had no insurance. Photo below made in 1896, presumably just before it burned; since the picture says this house was built about 1880.

Holder family and house. Clinton L. Holder, Father born 1845, Comanche Delaware Holder, Mother born 1857, Eulah Holder Morrison, Beulah Holder Nicholas, Charles F. Holder, Rufus I. Holder, Front Row: Lawson L. Holder, Gladys Holder Kibler, Nancy Holder Evans, Jerry Bledsoe. Below: Comanche Delaware Strait Holder & Clinton Lafayette Holder.

A Theft at Glen Eden
Crime Didn't Pay for this Thief– It Cost Him Everything

Denison Daily Cresset Oct 27, 1877 - A man named Mull loaded a bale of Glen Eden cotton on a wagon also belonging to Judge Porter, at his plantation in Preston Bend, and brought it to town to sell. The judge discovered his loss about daylight, and mounting a horse, started in pursuit. He arrived in Denison just in time to discover Mull in the act of disposing of the cotton and had him arrested for theft and jailed. **Another account of the apprehension stated that Mull was later taken from jail to the edge of town and shot.**

Lawsuit Results in Fisticuffs - Denison Daily Cresset

April 19, 1877 - From the Sherman Register.

A spirited fight occurred in the office of Judge Wilkins between one of the young members of the bar of this county - Mr. G. G. Randell, of Denison, and his client, a Mr. May. It seems that May had a lawsuit with Judge Porter (of Glen Eden in Preston Bend) in which he employed Mr. Randell.

The suit went against May, and he has since made very serious charges against Mr. Randell, and we are informed, went so far as to try to have proceedings instituted to strike his name from the role of attorneys. These charges came to the ear of Mr. Randell, and when ongoing into Judge Wilkins' office, he found May, and at once asked him if he had made the charges. After some words, May admitted that he had made the statements imputed to him and when he did so, Randell struck him, and the fight began in earnest. Around the room, over the chairs and the stove, the battle raged, Randell, getting in some telling blows on the frontispiece of his antagonist. They drew near the door, when May, being hard pressed and seeing his way out, broke for the opening, and as he did so, Randell planted his fist in the rear of May's head, and his toe under his coat-tail, and thus the fight ended with victory and vindication for the lawyer and an ignominious exit for May.   More with G. G. Randell…….

Team and Wagon Stolen From Preston Bend Auctioned Off Twice in One Day

The Galveston Daily News - July 1, 1884 - T. W. McMichael from Preston Bend came into Denison with two horses, a wagon and two children. The wagon and horses he sold at auction. Johnnie Hinds was the purchaser for $36. McMichael gave Johnnie a bill of sale for the horses and Johnnie bounced into the wagon and started to drive the team and the wagon to his farm.

He met G. G. Randell, who, after asking some questions of Johnnie as to his future, received the reply that Murray, of the Denison Gazetteer newspaper, had convinced him to take up the business of wagoning and that he had just bought this wagon and team to begin his business. Randell, in the inquisitiveness of his nature, and perhaps having his eye on speculation, asked what he had paid. When Johnnie replied $36, Randell at once offered Johnnie $10 more for his bargain. About this time John Cox, another speculator, came along and raised Randell $10. Another impromptu auction was underway! Randell then raised Cox a further $10, and Johnny took him up on the offer.

Randell took the lines and started to drive the team to his farm, when he was overtaken by a woman in hot pursuit after the wagon and team, claiming the property was her own; that her husband had stolen it along with her two children and skipped the country. Randell drove the team to Gilroy's stable to await a trial to determine the rights of property.

Nothing is known of the outcome of any attempt to capture McMichael and the children.

It could be imagined that since he sold the team and wagon in Denison near the train Depot, he and the children might have traveled almost anywhere on the train.

Another Stolen Horse "Fenced" at Preston Bend

Once again Preston Bend was a magnet for stolen horses. Due to its strategic position on the Red River near the Indian Territory, it was THE place to "fence" (pun intended) or sell stolen horses. Fort Worth Daily Gazette - December 8, 1884 - A young man named Hubbard Watson was arrested and charged with having stolen a horse from J. R. Wheeler who resided at Van Alstyne. The horse was disposed of to a person near Preston Bend, (what a shock!), but was recovered and returned to the owner.

Watson tried to make a break for freedom after his arrest but was soon captured after an exciting chase. Of course, he had tried to accomplish his escape on yet another stolen horse!

Longest Continuous Chase of Horse Thief Begins in Nebraska, Ends at Preston Bend – Magnet for Horse Thieves from Far Away!

Fall 1879 – Printed by B. C. Murray Sunday Gazetteer June 11, 1911 - The longest ride after a horse thief (in the writer's recollection) was in the fall of 1879. A thoroughbred horse was stolen from Fremont, Nebraska. The thief had about three days head start, as the owner was absent at the time in Omaha. The horse was valued at $2,000 and had made a record on the racing track.

One morning the thief presented himself at the home of the owner and claimed that he was an intimate friend; to confirm this, he related so many incidents that he removed all suspicion. He presented a letter that authorized him to bring the horse to North Platte, where he was to meet the owner. He left with the horse. When the owner returned home, the whole plot was disclosed as false and as a ruse to steal the valuable horse. He telegraphed along the line of the Union Pacific and then started in pursuit on horseback. The thief, having three days' start, crossed the line into Kansas, traveling by easy stretches.

When arrested by Grayson County Sheriff Everheart, he stated that he did not make over twenty-five miles per day, so as to save horseflesh and bring him in good condition to Texas where he had a sale lined up for him.

When the owner arrived in Kansas, he got the first clue of the stolen animal. When the man left Nebraska, he left an envelope that bore a Texas postmark, and the owner of the horse supposed that he would head for this state. He learned in Kansas that a man had passed through a certain section riding a horse answering the description of the one stolen. Hundreds of notices describing the horse and the reward were offered.

Grayson County Sheriff Bill Everheart received one of these notices.

The thief left Kansas and went to the Osage Nation and passed several days into a full-blood settlement on the Canadian River, where the horse was well fed and rested. It was there that the man received the first intimation that he was pursued. An Indian had been to the railway station and read the notice posted at the depot.

That night another horse thief rode into camp with a fine animal which had also been stolen in Kansas. The two started together for Texas. They were probably previously known to each other.

When they reached the Chickasaw Nation, they met an officer who attempted to arrest them. They promptly shot and killed him.

The new arrival (in the fight) was also shot, and when they reached Texas, he went to a cabin near Coffee's Bend, where he was cared for until he got well. After leaving Coffee's Bend, the horse thief started for Preston when Sheriff Everheart and the deputy, while riding through some woods, saw a man in the distance so faintly discernable that only keen eyes could have seen him. He was on the ground munching cheese and crackers. They rode up to him, and the sheriff immediately recognized the Nebraska animal, standing right there at Preston. The horse thief had drawn his pistol and backed up against a tree. The sheriff asked him if he had seen any cattle and dismounted. This remark caused the man to lower his gun. The sheriff asked what he meant by pulling his gun on him; that he was after cattle. The thief then went to his horse and mounted. He was leading the stolen Nebraska horse. The sheriff and the deputy got in ahead

of him and at the turn of the road held him up with their Winchester rifles. The thief at this point couldn't get away and was obliged to stay on the highway, owing to the wire fences.

The man and the two horses were taken to Sherman and the owner was communicated with. On a requisition from the governor of Nebraska, the horse thief was taken back, tried, convicted, and sent to the penitentiary for ten years.

This case was declared by the newspapers to be the longest pursuit after a horse thief ever known to that time. In the Osage country, the ma had purchased another horse and led the stolen animal. The horse was shipped back to Nebraska on a railroad boxcar. The owner in pursuit of the thief, had ridden down two horses and arrived at Sherman on the railroad. The thief was a man of about 30, from San Saba County and was the son of a prominent cattle raiser. He was mixed up with a gang of horse thieves who used to steal animals in Kansas and Missouri and sell them in Texas regularly.

Nefarious Doctor From Preston Bend – No Gentleman!

Denison Daily News March 11, 1880 - Officer Morrell returned from Sherman without the culprit he went after – Dr. Warren, who had two charges docketed against him in the mayor's court, one for fighting and one for carrying deadly weapons. Morrell captured his man, but before the arrival of the train for Denison he was taken from him by the sheriff, the grand jury wishing to interview the gentleman on the charge of forgery. It was asserted that he sold some hogs to auctioneer Bryant of Denison, and forged the name of the owner to the bill of sale. He was also charged with taking with him a pistol to which he had no legal right.

Dr. Warren formerly resided in Preston Bend, but as we learned from responsible parties, was forced to leave there because otherwise, in all likelihood, he would have met with rough treatment by the locals. It is said that he had been guilty of several suspicious transactions at Preston, and on various occasions had circulated reports derogatory to the good name of the young ladies at Preston Bend. This was an offense which never can be condoned by a true Texan or a gentleman.

He came to Denison only a few months previous. If the charges against him can be proven, the doctor will in all probability, soon wear the striped zebra suit issued to state pensioners at Huntsville.

Joe Meadows Store Robbed

Fort Worth Daily Gazette October 13, 1886 - Deputy U.S. Marshal Henry Hackney, who has been on the trail of wrong-doers for the last two weeks in the Territory, arrived in the city today with three United States prisoners, Charles Luttrell, captured thirty miles north of Paris, in the Choctaw nation, wanted for murder in Hunt County. Marshal Hackney turned him over to Officer McKay, who took him on to Hunt County. The next two are Hardy Henry and Bud Jordan, captured at Tuscahoma, Indian Nation, wanted for robbing the store of Joseph Meadows in Preston Bend, several years ago. One of these last two is said to be wanted in Missouri for murder; which one it is cannot be told at present. This is a good haul for Marshal Hackney and speaks well for his perseverance and vigilance.

– Eufaula Indian Journal Oct 21, 1886 - Hardy Henry and Bud Jergins/ Jordan were arrested at Tushka Homma last week, charged with robbing Joe Meadows' store at Preston Bend, Texas.

Joe Meadows at one time owned Glen Eden, he also operated a store, a cotton gin and a ferry service at Preston Bend and had a half interest in the White Elephant Saloon in Denison.

ARMED SHOWDOWN ON THE RED RIVER AT PRESTON BEND

Story from the Sunday Gazetteer. (Denison, Tex.), August 31, 1902 - There was a critical situation at Preston Bend. The Indian police and a number of others were driving cattle across Red River from the Indian Territory to graze for which they were paid $2 per head. The cattle had been ordered out by the U.S. authorities. Texas tick fever was a terrible problem in cattle and many states were banning Texas cattle from even entering their state in fear of spreading these ticks. (Late August in this area also usually means extreme heat and drought, which means no grass for cattle to eat – another bad problem for ranchers with large herds.) The people of Preston Bend objected to the presence of the cattle on their grazing lands, as grass was very scarce on their side of the river at the time as well. They wanted their grass for their own cattle. They took action under the leadership of Joe Meadows. A large number of armed men gathered at the river to prevent the passage of any more cattle, and after a parley between the factions on the North and South sides of the river, the Meadows party gained their point and there the matter ended. Perhaps the Indian police didn't consider $2 a head to be adequate compensation for dodging bullets from irate ranchers. Not what they signed up for! Maybe they crossed the cattle elsewhere.

VOODOO SPELLS AT PRESTON BEND

VOODOO Spell is Claimed by Her Husband to Trouble Ella Hudson.
April 20 -- Sherman Daily Register, April 22, 1887 - a black woman by the name of Ella Hudson was brought to the city by her husband, and tried before Judge Gregg and remanded to the Alms House, to await commitment to the Terrell Asylum. Apr. 21, Superintendent Wilkins notified Judge Gregg that she was becoming unmanageable and that she had torn every particle of her clothing off, notwithstanding the efforts of the guards and attendants to keep her from doing so. Judge Gregg went out and found everything as represented and took with him some

108

relatives of the unfortunate woman, and they managed to quiet her down and get her clothing replaced. Her husband is opposed to her being transferred from Sherman to the Terrell Asylum, and while he himself was the first person to report her strangeness, he denies she is crazy but lays all the trouble to "Voodooism," claiming that a spell has been put on her by a witch. He should be careful he doesn't end up at Terrell himself, either because of the authorities declaring him insane or the witch cursing him for exposing her!

The "Voodoo" Victim

The Sherman Daily Register, April 26, 1887 - Jennie Ella Hudson, the black woman from the Preston Bend neighborhood, who was convicted of insanity, but who was taken charge of by her husband, will be taken to Terrell at once. Dr. Wallace, of the Terrell asylum, sent a telegram to the county judge today stating that there was room for her.

The Sherman Daily Register April 27, 1887 - A black woman, Ella Hudson, who was recently brought in from Preston and convicted of insanity, was taken to the Terrell Asylum by **Officer Cam Whitesides** this morning at 4:25 o'clock.

She is very troublesome, and has to be carried almost bodily from one point to another. Her husband persisted to the last that she was not crazy, but that a "voodoo" doctor, alleged to hold forth in the Red River bottom, had put a "spell" on her. That reasoning probably didn't make much difference to the authorities.

"Arkansas Dude" Didn't Like His Name – At All

The Galveston Daily News, November 20, 1886 – Three Preston Bend families traveling together to Texarkana found out the phrase "Sticks and stones may break my bones, but words will never harm me" is just not true.

These three families, on their way to visit Texarkana from their homes in Preston Bend, stopped at Honey Grove at J. L. Toney's wagon-yard. A difficulty started between N. A. Sargent and J. B. Moore, resulting in Moore stabbing Sargent in the right breast just above the nipple to the depth of about three inches, and also cutting him in the wrist. Sargent's brother got a severe cut in the right hand in trying to separate them. Moore's brother and Sargent were brothers-in-law. The two Moore's and Sargent's brother had families with them. What caused the trouble? The parties were drinking, and it is said Sargent called Moore and Arkansas dude, and Moore began to carve him up for it. The wound was a dangerous one, but not necessarily fatal. I suppose the name wasn't THAT offensive to him.

Sunday Gazetteer June 25, 1905

Elder Noble, who for many years resided at Preston Bend, has, with his family, moved to Woodville, I. T., where he is engaged in merchandising. Mr. Noble still has his store at Preston, but his personal attention is given to the business at Woodville. Mr. Noble visited Denison this week.

A.G. Noble Store Burglarized

Burglars entered the store of A. G. Noble at Preston Bend and took a small amount of money from the cash drawer. They attempted to blow the safe, drilling a hole in the door by using gunpowder, but failed. A number of dry goods and groceries was taken. The Shawnee News December 7, 1908.

Man Wanted For Crimes in Preston Bend in 1884 Finally Resolved in 1914

Dallas Morning News 8 –12–1914 - A man 70 years of age, giving the name of Charles Coe, accompanied by District Clerk Sam K. Rudolph of Gainesville, and a son, Ben Coe, appeared at the Sheriff's office here and asked if there were any charges on the court dockets against one Charles Coe. Sheriff Lee Simmons and District Clerk Harve Taylor looked up the records and found that on March 15, 1884, the Grayson County Grand Jury had returned three indictments, two charging assault to murder and one arson, against a man by that name.

It developed that the aged man was Charles Coe, and thirty years ago, in connection with several others, he had been indicted on a charge of beating up some black men and burning a black schoolhouse near **Preston Bend.** Mr. Coe was not arrested at the time, and shortly afterward he read an account where one of the men indicted with him was sent to the penitentiary for life, but did not stop to read that it was for a killing, which had nothing to do with the incidents with which he was alleged to be connected. As soon as he read the man had received a life sentence, he walked out of his yard and was seen no more in this country. He figured he was next on the list to head for the pen! He left a wife and five children on their farm on their own. The wife reared the children, and a few years ago, the family moved to Oklahoma.

Mr. Coe stated that he had been in the Klondike most of the time since leaving Preston and had made good. Recently he took a notion that he would come back and face the charges against him. He was made very happy to learn that his wife and children, now grown, were not only glad to see him but had grown into such citizens that any man would be proud of them.

Sam K. Rudolph, acting as an attorney, made a motion in the 59th District Court that the indictments be quashed, and the cases dismissed, producing affidavits showing that all the witnesses were dead. Judge M. H. Garnett sustained the motion and Charles Coe walked out a free man.

He said; "For thirty years I have been a fugitive and have always been afraid lest the heavy hand of the law is laid on me. Today the air seems purer than it has ever been, the heavens brighter and people better. The rest of my days shall be spent with my family (in Ardmore). I am grateful to again be a free man. While I have never been behind prison bars, I have never been free for thirty years until today."

Although 70 years old, Mr. Coe was a fine specimen of physical manhood and looked like one would expect of the typical Alaskan gold miner, and judging from appearances, he should have many years ahead to enjoy with family.

The others who were tried in the 1880s for also participating in the crimes Mr. Coe was indicted for, were acquitted. Thirty years later, Mr. Coe was also, finally, set free.

Forced to Take His First Drink - Harry Hardenburg, of Preston Bend, 14 years old, was coming into town when he met three men going out. He saw they were intoxicated and when he met them, they stopped him and asked him if he ever had drunk anything. Receiving the answer that he had never taken a drop of liquor in his life, the men produced a bottle and told him to drink. He refused and the men took him from his horse, and putting a six-shooter to his head, told him to drink or they would shoot. The boy was frightened nearly to death and drank a copious draught of the whiskey. After he had done so, the men mounted him on his horse and allowed him to proceed on his journey. The boy arrived in town badly frightened and very much under the influence of the liquor. He went the home of J. E. Pollard, relatives of the family, where he told his story. The boy is the son of a widow woman living at Preston Bend. The three men were not known to the boy and the only description he could give of them was that they looked like Indian Territory people. - Dallas Morning News Oct 20, 1896.

CONRAD HARDENBURG,
Deceased.

G. H. BELL,
Deceased.

Above: James A. Bell and Caroline (Brown) Bell

All Not WELL at Preston Bend

Jes and Lou Gunter, who have been living on the Wilson place at Preston Bend, were arrested and put under $350 bond each for assaulting an old woman by the name of Brown. The difficulty arose from the two brothers getting water from a well after being forbidden from using the same. They were arrested in the Territory. - Denison Gazetteer, July 22, 1888.

Prisoners Captured at Preston Bend

October 1892 - Deputy Sheriff Jack Sims in company with deputies Lee and Henderson, captured Dave Vaughn and Sam Lyon, two of the ten prisoners who made their escape from the Sherman jail three days earlier. The arrest was made out in the Preston Bend country near the Red River at the house of a farmer named

Fletcher. Sims heard of the presence of the men by a note written by a party at Preston Bend. The officers arrived at the house sometime after midnight and when all arrangements had been made for a fight, Sims shoved open the door, jumped in and threw his pistol into the faces of Lyon and Vaughn while they still in bed. Steel shackles were on the men in a very few moments and before the men scarcely realized what was going on, they were safely out of harm's way so far as resisting the officers was concerned. Two buggies had been procured for the occasion and the three officers and two prisoners were soon en route to Denison. It seemed Vaughn had broken from jail bare-footed and his feet were sore due to his arduous journey of escape. The men were jailed in Denison and late in the afternoon were returned to Sherman via the train, to the relief of Vaughn's sore feet, where they were again placed behind the bars of the impregnable $95,000 jail.

It seemed the Grayson County jailer was "losing his grip" on the prisoners in his charge, since a few days earlier, even MORE prisoners had escaped and these men were captured out at Gainesville and returned (hopefully to stay) in company with a man by the name of John Watts, who got out through an open door and escaped once again.

Turnkey Sam McAfee, stated that before he left for supper, he locked the door to the rotary cells, but when he came back, it was standing wide open. Officers were sitting in their office at the time, but they did not know about the escape. Watts was charged with counterfeiting and Johnson with selling whiskey in the Indian country in violation of the federal law. The last escape was a mystery and many people were inclined at the time to lay the blame on someone at the jail for deliberately helping with it. From The Sunday Gazetteer (Denison, Tex.), October 23, 1892, and The Albany Weekly News Oct. 28, 1892.

Below: Grayson County Jailhouse in Sherman with the rotary cells, picture courtesy of Pat Revill of Sherman.

Below: Grayson County Courthouse in Sherman.

Former Grayson Co. Deputy Sheriff Is Shot 'by Woman

Bonham Daily Favorite Apr 8, 1932 - 36-year-old Ex-Deputy Sheriff Grover Bell at Preston Bend was until very recently, employed at a local filling station, was admitted to the Wilson N. Jones Hospital, seriously injured from a pistol wound through the abdomen. Physicians said he had a chance to recover following an operation. The complaint was filed about 10:15 a.m. Thursday in the Justice court of J. N. Phillips charging Mrs. Pearl Bennett with assault with intent to murder in connection with the case. The shooting occurred about 1:30 a.m. Thursday.

In a statement made to Criminal District Attorney Joe P. Cox and Sheriff Frank Reece Thursday morning, Bell said the shooting occurred in an upstairs apartment of a brick building at the corner of Rusk and Lamar Streets. He said the shooting followed a brief quarrel. The pistol was said to have been in a dresser drawer. One shot was fired. Bell walked a few blocks to an apartment on West Jones Street into which his wife and three children had moved only two days ago. His wife summoned a doctor, but the wounded man was carried to the hospital in a private car before the physician arrived.

The Sheriff's department was notified of the shooting and the police were asked to aid in the search for a woman. Mrs. Bennett was found at the house of friends near Payne, south of Sherman. In the apartment where the shooting is said to have taken place, was found on the floor an automatic firearm, according to Sheriff Frank Reece. The bullet passed through Bell's left wrist and tore a large hole in his stomach. Instead of striking his intestines, however, it struck his liver. The bullet was not removed in the operation. Mrs. Bennett had been living in Sherman several weeks, coming here from Waco, it was said.

116

Unfortunately for all parties, Grover Bell, shot on April 7th, finally succumbed to his gunshot wounds on April 19th. Therefore, Pearl Bennett was formally charged with assault to murder. Mr. Bell left behind a wife, two sons, and two daughters. His body was buried at Dripping Springs.

RECORD FREEZE Houston Post Feb 16, 1899

The heaviest freeze of the winter was reported from Preston Bend in the northwest portion of Grayson County. **Mr. Dave Fletcher**, a prominent farmer at Preston, stated that the water in his well at a depth of thirteen feet below the surface of the ground froze several inches thick. The Red River was reported to still be frozen. Wagons and teams were crossing the river on the ice making ferry service or bridges unnecessary. The river was frozen solid to the bottom. The Washita, another large river, was also frozen and hundreds of teams were crossing it. A boy was also reported frozen to death. While in camp on the Red River, a 5-year-old boy was frozen to death in an emigrant wagon. The lad was the son of B. L. Martin, a mover.

Bad Pie Stuffing Causes Expensive Beat Down

by Natalie Clountz Bauman Not liking the ingredients of the stuffing of a pie that he had purchased, a Preston Bend man beat the stuffing out of the man who made the sale of the pie to him. Surely a case of giving "bitter for sweet." This was revealed in a case that came up before Judge M. M. Scholl. The Preston Bend man was fined $17.50 on a disturbance charge. According to Judge Scholl, the Preston man should have beat the stuffing out of the pie that he purchased instead of the man who sold him the pie, and he would have found it a lot cheaper. The pie only cost a dollar, the stuffing he beat out of the man cost him a lot more. - From The Denison Press - March 8, 1935.

HIGHWAY ROBBERY – A REAL PROBLEM AT PRESTON BEND

ROAD AGENTS STRIKE AT PRESTON BEND

The Sunday Gazetteer, October 30, 1887 - Mr. J. D. Causey, a farmer who lives on Mr. A. Hall's place near Preston Bend, came to Denison on October 22nd and sold a load of cotton, receiving a check for $150. It was after bank hours when he got his check, so he took it to the grocery house of Brooks & Harris and had it cashed, and, after paying bills to the amount of $35, he started for home with the rest of the cash. As he reached the top of Rock Hill – a wild and rocky elevation in the road this side of the Porter place (Glen Eden) – he passed a man who nodded to him, and, having walked by, commenced to whistle. He had only got a few rods further when two men, springing out of the bushes at the horses heads, seized the reins and demanded his money. Mr. Causey replied that he had no money, but was interrupted by one of the robbers, who demanded with an oath what he had done with the money he got at Brooks & Harris's. A couple of six shooters were produced by the road agents, and he was made to disgorge his entire roll of money, amounting to $115, after which the robbers took to the woods, allowing their victim to proceed upon his way. Mr. Causey stated that the highwaymen were masked with handkerchiefs tied across their faces, but he thought they were black men. He thought he recognized one of them as being a blacksmith at Preston Bend, and upon returning home he secured the assistance of several neighbors, and proceeding to the house of the blacksmith, took him into custody. He, however, proved a satisfactory alibi and was released. Otherwise, there was no other clue as to the identity of the robbers except that they knew exactly where Causey had cashed his check in town.

Old Farmer Beats Off Two Armed Attackers on Preston Road
By Natalie Clountz Bauman

We have all heard of Preston Road. It has been a means of travel here for almost 200 years, and even longer, by other names. It has been used as an Indian trail, a cattle trail, a means of immigration by pioneers, and for one more thing – highway robbery.

You've probably heard of the Keystone Kops in the old silent movies who ran around in confused incompetency, incapable of accomplishing anything. This can also be true of some guys on the other side of the badge – Stupid Criminals. Some of these inept "Knight's of the Road" in the following true story thought they had selected an easy target for their crime - they were wrong, VERY WRONG.

An elderly farmer named Crabtree had a peculiar experience with would-be robbers in October of 1901 about dusk. It was not peculiar in that it was rare, this sort of thing happened all the time. It was peculiar in that the good guy won!

Mr. Crabtree had been in the city with a load of produce and started home in his wagon according to the Dallas Morning News. When about a mile and a half west of town, on the Preston Bend road, two men, one white and one black, ordered him to stop his wagon. They both had guns, but they could not stop Mr. Crabtree. Mr. Crabtree said later he had completed his business and had no need to stop and instead whipped his horses into a faster pace.

The white man attempted to get in the wagon, so Mr. Crabtree took his driving whip, the end of which was loaded with lead, and struck the man on the head. He fell off the wagon, and the black man struck Mr. Crabtree on the head with a pistol. Then the

119

white man who fell came back at Mr. Crabtree, and the two men assaulted him, striking him over the head with their pistols. (Bear in mind, Mr. Crabtree is armed only with a whip!)

They made no attempt to shoot him until Mr. Crabtree knocked one of them off the wagon the second time. They fired two shots at the old gentleman, neither of which took effect. The black man climbed up on the wagon again, placed the pistol close to old man Crabtree's side and fired. The bullet entered his coat and passed through his shirt and vest, blistering the skin on his abdomen as it grazed him, but doing no further damage. With a final heavy blow on the head delivered by the elder Mr. Crabtree, the black man fell off the wagon and did not renew the attack.

Two young criminals with pistols against one older farmer in a wagon with only a horse whip. Who would YOU have thought would win that one? Peculiar.

Both men decided to flee from the scene before further damage was done - to themselves - hoping for better luck next time, or maybe looking for hold-up classes.

Better yet, perhaps they contemplated a new line of work. (Perhaps their best career choice might have been clown college.) **For them that day, crime certainly didn't pay.**

Secret Game of Chance Is Itself Robbed at Preston Bend by Road Agents

Denison Herald and Whitewright Sun - Sep 10-13, 1923 - It seems even illegal gamblers hiding in a thicket in rural Preston Bend were not concealed well enough to escape the notice of two bold "stick-up men." Harve Odell of the Preston Bend community was shot in the right arm when a quiet game of chance was "hijacked" by two men who weren't invited to the party.

The boys were in the thicket when the game was suddenly interrupted, and the order was rudely given to "stick 'em up." Odell did not get his hands up as quickly enough, as one of the "visitors" thought he should, and the shot was fired. The wound was not deemed severe, except by Odell himself. He did, however, have bones in his lower arm shattered by the bullet.

The entire pot was secured by the two robbers, which amounted to $74.60. You expect them to steal money, what is not expected, they inexplicably gave their names, saying they were A. J. Moore and Doc Taylor. No one said criminals have to be smart, just audacious. They then escaped in a car until they got to the Red River where they engaged someone to row them across the river in a boat into Oklahoma. The man who transported them also reported them to the officers. Moore and Taylor were from Oklahoma and had been picking cotton in the Preston Bend community for a few days. Soon, word came from Durant, Oklahoma that the two men were under arrest there based on information provided by Deputy Sheriff O.F. Miles. Sheriff Everheart and Deputy Bart Shipp went to Durant and brought the prisoners to Denison where they were charged with robbery with firearms. The officers recovered $50 of the stolen money.

A third man, Lee Taylor, brother of Doc Taylor, was arrested also and charged with being a party to the holdup. It was stated that he acquired one of the guns in the holdup and received part of the money obtained in the robbery. Another man, Dan David was also charged in the highway robbery for harboring the robbers the first night after the robbery.

They rolled the dice but…… Their luck had run out. Once again… Crime did not pay.

HIGHWAY ROBBERIES (BY ROOKIES) a.k.a. Crime Didn't Pay

A farmer named James Simmons who lived four miles west of Denison reported being robbed of $3 by two armed footpads. They had doubtless followed him from town and attacked him on the road to Pottsboro. A few days earlier, Ollie Gare, who resides in the Choctaw Nation, while on the Preston Bend wagon road, en route home, was attacked four miles out of Denison by a man and boy who had followed him on horseback. The man held a cocked gun pointed at Gare while the boy mounted the wagon and went through his possessions for valuables. It was probably his first experience at robbery, as he betrayed extreme nervousness and only found a dime in silver, overlooking in his haste a tobacco sack containing the proceeds of two bales of cotton amounting to a considerable sum. - Dallas Morning News Oct 12, 1894

Denton County News, October 11, 1894 - Henry Schafer, who sold a bale of cotton in Denison an invested most of the proceeds, was held up by armed highway robbers near Preston Bend the same night. The robber only got $7.50. **Crime didn't pay – much.**

Highway Robbers at Preston Bend, Delaware Bend, and Martin Springs – Captured – They Pay High Price For the High Life

In this case, crime didn't pay, in fact, it cost the perpetrators a very high price – as it often does.

Deputy Sheriff D. Burris, in company with Deputy J. R. Dishner and Road Forman Hugh Bowen, went to Martin Springs, two miles west of Pottsboro, and arrested three brothers, John, Henry H. and Oscar Moss; bringing them to town where they were given lodgings in jail on the charge of highway robbery with firearms.

Above: Herman Thoma house in 1904 at Martin Springs

The Sunday before the arrest, a party of men were held up by two men with pistols, and were relieved of $485. The previous Sunday, a party of men at Delaware Bend were held up and robbed of over $900. Officers from Cooke county investigated the first robbery, while Deputy Burris was called upon to investigate several robberies they committed at **Preston Bend** on travelers passing from Texas to Oklahoma.

He set a trap for the men, and that Saturday, after getting everything in readiness he, along with the other officers, located the three men on foot near Martin Springs, their car had broken down. The lawmen got the drop on the robbers with a shotgun, so no resistance was offered by the men, even though all were armed with 45 caliber revolvers.

The men stated they were residing at Sherman, having moved there from Lawton, Okla. The officers stated the men confessed to holding up the Preston Bend boys, and that officers from Cooke county were coming to confirm their involvement in the Delaware Bend robbery.

They stole a great deal of money and may have lived "high on the hog" for a VERY brief period of time; but considering at the time, robbery with a firearm was a capital offense in Texas, they stood to pay a VERY high price – their very lives.

By December 7, it was discovered the three brothers arrested by Deputy Sheriff D. Burris and other officers were wanted on similar charges elsewhere. It seemed they had been identified as the men who had who committed armed robbery against people around Bonham as well. The three young highwaymen may have had dreams they were the next Jesse James and would be sailing down "Easy Street" soon with all their loot. They were quickly learning the hard way the truth of the old Proverb, "the way of the transgressor is hard." These "road agents" were about to find out how bumpy that ride was about to get!

Adapted from the Denison Gazette and Whitewright Sun - November 6-9, 1917.

Highway Robbery Didn't End "Well"

A young man named Fletcher Cobb was arrested near Preston Bend by Constable Creed Porter for robbing J. A. Daniel while he was en route home to Preston from Sherman with flour, bacon and other articles. Porter found sugar, coffee, and molasses in a ravine, and 200 pounds of flour in Cobb's water well where the robber had hidden them. From information in the Galveston Daily News, April 9, 1891, and Fort Worth Gazette April 11, 1891.

Not just horse thieves were attracted to Preston, but also car thieves, for the same reasons.

THREE MEN ARRESTED ON PRESTON BEND ROAD SUSPECTED.

MACHINE IS SEIZED

AUTHORITIES CLAIM FENCE IS LOCATED AT MADILL AND WICHITA FALLS.

BELIEVE PART OF AUTOMOBILE RING HELD IN SHERMAN

Denison Herald August 30, 1923 - Three professional automobile thieves were put in the custody of Sheriff Everheart's the result of some more quiet and clever work on the part of officers here the trio or apprehended on the Preston Bend road Friday night and taken directly to Sherman where they were grilled by the sheriff and his deputies. It was believed that some confederates would be located, so their apprehension was not disclosed until later. It was ascertained that there were probably no other members of the gang in this vicinity.

Officers were highly elated over their catch which they declared was the best and slickest piece of work since the apprehension of some notorious burglars here more than a year earlier. It was declared that the widespread theft ring of new automobiles in Fort Worth and the organization which they used to conceal their activities had been fully revealed.

Gamblers Had NO CHANCE at Preston Bend

Sunday Gazetteer, Oct 5, 1899 - The gamblers in Denison do at least give their patrons a chance for their money, but the thieving skin games at the fairgrounds were a sure thing for the operators. The Gazetteer learns that several young men of the Preston Bend district were fleeced out of as much as $50. You might say, "Call the sheriff, he will put a stop to this!" Maybe not. This was going on when the Sheriff of Grayson County himself was on the same fairgrounds. He was there all the time and the brazen con men still bilked the Preston Bend locals without fear of apprehension.

Games at the fair and the carnival are rigged and police are powerless to stop it? Say it ain't so!

(There should be a moral in that story somewhere, but you can figure it out).

Mr. Smith Finds Stolen Harness One Year Later

The Sunday Gazetteer. (Denison, Tex.), February 24, 1895 - Friday evening Mr. O.E. Smith of the **Preston Bend** community was in Denison and while passing through the vacant lot in the rear of the State National Bank came across a team of horses which were wearing a harness which he recognized as one which had been stolen from his barn about a year earlier. Officer Lee French was notified of the matter and in a short time the owner of the team, Mr. T. Ragsdale of the Indian Territory appeared. A complaint was filled out in Justice Maynard's court and Ragsdale was arrested, lodged in jail and charged with having stolen property in his possession. The harness was stored in the justice courtroom and the wagon and team were turned over to a friend of Mr. Ragsdale who had accompanied him to the city from the Indian Territory. The trial was set for Feb 25th.

State National Bank, Denison, Texas.

DOUBLE MURDERER HIDES AT PRESTON BEND

A father and son were shot to death in the Chickasaw Nation, in the Lem Reynolds settlement, about twenty miles northeast of Denison. An older black gentleman named Dawson, together with his family, had been residing in the neighborhood for a number of years and had accumulated considerable property. A few weeks earlier, another black man secured employment on a neighboring farm, and last week he and the Dawson family quarreled. The strangers appeared at the Dawson cabin and called the old man to the door, where he was shot down. One of Dawson's sons came to the door and two balls from a Winchester went crashing through his body, the young man falling across the body of his father. The slayer fled to an adjoining wood where he had hidden a stolen animal and escaped to the Texas side of the river. He has been traced to Denison and a posse accompanied by a deputy marshal, went out to the **Preston Bend country,** where it is expected that the murderer will be captured. An atrocious murder was committed in the Reynolds community just a few months earlier, so the neighborhood was very disturbed. Everyone always thinks the same thing – "It can never happen in MY neighborhood!" - Dallas Morning News Dec 6, 1892

SHOOTING REPORTED FROM PRESTON BEND –

Preston Bend was the scene of a shooting yesterday in which a pistol and shotgun were used. The matter, as reported to the officer is that M J. Wallace had an altercation with his father in law, Daley, in which Wallace shot at him several times with a pistol. No shot took effect. Later it is claimed a relative of M. J. Wallace, whose name is James Wallace, met Daley to the road, pointing a shotgun at Daley. Deputy James Dishner of the Preston Bend community arrested the two Wallaces and brought them into Denison yesterday afternoon. They waived examination before Judge Woodward and had their bonds set at $1,000 each which were met yesterday. - Sherman Daily Democrat November 23, 1920.

Preston Postmaster Walter Steel Accosted in Denison – By a Policeman!

Walter Steel of Preston Bend reported to the Sunday Gazetteer in the Sep 30, 1900 issue that while he and his cousin were passing down Main Street in Denison somewhere between Fox & O'Brian's and Madden's store about 12 o'clock the previous Wednesday night, on their return from the Fairgrounds, they were suddenly halted by a man who ordered them to throw up their hands. Asking for an explanation for such treatment, the man told Steel he believed he was the person who had insulted a woman, and that he had to go along with him, and furthermore, if he made much fuss about it, he would clap the irons on him.

Mr. Steel got very heated up by this time and told the officious gentleman that he was not big enough or man enough to make him follow him, nor clap iron him either unless he had a warrant and had some kind of authority behind him.

Just then Steel saw a friend across the street and called him over. This man told who he was and the would-be arresting officer retired, Mr. Steel says he demanded the name of the man who held him up, and he gave it as Walker, who said he was a policeman.

Mr. Steel was at that time the postmaster at Preston and a highly respected citizen who never insulted a woman, nor anyone else.

The moral of this episode is that officers who make a practice of arresting men on mere suspicion without warrants are liable to get themselves and their bondsmen into serious trouble.

At least the policeman and the department of those days didn't have to worry so much about false arrest lawsuits like today.

Compassion of a Doctor and The Cruelty of Another Man, Brings 2 People Together To Begin A Family

Alexander Morrison is the Doctor in this story and he was born in Scotland about 1813. He married Harriet Newell Deveaux/Devoe in 1839 in New York. His daughter Helena Alexandria was born on May 6, 1841, in Napoli, New York. His daughter Harriet Eugenia was born on November 20, 1843, in Sparta, Ontario, Canada.

During the time of the Texas Republic (1836–1846), the Morrison family traveled on a steamer on the Mississippi River, going to Shreveport, Louisiana. They traveled with a man named Dr. Stewart. Then the group traveled on by ox cart to Old McKinney in Collin County, Texas. One source says Dr. Morrison went from McKinney to Weston, in Collin County. He bargained for a headright and a little cabin from a man who wished to dispose of his right. They stayed there for several years, but the Reservation Indians came to steal cattle and horses and sometimes even to kill people. This convinced them to move away from there to Grayson County in 1852.

The Morrisons lived for a while at **Preston Bend,** on the Red River, where the doctor set up his practice. He was one of, if not the earliest physician in the area. On April 14, 1855, he sold his lots in Preston to James G. Thompson, the first county judge of Grayson County.

Since he was a pioneer, Dr. Morrison was able to claim a headright of 640 acres of land which is the Morrison Survey adjoining the old James G. Thompson Survey on one side, and James Ingram Survey on the other. Later he bought 100 or so acres of the James Ingram Survey. Around 1854, the family and their slaves moved there, staying throughout the Civil War. The farm was just north of where Pottsboro was later founded, with early census records listing Sherman as the post office for the farm. In the 1908 plat map, this area was defined as being part of "Georgetown."

Dr. Morrison came to Georgetown in 1854 where he farmed and practiced medicine. He came to Denison soon after the town was mapped out in 1872 and continued medical practice throughout his life. He still kept the land in Georgetown in his family even after his move to Denison, because in 1908 on the plat map, it all still belonged to his two daughters and his son Charley Morrison. He had two female children, Mrs. William Chiles, and Mrs. James Cummins, both of whom were at his bedside at the hour of death. Dr. Morrison's residence at the time of his death was 815 West Main which would have been across the street from the present Waples Methodist Church. Dr. Alexander Morrison died on March 28, 1891, in Denison and his wife, Harriett, died on Valentine's Day in 1882. Harriet became the first person buried in Fairview Cemetery. [Source: Sunday Gazetteer, Denison TX, March 29, 1891]. The cabin/house that Dr. Morrison built was the first built in Denison. After his death, Mr. Esler in Denison (who had the Esler Paint store on Main Street, which still stands) kept Morrison's cabin in his yard for years preserving it, trying to convince city leaders to preserve it for posterity but was unsuccessful. Sadly, he ended up using the logs of the house for firewood. Below: Dr. Morrison's cabin in Denison.

Dr. Morrison – a Georgetown & Preston Resident - Father of Charley Morrison (Mulatto)

By 1850, census records show Doctor Alexander Morrison had land in Grayson County, Texas as a physician and farmer. Dr. Morrison was a well-respected physician all over Grayson County, and at the time, the only one in the Preston area. In the early days of Preston Bend, slavery was legal, and there were hundreds of black slaves living in the Preston and Georgetown area. **But Dr. Morrison treated white and black patients alike.**

By 1850 Grayson County had a population of 2,008, most of whom had come from Southern states. The census enumerated 186 slaves, used mainly by farmers and stockmen along the Red River and its tributaries to raise grains and livestock, cotton being a minor crop in the area until much later.

There were probably some white men who had "romantic" relations with black slaves which resulted in children, some were with mutual consent between both parties, some may not have been. Dr. Morrison had come to Texas from Scotland, which was a very different culture. Dr. Morrison did have black servants, and a Morrison descendant, Jack Chiles, stated that they stayed with Dr. Morrison after they were freed by the government. He must have been good to them, and I also believe that he provided them a school on his land (per 1908 plat map). On Sep 15, 1855, a mixed-race baby boy was born named Charley Morrison. In the 1910 census, Charley was listed as a Mulatto, part white, Indian and black, according to his present family. He served as a houseboy since he was part white, according to his descendant Finus Roy Potts.

According to Jack Chiles' family information and Charles Morrison's death certificate signed by Dr. Freeman, and his inheritance from Dr. Morrison, Alex Morrison either had some sort of an affair with a lady named Janie Smith who was believed to be mixed race (black and Indian according to her descendants) with Charley Morrison being the son, because he gave him land along with his own two daughters after his death. Plus, it was Charley Morrison's own daughter Myrtle Johnson who provided information which listed Dr. Morrison as the father. Also, I spoke to James Clement, a modern-day Georgetown resident, and he recalled that at the time, local people were surprised to learn that this black family had received an inheritance of 50 acres from a white doctor who had other children, and thought he must be the father for this to have occurred.

According to military records, on August 6, 1863, Dr. Morrison, at age forty-seven, enlisted for six months in the Confederate army at Camp Stonewall in Collin County. He was a private in Company B, Cavalry, 15th Battalion, Texas State Troops, under Capt. John Goode; the company's ranks were drawn from Collin and Grayson counties. The doctor worked as a military surgeon during this time. Information from descendants Ray Potts and Newell Cummins stated that one of Dr. Morrison's servants, Charley Morrison, who was a houseboy in the doctor's house, went through the Civil War with Dr. Morrison as a personal servant. After the slaves were freed and the Civil War came to an end, the African Americans who had been his slaves stayed with him, probably working as sharecroppers.

Dr. Alexander Morrison's wife and daughters managed the farm while he was away serving the Confederacy. Soon after the war ended, both the Morrison daughters married Confederate veterans from Missouri. Helen Morrison, on August 24, 1865, married James Hunter ("Jim") Cummins (1842–1890), from Harrisonville, Cass County, Missouri. Harriet Eugenia Morrison, in 1866 married William Ballinger ("Bill") Chiles Sr. (1844–1900).

Alex Morrison was an extremely intelligent man, who loved reading and learning; and valued education for all people. He spent his life furthering education and it is believed he was instrumental in installing a colored school on his land at Georgetown. He was ahead of his time in seeing that "colored" people at the time had equal opportunities.

He also saw to it that his own daughters were well educated, something else that was not common at the time. Females were not encouraged to be scholars at the time. He even had hopes that one of his daughters would follow him in becoming a doctor. He often took his daughters with him on house calls as would-be apprentices.

His daughters were also well versed in the social graces. They were well known in society, both good dancers and went to many parties at 'Aunt' Sophia Porter's" (The History of Grayson County, Texas, vol. 1, published by Grayson County Frontier Village).

RESIDENCE OF MRS. HELEN A. CUMMINS, 1031 WEST BOND STREET.

1908 Plat Map for Georgetown below shows the only local colored school located on the land belonging to Charley Morrison, son of Doctor Alexander Morrison. Land just to the east and south belonged to the other heirs of Dr. Alexander Morrison – his daughters Helen Alexandria Morrison Cummings, and Harriet Eugenia Morrison Chiles, his white half-sisters.

Finus Ray Potts, a descendant of Dr. Morrison and Charley Morrison has some great stories about his ancestors which has been passed down through his family. He said he had multiple Native American ancestors who came west on the Trail of Tears. Janie Smith, who was said to be the mistress of Dr. Alexander Morrison, and the mother of Charley Morrison, was reported to be mixed race Native American and African from the island of Madagascar. He also stated that Dr. Morrison's white wife was aware of Janie and Charley.

Ray Potts told the interesting and tragic story of how Charley Morrison and his wife met each other. Lucy was a young servant at **Preston Bend** for one of the wealthy farmers there, whose name Mr. Potts cannot recall. But records indicate her last name may have been Young, which means she or her parents once "belonged" to a farmer named Young since it was the custom for slaves to take the last name of their masters. Lucy made the man angry with her for some inconsequential reason, and he hit her on the head with an axe and threw her out into a field to bleed to death. He ordered that no one was to help her. After dark though, some of the other servants sneaked out to get her and summoned Dr. Morrison to come to tend her to save her life. Charley came with him and their acquaintance began and grew into marriage and children. Charles "Charley" Morrison married Lucy Young (according to a Grayson County marriage license) in 1872 and one of their daughters was named Lillie Myrtle Morrison. She married Jack Johnson and they lived in Georgetown there on the site of the old colored school on her father and grandfather's land just south of present-day Reeves Road. The house where Myrtle lived was built in 1890 and as of today is still standing and is in surprisingly good shape inside and out, considering its age and its vacancy. It is located in the spot where the 1908 map says the colored school was located. One of Charley Morrison's daughters, Myrtle, continued to live in the home Dr. Morrison left

Charley near Pottsboro up until the 1980s. Below is the house in Georgetown where Myrtle Johnson lived, which still stands.

Charley Morrison (1855–1935) died of pellagra in Denison in 1935. His death certificate, signed by Dr. William M. Freeman, stated that Charley's father was "Dr. Morrison." His mother, another of the doctor's slaves, was Janie Smith (born in 1830). Charley's youngest daughter, Clara George Morrison Bell (1893–1960), was the mother of Charles Samuel Bell (1909–2008), a landscaper who worked for prominent white families in Denison for many years. His obituary said, "Charles would always look his best, even wearing a shirt and tie while working in the yard. He was proud of his profession and handed his knowledge and work ethic on to his grandchildren. . . . He was a faithful deacon for over 65 years at Hopewell Baptist Church. Charles was also a member of the H.A. Coleman Masonic Lodge, where he served as Senior Warden and Senior Deacon until his health failed." It has often been said that the African American founders of Hopewell Church came from Preston Bend. This makes sense because, in the earlier days in Preston Bend, there were many people of color, and the "colored" church there was very strong and active. When these spiritual people moved to Denison, they took their faith with them. Charlie Bell and Clara Morrison Bell are both buried in Jeremiah Cemetery southeast of Denison. They were among Dr. Morrison's descendants — **a family brought together by both cruelty and kindness.**

MORRISON – POTTS CONNECTION

Another part of Ray Potts family in Preston Bend, on the Potts side, was Randall Potts. He owned land on the Red River bottom. Bottomland made for excellent farmland, so there were some who covetously cast their envious eyes upon his place, wanting it for their own. One particular white man, thinking that a black man would make a vulnerable target whom no one would care about, he tried to lynch Mr. Randall Potts for his land. Well, Potts didn't go down without a fight, in fact, he didn't go down at all. There was a shootout and the Potts clan won, the covetous guy died. One casualty of the Potts family was a nephew of Randall Potts. In fear of being killed, he swam the Red River to Oklahoma and was never heard from by the Potts family again.

RANDALL POTTS – Resident of Preston Bend

Age 0 — **Birth**
abt 1868 • Texas

Age 2 — **Residence**
1870 • Precinct 1, Grayson, Texas, USA
Residence Post Office: Sherman

Age 25 — **Marriage**
1893 • Grayson, Texas, United States
Lizzie Huff
(1874-)

Age 32 — **Residence**
1900 • Justice Precinct 8, Grayson, Texas, USA
Marital Status: Married; Relation to Head: Head

Age 42 — **Residence**
1910 • Justice Precinct 8, Grayson, Texas, USA
Marital Status: Married; Relation to Head of House: Head

Age 52 — **Residence**
1920 • Pottsboro, Grayson, Texas, USA
Relation to Head: Head; Residence Marital Status: Widowed

Age 62 — **Residence**
1930 • Precinct 2, Grayson, Texas, USA
Marital Status: Widowed; Relation to Head: Head

Parents

Julias Potts
1830-

Emaline Potts
1834-

Spouse & Children

Lizzie Huff
1874-

Harry Potts
1896-

Shug Potts
1899-

Besie Potts
1900-

Lafayette Potts
1902-

Zeffie Potts
1904-

Randall Potts
1907-1971

Sam Edward Potts
1908-

Spouse & Children

Overton Potts
1911-

Ora Potts
1911-

Randall Potts' son Randall worked at Yellow Jacket Boat Company in Denison. His son Sam Edward was a Trucker. But…. Randall's son Harry is another story… but he isn't really a bad guy in this case.

Herb Jackson Goes to the Show Sherman Daily Democrat Jan 25, 1917

J. R. Dishner, D. L. Jackson, J. W. Fawcett and wife, E. P. Jackson and wife, J. W. Kennedy and wife, W. J. Fawcett and wife, Mrs. Belle Williams and Misses Mansker, Noble, Meadows and Buford and Messrs. Joe Meadows, J. D. Bell, Ross Meadows, Wash Fawcett and Herb Jackson saw "The Birth of a Nation" at the Star Theatre in Denison Saturday evening..... Mrs.

Herb Jackson Goes to the Pen Sherman Daily Democrat June 28, 1917

Two Years.
Herb Jackson pleaded guilty to a charge of burglary and was given two years in the state penitentiary.

Herb Jackson Goes to the Cemetery Denison Herald

FATAL SHOOTING PRESTON BEND June 3, 1919

Herb Jackson, a white man aged 26 years, who was reared in the Preston Bend community, was shot and killed by a black youth by the name of **Harry Potts**.

According to the story of **Randall Potts, father of the shooter,** who was brought to Denison and lodged in jail, the trouble came about in the following manner: **Potts and his son had gone to the home of Jim Roan, a black farmer, and neighbor of Potts,** to see about getting hands to help chop cotton. Jackson was at the place and it appears had some grievance against the elder Potts. He immediately started quarreling and finally knocked Potts down, either with his bare fists or with brass knuckles, and just as the man was getting up, Herb Jackson fired at him with a pistol. The bullet plowed across the Potts's face, cutting a gash in his cheek and across his nose, and the range was so close, his face was badly powder burned. At his juncture, Harry Potts stepped up, drew a pistol and fired on Jackson, two bullets taking effect, one in the mouth and one in the side, producing almost instant death.

Harry Potts left the scene and was not apprehended immediately. His father, who was suffering from the bullet wound in the face, made no effort to leave the scene. In fact, he claimed there should be no charge against him and he was brought to jail at his own request for protection, as he said he was afraid he would be killed if he remained in the neighborhood. He was brought in by local Deputy Sheriffs Jim Dishner and Bud Jackson, and a physician was summoned to dress his wound, which was quite painful.

Herb Jackson, the slain man, was unmarried but had a number of relatives in the Preston Bend community. He was found guilty of gaming and causing a disturbance in March 1917. He is said to have had trouble on two or three occasions and is also said to have been paroled from the penitentiary at the time of his death (that was true). Funeral services and burial were held at Preston under the direction of J. L. Swank.

Whitewright Sun June 6, 1919 - A complaint charging Harry Potts of Preston Bend with murder was filed in Justice R. A. McCrary's court at Sherman as a result of the shooting death of Herb Jackson, 26 years old, at Preston. Wasn't Harry just defending his father Randall Potts' life because Jackson shot at him first?

Another Tragedy Hits the Potts Family at Preston Bend

Denison Daily Cresset, August 31, 1875 - On Sunday evening, a black man named Shadrach Potts, living on the farm of Col. Massey, started on horseback for Denison. In company with his two children, he crossed a stream called the Little Mineral, but on arriving at the Shawnee, it was out of its banks, owing to the heavy rainfall, and he was unable to cross. He then abandoned the idea of coming to Denison and turned back to return home. When he arrived at the Little Mineral, it was also very high, but he determined to swim it, taking both the children with him. He rode the horse into the stream, but the water was so deep the horse lost its footing and commenced to sink. One of the children was swept away and drowned, and the other rescued by Potts. The body of the child was found in the bed of the creek Monday evening and was brought to Denison and buried.

They had not yet invented the term – "Turn around – Don't drown." Never enter a flood. Turn around, and go around, your life is worth more than the few moments you would save by hurrying through the water, like Mr. Potts. He turned around once, but took one chance too many.

Preston Bend Boy Critically Burned in Jail Fire

The Madill News November 13, 1908 - On an otherwise ordinary Wednesday night at 8:30 when the prisoners were usually preparing for sleep, they were instead crying out for help.

The jail was on fire. Men from the community rushed to the scene and found the doors all locked (of course, it's a jail, right!) and all the officers gone for the evening.

Three people could be seen through the window of the jail writhing in agony in the flames while the clothes burned from their bodies. This redoubled the efforts being made to break the locks on the outer doors. The groans, moans, prayers, and screams of pain from inside the jail made minutes seem like hours to the rescuers and added even more urgency to their mission. One man broke a window and the heavy screening on it with an ax and was armed with a fire extinguisher which he used to some effect on some of the burning men, though he was probably too late.

An Indian man named Walter Davis died of burns. Another Indian man named Seeler was burned but not seriously. Some others suffered from suffocation and smoke inhalation.

R. P. Potts, a boy of 14 years, was burned grievously and expected to die. Young Potts had a mother at **Preston Bend**.

The fire was believed to have started due to Walter Davis having set fire to the bedding in his cell.

Preston Bend Farmer Became Rich "Copper King" Told by Uncle Rip Aug 21, 1925

..... with a connection to the Potts family.

This is the true story of W. F. Green told by Uncle Rip of Preston Bend, (J. W. Fawcett) who prides himself in giving his readers the truth in everything, provided it has no connection with fish stories.

William Green was known as Bill, who with his brother Charlie, came to Preston Bend in 1873. Bill was a medium sized man with a pleasant face and laughing blue eyes that could change in an instant and like sharpened steel, go right through you. He dressed like all the young farmers – a broad-brimmed straw hat in summer, with a hickory shirt and generally a pair of homemade pants with lots of room to move, with more room to spare. The farmer's wardrobe was finished and considered ample when they put their feet into a pair of brogans. These shoes were very coarse in every particular, generally made from bull's hide leather, and oftentimes the leather was split, making two pieces from one thickness. These shoes resembled a wooden glut (a large wooden wedge) more than anything else.

That these brothers came from some northern state was easily discerned from their brogue (accent). Now Bill was domiciled at the home of **Hayne Potts,** known and beloved by all good citizens. He was an ex-Confederate soldier. Bill made a share crop, now known as fifty-fifty; Bill to do the work and **"Uncle" Hayne Potts** as we all called him, to furnish teams, tools, board, and bed. The teams consisted of a yoke of oxen - great, big, rawboned Spanish cattle that answered to the names of Broad and Berry. They were so tall, an ordinary man would tiptoe to see over their shoulders. These oxen, hitched with a log chain to a heavy, home-made plow, were used to prepare the ground for the crop, and in the fall, the oxen were hooked to a home-made wagon with wooden axles lubricated with pine tar taken from the tar bucket swinging from the coupling pole. The tar had a pleasant aroma that might be detected two hundred yards away, if to the windward. Now for the planting and cultivating of this crop, the motive power was a little Spanish mule that possibly weighed six hundred pounds. This little fellow's name was Pete. It wasn't his fault that he couldn't hear, for he too had been in the Confederate army, and it may have been shell shock that made him deaf, or it might have been because he'd left his teens some fifteen years before, as the gray hairs on his ears, legs, and flanks indicated. He was at least well up into his twenties. His body, like his mind, was never very active. Green hitched Pete to a clumsy affair called a bull-tongue stock, and this was home-made too. Now it was often said back then, by using a grass horse and a buttermilk man, what you would make a clear profit. Pete rustled his own living, until roasting ear time, and then generally helped himself while the folks slept. Green was sumptuously fed, for Aunt Pew, Uncle Hayne's wife, was a splendid cook, with an abundance of every necessity and many luxuries not now obtainable.

With these teams and tools, Green made 100 bushels of Irish potatoes, seven bales of cotton, and a good corn crop. The next year, Green confined his crop to cotton exclusively and made eight bales. This he hauled to Denison and sold to a man in or near the 200 block of Main Street by the name of **Goldsoll.**

Denison Daily Herald April 25, 1878

Hayne Potts knew the Goldsoll store had it all on the 200 block of Main Street in Denison; clothes, jewelry and they buy your cotton crop too! In the settlement for this last crop, Uncle Hayne claimed he did not get an equal division from Green. Both parties became dissatisfied, causing Bill Green to leave Preston. Uncle

Hayne Potts tried to keep track of Green (to collect what he felt was owed to him) and finally found he went to the army, then to the Rocky Mountains, and fought Indians. But Bill had an eye open for anything that promised wealth, for Bill often told the writer that someday he expected to be worth a million dollars.

Being in that new country, while with the army, this gave him the opportunity to examine the local minerals, using all his spare time for this purpose. Bill Green finally came upon a rich vein of copper. He marked the spot, as in three months, his time in the army would expire. After his discharge, he returned to this spot and found it, just as he had left it. Having saved his money while in the army, he went to New York City and interested moneyed men, forming a company and worked not only this vein but others too. Now Bill from Preston Bend became Colonel William P. Green and was frequently spoken of as the "Copper King," which this writer believes he deserved. Uncle Hayne Potts found in a paper, certain quotations from the copper market and quite often the name of W. P. Green appeared, and he was referred to as the Copper King. Thinking this might be his missing Bill Green, (who still owed him money), he wrote letters to his New York address, but to no effect.

Finally, he applied to A. S. Noble, who was at that time a merchant at Preston, then later the auditor of Grayson County, who suggested that he make out his bill, with the accrued interest, which was done.

Mr. Noble enclosed it with a letter to Colonel Green and requested Green's private secretary to see that it was delivered to Green, which must have been done, for in a reasonable length of time, there came a check for a little over $800, for this had accumulated, principal and interest, in the ensuing 34 years to reach the above sum, and a nice letter telling of some of Green's history since he was a cotton farmer in Preston Bend. He stated he had ordered that debt settled long ago and hoped the money might be a comfort to Uncle Hayne in his declining years, which it did prove to be, for in 1908, the Red River flooded out of its banks and rose up to the ceiling in Uncle Hayne Potts' home in Preston. He went to Pottsboro, bought a little home and died, and in about a year, his good wife followed him to heaven.

A. G. Noble   *A. S. Noble*

A. G. NOBLE & COMPANY

General Merchandise

Implements, Undertakers' Supplies

Etc.

PRESTON   ::   **TEXAS**

1908

Colonel Green finally became immensely wealthy, with mining interests in the United States and in Old Mexico, with railroads through that republic, as well as oil interests. It was around 1910 or before when the writer read an article saying that W. P. Green, the Copper King, was killed down in Old Mexico. His driver lost control of a pair of spirited horses and the vehicle was torn in pieces - but not before he paid the debt he owed Uncle Hayne Potts of Preston Bend for 34 years.

So ended the life of the old Preston Bend farmer, Bill Green who became the Copper King.

Next is another version of the same story with a few different details a few years later:

145

Haynes Potts and Bill Green - The Swindler Who Became a King - A Strange Story of the Indian Territory Days

William R. Strong came to Indian Territory in the 1870s and in 1931 was living comfortably on his southern Oklahoma homestead, near Preston Bend. Mr. Strong was past 70 years of age, when relating this story and well remembers and fondly recalls the scenes of early days when the now highly developed State of Oklahoma was wild and primitive, exuberant with tall grasses, clear running streams, and virgin timber. He says it was beautiful to behold all this natural beauty before man plowed up the land, cut down the trees and built towns and cities in it.

Wild buffalo, deer, and turkey were there by the thousands. You did not have to be an expert hunter to kill all the game wanted. Living in those days was a simple matter, said Mr. Strong. With little help, a man could build for his family a log cabin out of forest trees that cost him nothing, just his own labor. If well built, the cabin of two or three rooms could be made as comfortable as any home of today. The rifle and an abundant variety of wild game just about solved the food problem. As for clothing, those who did not want to wear home-spun clothes could be well dressed and quite comfortable in the furs of wild animals. Pants made of deer robes or buffalo robes were stylish and becoming, thinks Mr. Strong. He also thinks pioneer folks got along about as well as folks of today. "In most ways, they were a lot happier," he said, "less envious, less selfish, and less snobbish."

When the Strongs established their home near Preston Bend, on the north side of the Red River at THAT time, they had few neighbors. One of the nearest neighbors was the Hayne Potts family, who lived just across Red River on an 80-acre farm.

In the fall of 1884, a black jaundice epidemic swept that part of the country, which was on the borders of the lowlands of Red

146

River. Not much was known about black jaundice in those days or how to treat it. ("Black jaundice" usually refers to what is now known as Wiel's Disease. This viral disease is caused by a germ found in the urine of cattle, horses, dogs, and rats.) As a result, the dread disease almost wiped out the Strong and Potts families, proving fatal to all five children in the Potts family and to all children in the Strong family except one. Mary Lee Strong survived the disease. The loss of all their children left Mr. and Mrs. Potts sad and lonely. About this time, a young man, 25 years of age, appeared at the Potts' home and asked for work. He was a stranger in the community, but strangers were always welcomed without question in the best pioneer homes of Preston and the old Indian Territory. Suspicion or mistrust were not traits of the pioneer. Mr. Potts employed the stranger to put in a share crop on his farm.

"About this time a young man appeared at the Potts home and asked for work"

All went well, for a time. The young man was of good habits and a hard worker, though not a good mixer, remaining aloof somewhat and taking no part in the social activities of the community.

The season was good for all crops and the cotton yield was heavy. The nearest cotton market was Denison. As fast as Mr. Potts' tenant gathered his cotton, he would have it baled, haul it to Denison and store it, saying he intended to hold it for better prices. Mr. Potts fully trusted the young man, never doubting that he was honest and that his judgment was sound as to the best time to sell the stored cotton.

Finally, the young tenant picked his last bale of cotton, had it ginned and hauled it to Denison. By now he had in Denison twenty bales that he gathered from the Potts farm. He asked buyers to bid on the cotton, accepted the highest bid, sold the entire twenty bales, put all the money in his pocket and skipped out for parts unknown – **especially unknown to Mr. Potts!**

Several days elapsed before Mr. Potts found out that he had been swindled of his part of the cotton crop money. It was a severe blow to Potts and his good wife, who were relatively poor and had gone into debt in order to finance the young tenant. Officers worked hard on the case but were unable to locate the defaulter. His disappearance remained a deep mystery until twenty-four years later when his whereabouts were discovered through a newspaper advertisement. While Mr. Strong was reading a newspaper one day, he noted that the name of Potts' former tenant farmer appeared in an advertisement featuring copper mining stocks. An investigation followed which linked the name in the advertisement with a well-known **millionaire** who had made a fortune out of mining in Mexico and was now living in New York City. Mr. Potts addressed a letter to the millionaire in which he inquired if he were the young man who had raised a crop of cotton on his Indian Territory farm twenty-four years ago. No reply came to this first letter. A second letter was written by Mr. Potts and addressed to the millionaire's secretary in which he politely reminded the secretary that unless an answer was received soon to his second letter, he intended to turn the entire matter over to the authorities and demand a full investigation. In a few days, a draft was received by Mr. Potts from New York covering the entire amount of the tenant's deficit with 8 percent interest added for the full period of twenty-four years. The total amount was $1,800.00. But Mr. and Mrs. Potts have long since died. They were dear friends of Mr. and Mrs. Strong, and while recalling them as their first and nearest neighbors, Mr. Strong told the strange story of the defaulting tenant farmer. - Eufaula Indian Journal November 19, 1931.

The Sunday Gazetteer (Denison, Tex.), August 19, 1906

An old account book, the property of A. D. Budlong dealer in hides and furs, has just come to light. It shows that in 1873, 51,000 buffalo robes were received here from the region beyond Jacksborc, about 100 miles distant from Denison. In the same year a few buffalo were seen in the Preston Bend district. It is supposed that they had been chased to the settlements by the Comanches.

HOT PORK Dallas Morning News, Jan 30, 1886 - B. B. Perry of Preston Bend was taken before Judge Adams and bound over under a bond of $200 to appear to answer the charge of hog stealing. **AND MORE HOT PORK** - Dallas Morning News May 19, 1890 - **Bill Potts,** a black man living eight miles northwest in the Preston Bend Community, came to town and offered a large quantity of bacon and lard for sale. The fact was reported by merchants. Later in the day, Farmer West, also of the Preston Bend neighborhood, came in and reported to the officers the depletion of his smokehouse. In the meantime, Sheriff McAfee arrived from Sherman and an hour later, Potts was behind the bars in the city jail. Two other men were implicated in the burglary, but have evaded the officers.   The Sunday Gazetteer. (Denison, Tex.),   August 10, 1890 -   **Bill Potts** of Preston Bend was arrested and lodged in jail in Denison at the instigation of his bondsman, as they intimated a desire to released from his bond.   Potts was charged with several high crimes and misdemeanors. He was expected to remain in jail without bond until the meeting of District Court in September, and afterward, the prospects were that he would spend a number of years at Huntsville prison.

Former Preston Bend Resident and Son Dead Under Much Different Circumstances

Rev. G. Beauregard Potts, a well-known black Baptist preacher, died very suddenly at his home on a farm about 5 miles north of Sherman, in the Iron Ore settlement. He was in apparent good health up until a few minutes of his death. He worked all day in his own cotton field the previous day, not complaining in the least.   He was suddenly attacked with congestive chill and although Dr. A. N. Prince was immediately summoned, Rev. Potts died before the physician could reach him.   Rev. Beauregard Potts' sudden death recalls the recent tragic ending of the career of his son, Leonard Potts, who was riddled with bullets by a posse in the Red River bottoms near Woodland, a little inland settlement north of Detroit, Red River County, on the afternoon of August 5, just one month to the day before his father's death. Rev. Beauregard Potts was an industrious, law-abiding citizen and the boy, Leonard, while he lived in Grayson County was looked as a peaceable young man. In fact, he never had any serious trouble until that which brought him to his death.   Rev. Beauregard Potts was 50 years old, a native of Grayson County, having been born in Preston Bend March 12, 1862. While he was a hard-working farmer, he was also an ordained Baptist preacher and had held services for years in the old black church house known and Honey

Run in the vicinity of where he lived and where the death occurred. Only recently Rev. Potts had been preaching at a protracted meeting being held in the Iron Ore community and his sermons were listened to by the black and white community alike. He was a member of Prince Star Lodge No. 196, colored Masons, and of Caney Commandery, Knights Templar. He was buried at the Iron Ore cemetery.

More Theft

The Sunday Gazetteer. (Denison, Tex.), June 15, 1890 - Fred Young, a black man from Preston Bend was arrested and taken before Judge Cook on a charge of burglary and two charges of theft.

Guilty of Purse Theft, Present During a Death at Preston Bend

Sherman Daily Democrat, February 6, 1917 – Luther Brown, a black man was found guilty of stealing a purse containing $10 which belonged to I. G. Kay. He was sentenced to six months in jail in the county court. Mr. Brown is the man who was in the tent with a man who was killed in the "good roads" project camp near Preston Bend some months previous. It was not mentioned if he had any culpability in that case.

Slander ... Then Jail-Breaking May 11, 1888,

Deputy Sheriff McAffee, accompanied by Constable Porter of Pottsboro, arrived in the city with Leroy Henderson whom they lodged in jail. Henderson was convicted on a charge of slander several months ago, and while at work on the county farm serving out his fine, made his escape and remained at large for several months till yesterday when officers arrested him at Preston Bend, this county.

Fort Worth Daily Gazette

Above are coyotes killed by ranchers to protect their livestock along the Red River in 1966. At that time, there were only coyotes still existing in this area, and there were bounties paid on them by the government. In the 1800s, there were many wolves which roamed the woods.

Dallas Morning News - Jan 23, 1892 - In the celebrated wolf scalp case of Vaden vs. Grayson county the court granted the plaintiff a new hearing on the ground that the word "lobo," which appears in the stature, was a Mexican word and really meant any kind of a wolf except the coyote.

Charles Harrison of Preston Bend was put in jail in default of two bonds of $1,000 each, in cases where he was charged with assaults to murder Officers Hackney and Ford of Dension. One day later.......Charles Harrison and Sam Smart came to Denison on the train from Pottsboro and after getting full of bad whiskey, proceeded to paint the town red. A number of shots were discharged in Ed Ford's saloon on South Austin Avenue, and a few moments later, both men were arrested and jailed. - Sunday Gazetteer January 24, 1892

3. THE STORMS OF LIFE...DIDN'T PASS PRESTON BEND BY – NATURAL DISASTERS

PRESTON BEND TORNADO DRAINS LAKE DRY

By Natalie Clountz Bauman

On May 2, 1893, a twister that went through Valley View paid Grayson county a visit. From the narrative below, it can be seen that people then were still very unfamiliar with the workings of these destructive storms.

Ben Perry of Preston Bend told of a disastrous tornado which came through just before sunset. Preston is remote from railroad or telegraph communication, and while in this county, it is at the extreme northern reaches of the county. It is nearly, if not quite twenty-five miles from Sherman. The path of destruction was only about 100 yards wide and in that width, everything was swept clean. It came from the southwest and moved toward the northeast. A house on the Bennett farm was torn down and a house on the Maxwell place, was torn into kindling wood, but not one of the occupants was hurt. Joe Combs' place was torn to pieces and Mrs. Combs hurt on the neck. A little baby was blown fifty yards into a brush pile, where it was found uninjured. A dead goose and a dead cat were found on either side of the child. The fowl was picked nearly clean of its feathers. Alfred Smith, two other young men, and their sister saw the tornado approaching and did not succeed in getting entirely clear of its path and were

153

all slightly hurt. Mr. Ferry, in describing the action of the storm, says that at the top there was a very black cloud, very closely resembling a volume of smoke from a large smokestack. At the bottom of it was the deadly funnel. Though the main path was not over 100 yards wide, timber for twice that distance on either side was damaged and twisted. There seemed to be a powerful suction in the main body and wagons and other objects at some distance were almost drawn into it. Stumps were literally blown up and the earth rolled up in mounds. The crops over which it passed are mown down and scorched.

Information from Woodville, Indian Territory (just to the north across the river from Preston) has come in, to the effect that about sunset, the cyclone struck that place. The residence of a man named Voss was completely wrecked as was that of Ed Hollinger, whose family saw the storm approaching and escaped to the stormhouse of a neighbor and were not hurt. The residence of Ben Rubes and John Thomas were wrecked, but no one was injured. Fences, outhouses, etc. were completely obliterated and not a piece of timber of several of the houses could be found within a quarter mile of where they previously stood.

Perhaps the most astonishing fact: Burke's Lake, on the Texas side of the River, was left comparatively dry, the cyclone siphoning up and carrying the water off in the shape of a water-spout.

The Woodville correspondent of the Denison Herald says: "The first place it struck squarely was that of R. W. Voss. His house was completely destroyed, no two pieces of it being left together. Two of his horses were badly injured. The family barely escaped by running out from the house. His wagon was literally torn to pieces and scattered along the track of the storm. It next struck S. D. Hollinger's place, one-half mile further on, where equal ruin was wrought. Hollinger's family saw the cyclone coming and ran to a near neighbor's, taking refuge in a stormhouse. Next was Ben Ruth's house, which was torn down. He and his family were in the house, but strange to say, none of them were hurt. Mr. Thomas was the next sufferer. Two log houses at his place were blown down, but not being in the path of the storm proper, were not so badly wrecked as the others. Trees, fences, chickens, geese, hogs, birds; in fact everything in the path of the cloud monster, was torn, twisted, mangled and piled together in its path, leaving a scene of chaos terrible to look upon."

As the people of the time expressed, the most amazing thing to this writer is the fact that a Lake was sucked dry by the tornado. I thought that was only the stuff of urban legends. Apparently, truth really is stranger than fiction!   -From a story in the Dallas Morning News on May 2, 1893.

Destructive Wind Storm   Denison Daily Herald June 2, 1905

Preston suffered considerably from the recent storm. Several houses were blown off their foundations. Fred Worbe's house was rendered almost uninhabitable. Tom Harris' house was demolished considerably. The east end of the M.E. church was blown away and the derrick at the oil well was blown down. C. S. Meadow's store was blown off its blocks. Timber is scattered in every direction. Red River is higher than it has been for years.

Tornado and Flood Takes Preston Bend Lives

The Peoples' Voice (Norman, Okla) May 29, 1908 - A cyclone (tornado) struck southern Oklahoma and thirteen sight-seers from Preston Bend on Red River were watching the dividing floods of the river from an island in the vicinity of Colbert. They were swept away by a flash flood of water which engulfed the island and all were lost. The loss of life and property was heavy in Oklahoma.

Severe Hail Storm at Preston Bend

Dallas Morning News, March 15, 1904 - Farmers from the country west of Pottsboro and extending into the Preston Bend section reported a very severe hailstorm. W. B. Golden, who resides three miles west of Pottsboro, says a very heavy hailstorm did considerable damage at his place. All window lights on the west side of the house were knocked out and all the roofs on the south and west sides of the houses were demolished, so heavy were the hailstones and so terrible their velocity. Young trees were literally whipped to pieces.

Ike Clements, on the Preston Bend road, reported a very severe hailstorm, damaging roofs and windows and killing chickens in the barnyards. W. S. Reeves reports damage to window lights and roofs, and barnyard fowls killed by the terrific hail.

Ed McLean, living about five miles west of Pottsboro at Willow Springs, reported serious damage in his neighborhood. The windows on the west side of the house were all broken out, and roofs on the west and south sides of houses were damaged so that buildings will be reroofed. W. B. Chiles, living west of Pottsboro, reported a very heavy hail and considerable damage.

W. B. Coonrod reports roofs severely damaged, window lights were destroyed and chickens killed.

This reminds the writer of a horrendous hailstorm which attacked this same area in 1996. Those hailstones were larger than softballs and had spikes all around the hailstones. We were in a cellar and it sounded like someone was throwing bricks on to the door. Being outside the door would have been deadly. This was the worst ever experienced in my lifetime and I hope to never see it again.

If a Tree Falls in Preston Bend...... Will it land on someone?

Dallas Weekly Herald March 02, 1878 - While an Indian man was chopping wood near Preston Bend, a tree fell on him and crushed him to death.

Denison Daily News   June 5, 1880

On Thursday a young man named Hancock, living near Preston Bend, was seriously injured by having a tree fall upon him while chopping it down. His spine was injured and his lower limbs paralyzed.

Denison Daily News August 15, 1879

It is reported that while some workmen were engaged in putting up the frame work of a new building near Preston Bend, the timber gave way, precipitating a carpenter named Watkins to the ground and breaking his neck. The deceased leaves a wife and ten children. in Sherman.

DEADLY LIGHTNING STRIKES AT GLEN EDEN

Don't take shelter underneath a tall tree in a lightning storm, you may not live to regret it, and you wouldn't be the first.

May 2, 1878, the Denison Daily News brought the story to the world that tragedy had struck with a flash of blinding light and an ear-splitting noise that shook the earth.

Mr. Barbour was a relative of Judge Porter of Glen Eden at Preston Bend. He reported to the News that on that Tuesday about mid-morning on Judge Porter's farm, there was a terrible lightning storm. Several hands were out in the wheat field working when this storm came up.

Two of the workers were black men, Jasper Gray, about 40; and Robert Bohannon, about 25 years of age. Bohannon had lived here for a long time and had a family. Jasper Gray recently came to the area from Mississippi. They sought shelter under a large tree and stood just outside of the field, waiting for the storm to pass to resume their work.

There was a vivid flash of lightning followed by a tremendous thunderclap almost immediately after the lightning struck the tree the men were standing under.

The other hands, who were not more than thirty or forty feet away, felt the tremors in the ground and saw the two men fall to the ground.

They immediately ran to their assistance and found Mr. Gray lying on his face eight or ten feet from the tree, quite dead. Mr. Bohannon was lying on his back, and on being taken hold of, showed signs of animation. He soon recovered sufficiently to talk and asked if they had been struck by lightning. Mr. Barbour said, "Bob, you are all right." "Yes," said he, "I am all right," and asked for a drink of water. It was offered him in a jug, but he could not drink it. While someone was going after a cup, he said, "Boys, straighten out my legs," and then with his tongue protruding from his mouth, died immediately.

Strange to say, the lightning left no marks of violence on either body, although the tree they were standing under and which the lightning struck, was considerably shattered.

Lightning Strike Causes Mass Baptism on Little Mineral at Preston - Denison Daily News July 23, 1878

There is a great religious revival occurring among the black people at Preston Bend. This happened because a few weeks earlier, two of the workers on Judge Porter's place were killed by lightning.

A day or two after that, a team ran away and broke another black worker's leg.

The people there are very superstitious and interpreted these occurrences as special visitations of Providence expressing His displeasure at the spiritual condition of His church at Preston Bend, and the result was that nearly all the black people there experienced renewed religious fervor. The black preacher at Preston was kept busy baptizing the converts. Twenty-eight were immersed in Little Mineral just the first Sunday, with more expected later.

Bad news ══▶ Good News.

PECAN TREES IN PRESTON BEND IN DANGER OF BREAKING

Why? The Dallas Morning News reporter on Oct. 5, 1897, was in Preston Bend and found the pecan trees so laden down with nuts until they were bending to the ground in some places under the heavy load.

He had never seen such a crop of pecans in all his life in Texas. Red River bottom for twenty miles was seen to be rich in pecans. (It still is to this day!). Some years, it is true the harvest of pecans, or any nut, is particularly heavy as it was in 1897.

Post-Independence Day Fireworks at Preston – But NO Cheering

Denison Daily Herald, July 6, 1905 - There may have been many beautiful fireworks displays around Preston and along the Red River on the 4th of July to commemorate America's Independence from England. These were eagerly anticipated by all and much appreciated. However, nature itself put on a most unwelcome light show the next night.

About 8 o'clock pm, a storm that looked as if it might easily develop into a cyclone (tornado) passed down the Red River. The storm cloud gathered somewhere near Preston Bend and swept steadily down the river, breaking and disappearing in the east within a few minutes after it first appeared. Branches were torn from trees as the storm passed, but no serious damage was reported. Of course, the lightning put on a fearsome, but glorious display.

RED RIVER FLOOD OF 1 8 4 4 & 1 8 4 9

Mrs. Sophia Porter of Preston Bend related the story how in 1844 the rise in Red River reached her dwelling, and she sailed out of the front door of her home in a skiff. Pioneer women had to be adaptable, tough and resourceful. Sophia certainly was all that.

One of the worst floods on record of the Red River happened during what was obviously the remnants of a tropical cyclone during August of 1849. Although it is doubted that flows exceeded the floods of 1892, 1908 and 1945 due to the log raft, nevertheless, this flood changed the streambed of the Red River to its present course. - Denison Sunday Gazetteer April 11, 1897.

The First Lake Texoma in 1899

Sunday Gazetteer (Denison, Tex.)   July 9, 1899 - The first Lake Texoma formed on its own during the 1899 Red River flood. This one, however, was not **west** of Denison but was **east** of Denison. The high water in Red River at that time formed a lake east of Denison of about **20 miles** in size. The lake was very deep and alive with many fish. All this without the benefit of a dam!

Yet ANOTHER Epic Flood in 1899 Dallas Morning News Nov 23, 1899

Red River was on the biggest rise it had in eight years previous. It broke the record of the previous July when it overflowed its banks and threatened a flood in the river bottoms causing a great deal of damage before it recedes. The rise in the river reached almost bank full with the result of the cessation of all ferry transportation across the river with even railroad bridges being threatened. For several days the river rose as a result of heavy rains in western Texas to reach the high water mark for the past eight years, until the lowlands in the river bottom were under water, covering many farms. The Washita is on one of the biggest rises in its history and threatens to go even higher. This, combined with the heavy headwater rise, and the full condition of the streams from local rains, will give it the biggest floods it has had in eight years.

News from **Preston Bend**, above the mouth of the Washita, is flooded to the effect that the Red River is considerably out of its banks, there caused by the backwater in Red River, there being a gorge of water at the Washita's mouth. From Preston eighteen miles northwest to the Yarnaby community, twenty miles east of the city, the reports are that the bottoms are submerged and that several thousand acres of land are under water, and that already there has been considerable damage done. The people who live in the lowlands are getting out of the way of the water and preparing to save their property in the event it goes higher, but so far, no great damage has been done except to ferries, fencing, and crops along the banks of the river. The people from **Preston Bend** reported that the water had backed up upon Mineral so they cannot cross the bridge. Fields in that vicinity are covered with water to several feet in depth. The flood there is the highest in fifteen years.

It is feared the flood may exceed the great flood of 1876. It is still rising and still overspreading the countryside. It is feared that the railroad and wagon bridges north of Denison will very soon be endangered by debris in the water. Only two miles northeast of Denison, the floodwaters were spread out over the river bottoms until it reached a width of a mile and a half with a raging current carrying entire large trees uprooted by the flood. These trees are the culprits likely to take out the bridges.

Denison Sunday Gazetteer November 26, 1899 - Red River and the Washita in the Territory partially overflowed their banks and considerable damage was done to farming lands. Red River was at its highest since 1891 and the Washita was reported to have been the highest ever known to the oldest inhabitants. Many farms were inundated on the Washita and the Blue Rivers. A large

162

number of cattle were drowned. People living in the lowlands were obliged to move to higher ground. A considerable amount of corn in the river bottoms which had not been gathered was lost. All ferry communication with the Territory was cut off. **At Preston,** the water backed up and overflowed the bridges at Little Mineral and Big Mineral. Paul's Valley on the Sante Fe was under water for several days. On November 22, about midnight, the water in Red River began falling rapidly and the worst was over. By the 26th, the Washita and Blue were back in their banks and all bridges were intact, although much driftwood clogs the River. The Red River was at one time within four feet of the railway bridge. **Further tragedy averted..... THIS TIME.**

Dallas Morning News Oct 2, 1900; Oct 1, 1904

RED RIVER IS RISING.

At Several Points Below Denison It Is Almost Out of Its Banks.

SPECIAL TO THE NEWS.

Denison, Tex., Oct. 1.—Red River is on a boom. There has been a rise of from six to eight feet in the river since Saturday night. This morning at a point seven miles east of the city the river was falling slightly, and at a point six miles west it was rising. This represents a distance of about 100 miles of water At Preston Bend the ferry boat was carried off in the flood this morning, and the river lacked but about three feet of being out of its banks. At a lower point on the river it lacked but a few inches of being out of its banks. The most of the rise seems to be from the headquarters in the Panhandle country.

If the river continues to rise till midnight, thousands of acres of bottom land will be flooded and a vast amount of cotton in the fields in the bottoms will be ruined.

RISE IN RED RIVER.

Several Ferries Discontinued on Account of High Water.

SPECIAL TO THE NEWS.

Denison, Tex., Sept. 30.—Red River was still rising this morning and the ferries from Preston Bend to Bloomfield are not able to cross wagons. Farmers are compelled to drive a round-about way and cross at the wagon bridge on the Colbert and Denison road.

The ferries which have been discontinued on account of high water are Preston Bend ferry, Rock Bluff ferry, Baer's ferry, Blue Bluff ferry, Carpenter's Bluff and Bloomfield ferry. The high water is said to be due to heavy rains on the headwaters of the river.

1908 RED RIVER FLOOD CREATES NEW LAKE, Again

River Changes Course - Land Which Once Was Texas, Now in Oklahoma.

There have been MANY floods on the Red River, but 1876 and 1908 were GREAT floods of the Red River. In 1899, the floodwaters backed up to the extent that there was a large lake formed along the River.

These floods, which came with fearsome frequency, had been causing catastrophic damage and loss of life for decades. 1908 was the last straw. This flood created a great lake along the River which eventually led residents to create a flood control reservoir, the lake we now know as Lake Texoma.

The newspapers in late May 1908 stated that the flood loss in Preston Bend from that catastrophic flood would at a very conservative estimate reach $100,000. From fifty to sixty families, who were renters, were absolutely destitute with not even a shelter. Without exception, their flight from the flash flood was so precipitate and under such dire circumstances that none of the kitchen or household effects could be rescued. They were fortunate to be able to escape with their lives.

As in 1899, the flood had formed a great lake around the river at Preston Bend and at other locations in the county. Preston Bend was covered by fifteen feet of water in 1908, 35 years before Lake Texoma existed.

Red River flood courtesy of Frontier Village Museum

Claude C. Lamberth, one of the greatest landowners in the Preston Bend country and who had 800 acres under water, had just returned from the scene, and said of the situation: "It is impossible to get within less than two miles of the main channel of Red River and most of the inspection has to be made through field glasses. Parties who tried to go across in boats were stopped quite a distance on this side of the ridge, which for the first time in more than sixty years is underwater, by the torrent which was hurling and whirling along huge trees like they were mere straws. Sixty-five years earlier, (1843) the slough was the main channel of Red River and there are many reasons to believe that when the flood subsides that the river will have returned to its old channel, throwing everything beyond the ridge into Oklahoma, at least 2,000 acres." Around the old channel, the water had to travel six or more miles while after the flood, it appeared to be racing through the slough or old channel, reaching the old channel again in less than three miles. The break through the ridge by which the flood entered the slough was near the Haynes Potts plantation at Preston Bend. Among those who would have large tracts of land providentially transferred from one State to another if the river's course swings to the cut-off channel, were Claude C. Lamberth, Haynes Potts, John Jackson, Joe Combs, W. C. Jolliff, and **James Jackson**. **James Jackson** had at that time been a citizen of Grayson County and Texas for sixty-five years. If after the water went down, he took up his old residence, he would be a citizen of the new state of Oklahoma (formed in 1907).

Nothing has changed in the last one hundred years. Warnings at that time were issued to the police and deputy sheriffs on duty stating that all those found looting homes in the area affected by the floods were to be shot on sight. Many entire houses were swept down the river. All the buildings at the town of Preston Bend were gone, washed down the river whole or broken up by the force of the water. Many people at Preston were feared lost in the flood. It was reported that two men lost their lives a few miles beyond the upper bend of the River, the names of the victims were not known. Tragedies like these drove the citizens of the area to eventually build the Denison Dam to attempt to mitigate the impact of future floods on the Red River. So far, the plan has been a great success.

Bridges out – take the ferry. Still House Ferry at Rock Creek on T. A. Davis place, from Frontier Village Museum donated by Bill Kirby.

Below: Red River flood comes inland, all the way up to the top of the electric poles, from Frontier Village Museum.

1908 postcards of the flood on Red River

Above: the wagon bridge with demolished house;
Below: houses washed down the River

Dallas Morning News May 28-29, 1908

Houses Washed Away in Flood -

The heaviest rain that has fallen in Grayson County for many years began here on Saturday afternoon and continued up till nearly noon Sunday. All creeks near Sadler and points north and east were higher than they have been in many years and as a result, nearly all the crops on the bottom land are ruined. Several head of livestock were drowned. Red River to the north, is reported to be higher than it has been in thirty years. It is said that many farmhouses have been washed away. In Preston Bend, the damage is very heavy, and the river threatens to change the channel there, which would transfer about 1,000 acres to Oklahoma.

McKinney Daily Courier Gazette May 28, 1908

Immense damage has been done by the overflow of Red River on the north. Many farms formerly in Texas are now in Oklahoma, as an entirely new channel has been made by the river. The famous Preston Bend district, noted for its fine cotton farms, is entirely submerged under fifteen feet of water. Thousands of acres in that garden spot of the Red River valley is one vast sea of water.

The loss of crops is simply appalling. The entire valley to the Cooke county line is under water. It is believed that what is left of the railroad bridge is several inches out of plumb. The new channel cut by the water will make some astonishing changes and not only the railroad bridge, but the wagon bridge, may be rendered useless and necessitate new structures.

Ardmore Daily Ardmoreite May 28, 1908

The Frisco people expect to be able to get trains into Madill from the north soon, as it is believed that only a few hours' work will be necessary to repair the washouts along the track between here and Francis. It will probably be weeks, however, before trains can be run across Red river between here and Denison and the North Canadian, north of Francis.

Washita Falling Rapidly.

Aylesworth, Okla., May 28.—The Washita at this point has fallen five feet since 5 o'clock yesterday afternoon.

Postcards of Washed Out Railroad Tracks on Red River
May 30, 1908

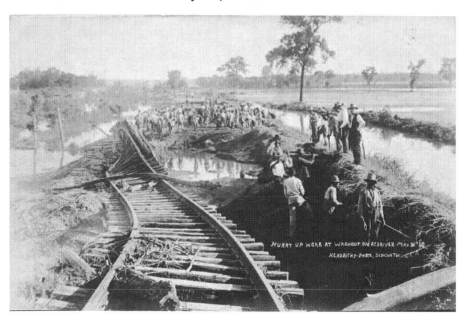

Rebuilding washed out Red River bridge June 1908

RIVER CHANNELS ARE CHANGED, BRIDGES ARE OUT

This whole section of the country is flooded. Although the water is rapidly receding, conditions are such that little information can be had from along the river. Two sections of the Frisco-Katy bridge across Red River between Oklahoma and Denison are gone and the division superintendent of the Frisco, who is here from Francis, says that in his opinion it will be from twenty to thirty days before the Frisco will be able to resume service in Texas. The channel of Red River has changed from bridge to Warner Junction, at Old Denison, about one-half mile south of the former course of the stream. The Washita has also changed its course above its mouth, a new channel being made about a half mile farther west.   House after house was swept down the river, all of the buildings at Preston Bend on the Texas side of the Red River were gone and was assumed that many lives were lost. It was known that a young man named Cleve Johnson was drowned in the flood waters.   Even in that time, hundreds of thousands of dollars of damage was done by the high water. The telephone and telegraph poles which supported the wires across the Red River were wiped out. The railroad trestle of the Frisco on the Washita near Woodville north of Preston was gone, although the bridge was still standing. The trestle was a very long one and considerable time would be required to replace it. More than a quarter of a mile of track near Red River was also gone. The Platter cut-off, the connecting line between the main line and the A. & C. was put out of commission. The Red River changed its course at the point where the Santa Fe crossed. The new channel of the river was then on this side of the bridge, leaving the bridge on the Texas side of the river. – Information from the Daily Ardmoreite May 28, 1908.

1908 Flood – A Mixed Calamity

Crops were destroyed, but the land was made more valuable by the flood! The old saw that "it is an ill wind that blows nobody good" has again been demonstrated. Claud Lambreth of Sherman owned 700 acres of land in the Preston Bend country on Red River, and during the 1908 flood his farm was covered with water from a depth of two to nine feet and his crops totally destroyed. Afterward, however, since the water receded, it developed that the rich deposits that had been left on his land made it even more fertile and served to increase its value by $10 per acre. Bad news first, good news later. - Denison Daily Herald, June 3, 1908.

WATER SHORTAGE AT PRESTON DUE TO 1908 FLOOD

One other ironic result from the flooding at Preston Bend is that many water wells and spring fed ponds were of course submerged and filled with contaminated water, making them unsafe for human or animal consumption. Some of these water sources were entirely washed away by the violence of the flood. It seemed a water famine at Preston Bend had been brought on by TOO MUCH water. - The Savoy Star, Savoy, Tx, June 12, 1908.

Flood Causes Extreme Suffering

R. P. Elrod, special agent for the United States Department of Agriculture, reported that in Preston Bend, as in the many areas along the Red River and even in the State, the flood had caused such catastrophic loss of food crops and animals that families were becoming destitute and in need of immediate aid for food, household goods and medicine. Most of Preston Bend's families had lost everything. Many generous people came forward to help those who were affected by the flood. Some farmers were seeking work on farms outside the flooded area, some were hoping to be able to replant that year. - The Denison Daily Herald, June 16, 1908.

SICKNESS AT PRESTON BEND

PRESTON BEND MAN DIES FROM HORSE DISEASE

Think a human can't catch a fatal disease from a horse, think again. It happened at Preston Bend. Dallas Morning News - Feb 6, 1894 - John Mayrant, a well known young farmer who died at his home in Preston Bend, was afflicted with glanders according to his physicians and gave it as their further opinion that he had contracted it from a sick horse with he had been attending on the farm. The neighborhood is considerably wrought up and as there are several sick horses in the community, an investigating committee has been appointed by the county judge to go out and examine all sick stock for traces of glanders. Sunday Denison Gazetteer Sept 23, 1894 - Glanders is reported among the horses in the Pottsboro neighborhood. A special commission appointed by Judge Wood is investigating the matter. Sept 30, 1894- The commission sent to Pottsboro report they found the disease in horses to indeed be glanders. Horse owners must be on their guards to prevent further spread of the disease. According to the Veterinary Manual – "Glanders is a contagious, acute or chronic, usually fatal disease of Equidae (horses, mules, donkeys) caused by Burkholderia mallei and characterized by the serial development of ulcerating nodules that are most commonly found in the upper respiratory tract, lungs, and skin. Felines and other species are susceptible, and infections are usually fatal. The organism is infectious for people, with a 95% fatality rate in untreated septicemia cases, and is considered a potential bioterrorism agent. Glanders is one of the oldest diseases known and once was prevalent worldwide. It has now been eradicated or effectively controlled in many countries, including the USA."

Ride with caution!

Malarial Fever at Glen Eden

Malaria causes symptoms that typically include fever, tiredness, vomiting, and headaches. In severe cases, it can cause yellow skin, seizures, coma, or death. Symptoms usually begin ten to fifteen days after being bitten by an infected mosquito. If not properly treated, people may have recurrences of the disease months later. Yes, Preston Bend was plagued by malaria-carrying mosquitos which bequeathed their infected parasitical bites on whomever they could – even the rich and influential. Sunday Gazetteer - September 28, 1884 - Judge Porter and his wife Sophia, of Glen Eden at Preston Bend, were guests of Mr. Sam Hanna. What makes this worthy of note is they were finally able to be able to be out visiting after a serious attack of malarial fever.

1938 - RED RIVER DAM WILL AID MALARIA CONTROL

A minor but no less concrete benefit considered by army engineers in appraising the Denison Dam project was the control of malaria. The principal breeding place of the Anopheles mosquito in the area below the dam site, the engineers found, is in pools of water left standing after the river overflows or cuts new channels.

Flow regulation through the Denison Dam will restrict the river to its channel and this eliminate the mosquito breeding places. Local measures of mosquito control then will be more effective.

The next year after the malaria story at Glen Eden .....

Huge Ears of Corn and Cholera at Preston Bend – Good News / Bad News

1885 – Judge Porter of Preston Bend, was in Denison and placed on exhibition at Porter's grocery house several ears of corn – the largest that had been seen in the area. Preston Bend is a river bottom area with extremely fertile soil. It was supposed at the time that even the fertile prairies of the great corn-producing state of Illinois never raised such enormous ears. One of the ears of corn was nine inches in circumference.

All was not rosy at Preston Bend, however. The Judge stated he had lost nearly all his hogs from cholera, and people who lived in the Indian Territory near Preston Bend had met with the same misfortune. When the hogs died, they cracked open, and they were sick only a short time before that horrific occurrence. In Jan. 31, 1886, the Sunday Gazetteer reported Deputy Constable Gardner arrested a man residing near Preston Bend for stealing hogs there. Not a good idea, I wonder if he got sick?

The Hog Cholera Plague at Preston Bend

The Sunday Gazetteer (Denison, Tex.), January 12, 1908 – It was reported: "the plague" among swine in Oklahoma and in Preston Bend had at that time killed many hogs in a short time. R. P. Elrod, a hog raiser of Preston Bend, lost twenty-three hogs himself and said that several of his neighbors had experienced even heavier losses among their herds of swine. The disease directly affects the lungs of swine and is said to be quickly lethal to pigs under 18 months.

A source of the disease was transmitted to humans in those days by a source, either water-borne or occasionally food, contaminated with V. cholerae can easily and rapidly transmit the cholera-causing bacteria to many people.

Glen Eden and Sophia Coffee Butts Porter

Order of Ownership of Glen Eden:

1843-1848 - Holland and Sophia Coffee   1848-1865 - Sophia Butts   1865-1897 - Sophia Porter

1897 - Mary Elizabeth Jewel Mosely

Joe Meadows; then his son Exey Meadows - Walter and Della Leverette become tenant farmers under the ownership of the Meadows family in 1936 until 1942 when the house is deeded to Judge Randolph Bryant – Then Glen Eden is torn down the be moved, then part of the logs are burned.

Mrs. Nellie Chambers (bought what was left of the logs and built cabins) Lastly: Frontier Village of Grayson County (moved cabins to Loy Park site at the Frontier Village collection of pioneer houses.)

Exey Meadows in about 1915 from the Frontier Village collection

The Boy Who Named Himself at Preston Bend

The Leverette family (with Walter and Della as the parents) crossed the Red River in 1908 in Shreveport over a bridge in a covered wagon. The only bridge at that time was a railroad bridge. They got halfway across and a train was coming from Texas, but it stopped and waited for them to cross. They remembered the sounds the wagon made as it passed over the bridge and it made them very afraid.

They first settled in Mount Vernon and then moved to Grayson County in Dec. 1916, moving to Sherman. They lived in a house on a corner lot on Cherry Street for a short while until their farm on the Stroup place east of Sherman was ready to move into. It was across the road from the Matt Hix place. This is where one of the people who became embroiled in tragedy was born – Bobby Joe Leverette - on August 2, 1924. However, at this time, he was not known as Bobby Joe. He was the thirteenth child in the family and was not officially given a name except his early nickname which stuck with him – Sonny Boy. This remained his name until Sonny Boy was about four years old. One day he was asked his name on the porch of the Hix house and he announced his name was "Bobby Joe." From that time forth, it was his name. **He was the boy who had named himself!**

They had a total of thirteen children, two of the girls died as babies in 1901 and 1904. One of the girls' name was Mildred, the other never received a name, but is merely known as Baby Girl Leverette. About 1929 or 1930 they moved to the "Brown house" just east of Preston Bend, owned by Clarence Scott, the one-time Mayor of Denison and lawyer Ross Stoddard, who were brothers-in-law. Mr. Leverette had several cows, farmed 200 acres and was an itinerate preacher. By 1936, the Leverette's became tenant farmers for Exey Meadows and moved onto that property and into the Glen Eden mansion. **The Leverettes were**

the last residents of Glen Eden of Preston Bend, the most famous house in the County. Information courtesy of Becky Muse Duncan, with information also from her Uncle Joe Leverette in Dallas.

Leverette Family circa 1907 – Parents – Walter and Adella, older boys – Floyd and Fred, Front – Otis and Gladys. Picture courtesy of Becky Muse Duncan – the great-granddaughter of Walter and Della Leverette through their oldest son Floyd.

Glen Eden Residents – The Leverettes – Suffer Tragic Year in 1938 - Four Close Family Members Die in Less Than 3 Months

1. **Former Preston Bend Woman, Daughter of Walter and Della Leverette, Dies from Car Accident June 22, 1938**

Alyene Leverette

178

Joyce Alyene "Aly" Leverette was born March 29, 1915, at Mount Vernon, Texas. When her parents lived at Preston Bend, she graduated high school at Woodville, Oklahoma, just north of Preston. For a time she worked in Wichita Falls, Texas as a nanny for Tom Hunter's daughter Helen. He ran for Governor. Alyene came back to Denison to work for Louie Bouray in the DeLuxe Café as a hostess. On June 22, 1938, they went to Dallas to pick up a new car he had bought and Alyene went to drive his old car back to Denison. On the way back on Hwy 75 between Anna and Van Alstyne, there was of course, even then, construction on that road. Mr. Bouray passed her and she went off the road, over-corrected and lost control of the Ford car she was driving, crashing head-on into a Lincoln Zephyr.

The 22-year-old died shortly after reaching the hospital, putting a tragic end to a promising life and beginning a series of excruciating calamities for the Leverette family.

2. Sister of Della Leverette, Thula Jane Causey Ivey, Dies August 16, 1938

3. Preston Bend Boy Dies From Lockjaw - Tetanus- Sept. 6, 1938 – Because of a Small Scratch!

Are you up to date on your tetanus shot? If not, beware. The disease is also called lockjaw because the most common early symptom is a stiff jaw, which can become "locked." It is a bacterial infection that causes painful muscle spasms throughout the body and can lead to death. Tetanus can enter the body through a tiny cut or scratch.

179

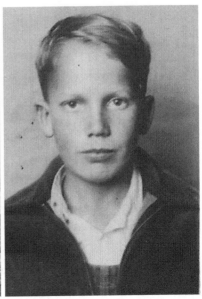

Above: Sonny Boy and Iva Lou Leverette; Sonny Boy / Bobby Joe Leverette. Courtesy of Becky Muse Duncan – great-granddaughter of Walter and Della Leverette through their oldest son Floyd.

The Denison Press on September 6, 1938, reported that Bobby Joe Leverette, 14, died that Tuesday morning at 1:30 in Sherman of lockjaw after a five-day illness. Bobbie had been in the hospital there two days, coming from his home in Preston Bend. Bobby's arm became infected from a small scratch received in the family's barn a month earlier, developed blood poisoning, and became seriously ill on Sunday when lockjaw began to show its effects.

It is so ironically tragic, the tetanus vaccine was developed in 1924, the same year Bobby Joe was born. It had begun to be produced in 1937 and 1938, the same year Bobby Joe died, but was not widely disseminated until the late 1940s and 1950s. Tragically it came too late for young Bobby Joe Leverette who probably never had access to the tetanus vaccine in the rural community of Preston Bend.

His parents are Walter J. and Della Leverette of Preston Bend. He was born in Grayson County August 2, 1924, went to school at Preston Bend and Woodville and was a member of the Baptist church. Burial was at Bethany Cemetery in Sherman.

Becky Muse Duncan said: "My Uncle Joe Leverette and Bobby Joe were only (born) about 5 years apart. Uncle Joe and my mother Margie both remember playing with him and Iva Lou Leverette at Glen Eden."

4. A Few Days After Bobby Joe's Death, Della Leverette's Mother Nancy Jane Died on Sept. 15, 1938

Della grieved so much that summer – crying so much and so long from all the tragedy that had suddenly struck her family, causing her eyes to be constantly swollen and inflamed, that it was believed that the nerves in her eyelids were destroyed which rendered her unable to open her eyes except in the most extreme circumstances. Later, if she got extremely excited or upset, she could open them.

Tragedy had left its mark on this dear lady, as it often does on us all.

Left: Walter and Della Leverette; Right: Della. Courtesy of Becky Duncan

181

Yet one more loss was to come for this family and for many others...

5. The Leverette Home Glen Eden, Was About to be Covered by a Permanent Flood – Lake Texoma

By at least 1940, the Leverette family would have been informed by the Corps of Engineers they had to move away from Glen Eden because Preston Bend was to be flooded by the new Lake. By 1942, Walter and Della made their last move to 1225 W. Hanna Street in Denison, to the only house they ever owned, where they spent the remainder of their lives.

The family then gathered before they had to say goodbye one more time to a place in which they had bestowed much work and worry and created many memories, both good and bad. They memorialized this farewell with pictures of Glen Eden.........

Below: Glen Eden, Preston Bend. Home of Walter Leverette Family 1936 to early 1940's courtesy of Becky Duncan.

Below: Glen Eden's smokehouse during the time the Leverette family lived in the home, courtesy of Becky Muse Duncan.

Glen Eden, At Preston Bend, Home of Walter Leverette Family 1940 courtesy of Becky Duncan.

Walter Leverette and border collie at Glen Eden courtesy of Becky Muse Duncan.

Ardmore Daily Ardmoreite   August 25, 1903

Fire at Woodville.

News has been received that the house occupied by R. D. Murphy at Woodville with contents, was totally destroyed. R. D. Murphy carried insurance on the contents, but the house was owned by Joe Meadows of Preston Bend and he carried no insurance. The fire originated from an oil stove and the kitchen was in full blaze before it was discovered, it being about 5 p. m. Mrs. Murphy barely escaped with her two babies and saved nothing.

Preston Fire   Amarillo Daily News   Dec 7, 1945

Officials Find Charred Body of Boat Watchman

SHERMAN, Dec. 6 (AP)—The charred body of Jake Millikin, 80 years old, boat watchman at Lake Texhoma, was found in the ruins of his one-room cabin on Preston Bend Peninsula and Justice of the Peace Jess Wall said today the man apparently died Tuesday night when flames destroyed the building.

4. Calamities & Accidents Plague Preston Bend

Denison Daily News July 7, 1875

Drowned.

We learn from a gentlemrn residing at Preston's Bend that a man named Turner was drowned about sundown Sunday night while bathing in Red River, just above the Washita, two miles west of Preston. It is supposed he was drawn under by a gar, as he called out for help as he was sinking, and one of those fish was seen in the immediate vicinity a few moments afterwards. His companions who were also bathing, went to the spot where he disappeared as soon as possible but could not find him. Search was was made for the body along down the river for some distance all the next day but without success.

Coffins and Skeletons in the River!

High Water Unearths Coffin in Red River

Denison Daily Herald   May 22, 1878 - A group of gentlemen who visited the Red River informed the Herald that the water was so high it had almost reached the railroad bridge and continued to rise. October 14, 1878 - A coffin containing the remains of a child was found floating in the Red River near Rock Bluff near Preston. Not what you want to see when out fishing.

The Sunday Gazetteer. (Denison, Tex.), April 17, 1892

Boy Drowned.

Sunday morning last Eddie Russell and Willie Adair, lads living on their father's farm in the Preston Bend neighborhood, went down to a stream to spend the day fishing. The Russell boy ventured out on a log over a deep hole of water; the log gave way and Eddie found a watery grave. His companion was powerless to render assistance, as he was only seven years of age.

Ardmore Daily Ardmoreite June 14, 1905

Drowned in Red River.

While bathing with two companions in Red river, opposite Old Preston, John L. Thompson was drowned Saturday evening. It is said the three young men were crossing the river on a log and young Thompson quit the log to swim about thirty yards to the shore, but sank and his companions were not able to rescue him.

The body was not found until Sunday evening and was badly decomposed. He was buried last night at Coffey's Chapel in Preston Bend. His father A. O. Thompson, lives at Preston, Texas., having lately moved there from the Indian Territory.

Skeleton Found on Red River Near Preston

Sunday Gazetteer - November 15, 1885

Portions of a human skeleton were found on a sandbar in Red River Tuesday, near Rock Bluff Ferry. Mr. Taylor, our informant, states that he thinks the skeleton is that of a man named Bush, who drowned about three years ago.

And ANOTHER man named Bush years later .... Apr 1921

BODY OF FRANK BUSH LOST IN SWOLLEN RIVER

COMPANION NARROWLY ESCAPES DEATH NEAR BAER'S FERRY. MEN WERE ON FISHING EXPE-DITION.

While assisting in running a trotline on Red River, near Baer's Ferry at 12 o'clock, Frank Bush, aged 47 years, who was rowing a boat, was drowned when the boat was caught in the swift current of the stream. Claude Tignor, who was running the line, was thrown into the river but escaped. Only the two were in the boat. A group went out in Red River to fish, and the two men had gone to the trotline to see what had been caught. Red River was up several feet as a result of recent rains and the current was always very swift. At the point where Mr. Bush drowned, the water was nine feet deep and reported to be very swift. It is said that the body never appeared after he went under the water. Tignor had to put up a hard fight against the waves before he was able to get out. On seeing their friend down, immediate effort was started to recover the body. Parties were sent on a special trip to Denison to bring the news and secure more formidable means at locating the body. A brother of the drowned man enlisted the services of

George Shields, who has given assistance before in locating drowned bodies in Red River and help was sent immediately, fully equipped for finding the drowned man. Word was sent down the river as far south as Bryant's Ferry to be on the lookout for the body of Bush. The drowned man was unmarried and was for several years engaged in the grocery business in West Denison. He had lately been buying and selling cattle.

TWO MEN DROWNED IN RED RIVER

Denison Herald, April 24, 1921 - A man said to have been George Smith, a resident of Oklahoma near Preston Bend, was drowned in Red River Thursday, according to reports. It is said that Smith was fishing when his boat overturned, and he drowned instantly.

The river is falling rapidly, and watch parties are lined up along the stream between Preston and Bonham keeping a close watch for the bodies of Frank Bush, drowned early in the week, and George Smith, drowned Thursday. Relatives of Mr. Bush have offered a reward of $100 for the recovery of his body. George Shields and a number of men left at noon today for the Colbert bridge, as it is believed that the body of Frank Bush is liable to float at any time now and a very close watch will be north of the city.

Drowning at Preston Bend section of Lake Texoma
Ardmore Daily Ardmoreite June 17, 1946

Two Men Drown In Lake Texoma

DURANT, June 17.—(AP)—An outing for employes of the Abe Ross Truck company, Denison, Texas, ended in disaster yesterday as two men were drowned when rising wind capsized their rowboat near the Preston Bend section of Lake Texoma.

The dead were Harmon Glenn, 30, Madill, and Vadis E. Shaw, 25, Denison, both employes of the company. A third occupant of the boat, Boyd Jacobs, Pottsboro, Texas, escaped drowning by clinging to the overturned boat until rescued.

Corsicana Semi Weekly Light   June 18, 1946

Search continues today for the body of Harmon Glenn, 30 of Denison, Tex., and Madill Okla. who was one of two drowning victims at Lake Texoma Saturday night.

The body of Vadis E. Shaw, 25 Denison, was recovered yesterday.

The two were employes of the Abe Ross Truck Co. of Denison and were attending a company fishing party and picnic. A rising wind and waves, capsized their rowboat near the Preston Bend section of the lake.

A third occupant of the boat, Boyd Jackson, Pottsboro, Texas, escaped by clinging to the capsized boat until help arrived.

PRESTON BEND MAN GETS WILD RIDE

Sunday Gazetteer, January 24, 1886 - A gentleman residing in the Preston Bend neighborhood, whose name was not known was on his way to Denison. When a short distance outside the city, his horse became frightened and ran away with the buggy. In its flight, the horse ran over a cow, giving her such a jolt that she thought she was going to Denny's meat market. On went the horse in his wild, frantic and mad dash until he ran through a gentleman's gate and broke the buggy into atoms, and amazingly only slightly injured the gentleman.

A Fatal Mistake - Dallas Weekly Herald September 13, 1883

John May, a farmer living near Preston Bend, took morphine, believing it to be quinine, and died before medical aid could reach him. He was for a long time an Adams Express wagon driver here, and as such, was known to many all over the state.

August 31, 1886

A little girl, the daughter of Mrs. Lasher, of Preston Bend, was bitten on the hand, Sunday by a rattlesnake, the bite coming very near being the cause of her death. Mrs. Lasher happened to have some whiskey in the house, which she promptly gave the child, at the same time tightly bandaging her wrist to prevent circulation of the poison through her body, and thus saving her life till a physician arrived. When last heard from, the little suffer-
Snake Bite! er was improving.

Denison Press

A Fierce Battle With a Wild Cat on Red River

Denison Daily News January 23, 1880 - There was a desperate battle between man and beast near Preston Bend on the Red River. An Indian man named John Waite, accompanied by another man, went in pursuit of some stray cattle. While passing through the woods, the men separated. Waite, with two hounds, kept close along the river. Having gone a short distance, the dogs were heard barking fiercely. Waite went in the direction of the barking and soon came upon the dogs, which were engaged in a fierce encounter with a wildcat.   He took his rifle from his shoulder, and taking deliberate aim, pulled the trigger. The cap exploded, but the gun failed to discharge. He placed another cap on the tube and the second time pulled the trigger with the same result. The gun would not go off. By this time, the dogs were badly whipped, and whining and limping, made their escape into a thicket.   The wildcat then sneaked slowly through the bushes toward the river.

Waite was determined to capture the animal, and imagined that he could conquer it by beating out its brains with the butt of his gun. He started in pursuit and soon overtook the animal, which stopped when Waite approached within a few feet of it. The man cautiously took one step after another, when suddenly, and with eyes gleaming like balls of fire, the animal turned and made a spring, landing upon the shoulders of Waite, and soon succeeded in inflicting several ghastly wounds upon his face. His body was also lacerated in a terrible manner, with his clothes being torn to shreds. After a fierce struggle, Waite succeeded in loosening the cat's hold.   **It seems the cat won this round of combat, having driven the dogs running from the field of battle and leaving its human opponent alive but very much worse for wear. The victorious wildcat seemed to emerge virtually unscathed, ready to fight another day.**

CHILD CRUSHED BY COTTON FRAME

On Oct 16, 1896, the six-year-old daughter of Wilson Combs was killed at Preston Bend. A cotton frame rolled off a wagon on to the child. - The Sunday Gazetteer Oct 25, 1896.

WATKINS GIN BURNED – TWICE IN TWO YEARS
- Denison Daily News Dec 5, 1874, & Dec 20, 1876

1874 - Mr. William Watkins' cotton gin, in the Nation, three miles from Preston, was destroyed by fire last Tuesday night. Fourteen bales of cotton were also consumed. The gin was a total loss. It was rented by Mr. Jim Shannon, and we suppose most of the cotton destroyed belonged to him. The fire was caused by a kerosene lamp.

1876 – William Watkins' mill and cotton gin, opposite Preston Bend, at the mouth of the Washita River, in the Chickasaw Nation, was burned about noon Saturday. The building and contents were entirely destroyed with a loss estimated at $8,000 with no insurance. Mr. Watkins returned from the south Sunday to find his property in ashes. He thinks the fire resulted from a match being run through the gin, with friction causing it to spark. But the engineer is of the opinion it was ignited by sparks from the smokestack. It is a severe loss, not only to Mr. Watkins but to a large neighborhood which depended on it.

CRUSHED STEELE HAND - Denison Daily News Nov 11, 1874,

Mr. G. W. Dismukes, informs us that there are fears that Mr. Algernon Steele, who had his hand crushed in the steam cotton gin at Preston Bend last week, will lose his hand. The hand was caught in the saws, cutting off the middle finger and tearing out the tendons as far as the wrist. Dr.'s Frazier and Williams are tending to him and still hope to avoid a resort to amputation.

Denison Sunday Gazetteer Jan 4, 1891 - Algernon S. Steele, who has resided at Preston Bend over forty years, died suddenly yesterday of heart disease.

WALTER S. REEVES GIN BURNS   October 5, 1897

Walter Steele came in from Preston Bend and brought the news of the burning of W.S. Reeves' gin, three miles north of Pottsboro this morning at an early hour. The gin and all the machinery was a total loss, valued at about $3,000. About 100 bales of cotton and about $1,000 worth of cotton seed were destroyed. The fire is thought to have caught from a match in the cotton. The lint caught fire in one of the gin stands and the fire spread through it like it was gunpowder. The building and machinery were insured for $2,000, about half the value of the loss, with no insurance on the cotton and seed.

Preston Bend had not had a great time with cotton gins. The Watkins family had their share of misfortunes, as has already been seen.   William Watkins' son Almarine Watkins was the victim of a very sensational murder case described in this book. The Steele family's bad luck with working on cotton gins also continued and grew worse.

Gin Blows Up - Sept 16, 1896 - The Noble cotton gin at Preston Bend blew up and killed Mr. McSwain and a young man.

Henderson Mangus Cotton Gin – Here Today, Gone Tomorrow

In 1899, the brand new Henderson & Mangus Cotton Gin was set to open. Mr. Mangus got two or three fingers nearly sawed off Friday, on the first day's run, and his son was thrown off a wagon two weeks earlier and pretty badly hurt.   (Seems like Mangus was getting a hint with all the calamities befalling him and his family, that he might want to make sure the gin was safe.)

On September 25, 1899, at about 1:30 pm, the boiler blew up, completely demolishing the boiler and press rooms. It was reported the blast was so strong, it was heard for miles.

Engineer Grant Conder was a young single man who had moved here from Illinois three months earlier. Algernon "Munn" Steele was the new pressman on his FIRST day at work, who had a young wife, Callie and young sons. Conder and Steele were both horribly mutilated and killed instantly.

After all this, Callie moved with her sons back to the area where her parents lived in Anderson County, Texas. But by 1911, once she had raised her children, she was still so despondent, she committed suicide at her home on Rainey St. by shooting herself in the center of the forehead. Her second cousin in law, Thad L. Steele found her. She was 5' 4" and dark complexion. The inquest was held Dec 17, 1911, by Dr. E. W. Link, hopefully bringing an end to the victims of that terrible accident.

The explosion from 12 years earlier was still echoing and taking its toll on people's lives. Time did not heal the wounds. For this family, the tragedy was not over and never forgotten.

Above: William Henderson and Mollie Mangus Henderson

195

STEAM THRESHER BLOWS AT PRESTON

Sunday Gazetteer. (Denison, Tex.), August 16, 1885 - A steam thresher and a quantity of wheat were consumed by fire on Mr. F. M. Utiger's farm, near the Preston Bend road, last week. A party was engaged threshing and the fire caught from sparks from the smokestack. Mr. Utiger estimates the loss of grain at about 250 bushels. Since the patentee of the thresher guaranteed that there is no danger from sparks with their machines, he will probably have to foot the bill for the losses.

Below is an example of threshers like the ones spoken of in the previous article:

THE HOWE ENTERPRISE, THURSDAY, FEBRUARY 19, 1970

THRESHER CREW — On machine: Arthur Sanders, Robert Savage, Ernest Jorden, Loren Tolbert, Henry Harrison, Jim Harrison; standing, left tfo right, Red Lewis, Arthur Sanders, Mr. Strawn, Macy and Cecil Swatszell, Frank Day, Lonnie Morrison, Ernest Strawn and Irving Morrison. Sitting: George Savage, Harrison Jones, Doug Savage, Mr. Speck.

Denison Herald April 21 & 24, 1921

PRESTON BEND MAN KILLED BY TRAIN

JOHN JACKSON AND Y. D. MYERS OF WOODVILLE, OKLA., DIE IN CRASH.

John Jackson, born in 1859, a farmer and substantial citizen of Preston Bend community, was instantly killed at Granger, Texas Wednesday afternoon at 3:30 when the truck in which he was riding was hit by a Katy passenger train. Also, Y. D. Myers of Woodville Oklahoma, who was with Mr. Jackson, was killed at the same time. Information from the Jackson home at Preston Bend Thursday morning is to the effect that Mr. Jackson and his traveling companion were making an overland trip to Corpus Christi and other port towns, intending to be away for some days on a fishing trip. Both of the men were lovers of the outdoors and camp life. They left home on Monday on the trip. From papers in the pockets of Jackson, his home address was learned, and relatives informed of the tragedy. The accident happened while the truck was making a crossing about three miles north of Granger, the truck being completely wrecked. Relatives learned that the place where the two men were killed was in a level and open place and they are at a loss to understand why the train was not noticed. Another peculiar thing is that the bodies of the two men bear no cuts or bruises made by the train, except a small scratch on the nose of Mr. Myers. The neck of Mr. Jackson was broken, but there was not one scratch on his body. One body was picked up on the north side of the track and one on the south side. Mr. Jackson was survived by his widow and two sons and one daughter. He moved to Preston Bend from Woodville, Okla. There was a double funeral for the two men at the Preston cemetery directed by John L. Swank and attended by hundreds of people from both sides of the river - Woodville, Oklahoma and Preston Bend.

Dallas Morning News   May 10, 1904 - W. H. Maratta fell under the wheels of a passenger coach at Vincennes, Indiana and was so badly injured that he died within a few hours. His burial will be at Preston Bend Cemetery with Rev. G. P. Fry, pastor of the First Methodist Episcopal Church conducting the services.

Palestine Herald-Press Sep 1, 1905 - Mrs. Lizzie McDonald, an aged lady, was run over and killed by a Katy passenger train. Her body remained on the track for three hours before she was discovered. She had wandered away from home onto the track where she was struck. The lady was a pioneer.

The Steamboat Annie Peruna of the Red River – "Annie P" - A Cursed Craft

Denison Sunday Gazetteer August 13, 1905 - The Annie Peruna is certainly an ill-fated craft. At her completion celebration, a man was stabbed to death. When she was launched in Red River she went to the bottom and now a passenger on the way to Gainesville is taken sick and died. Commodore McAleer had better put her out of commission or change the name.....

The Sunday Gazetteer, July 2, 1905 -

A MAN KILLED CELEBRATING THE ANNIE P.'S COMPLETION

Last Saturday night a general jubilee was held in Sugar Bottom, the occasion being the completion of Lon McAleer's Red River steamboat packet, the Annie Peruna Jr. About midnight the crowd became very hilarious, not on the premises of Mr. McAleer but the streets near the Katy crossing. It is alleged that a number were fighting drunk, at any rate, a general mix up took place and during the melee, a young man named Jack Glover, who resided on West Nelson Street, was stabbed in the abdomen. Glover lingered till Tuesday night when he died. A young man named Tom Smith, son of horse trader Smith was arrested on the charge of doing the stabbing. Smith was taken over to the Sherman jail. It is stated that before Glover died, he declared most emphatically that Smith was innocent, that he knew who inflicted the fatal wound but refused to divulge the name. There are a great many conflicting versions of the affair and it is going to be a hard matter to place the guilt where it properly belongs. It is stated that there is a young woman at the bottom of the affair and that jealousy prompted the murder. The county attorney has been over, and will no doubt get at the bottom of the facts.

A gentleman who was at the bedside of Glover Sunday night informs the Gazetteer that Glover declared most positively that he did not know who cut him with a knife, that it was wrong to hold Tom Smith, that an injustice might be done an innocent man. Two other parties who were present when the disturbance took place state that it is impossible to determine who cut Glover. It was quite a long time before Glover realized he had been stabbed.

El Paso Daily Times, July 6, 1905

The Annie Peruna has been Togoed. Without an intimation of impending disaster, McAleer & Ford, its builders and owners, serenely pushed the little craft into the waters of Red river, only to see it turn turtle and plunge to the bottom of the stream. The reason for this is ascribed to the fact that the gasoline engine built on the boat does not occupy a central position and when the launching was made the vessel careened and went down. The Annie Peruna has been rescued and the trip to Shreveport will be started just as soon as the position of the engine can be changed.

Thomas E. Horan Dead

He started for Gainesville but was stricken down on the unlucky Annie Peruna steamboat.

Sunday Gazetteer, August 13, 1905 - Thomas E. Horan died an unexpected death in the family's rooms above his business on the 400 block of West Main street Sunday morning. On the previous Thursday, Mr. Horan was in excellent health and good spirits. He was looking forward to leaving the next morning on a trip as the guest of Lon McAleer on a river voyage to Gainesville and return home to Denison by railroad. It turned out to be a fatal journey because in less than four days he would be a dead man. "Tom", as his many friends knew him, left Denison Friday morning on the Annie Peruna for a point on the river north of Gainesville.

Lon McAleer, Bert Ford, and Jim Cash, who worked for Mr. Horan, and a few others, were on the boat. The Annie P. started out very well and was predicted to make a quick trip to Gainesville. As a matter of safety, it was decided to tie up early in the evening since the river was quite "snaggy." A short distance above **Preston Bend**, the stop was made, and all hands turned in quite early. Mr. Horan at that time seemed quite tired and by the next morning, he was delirious and in a short time, passed into a coma.

A launch was dropped down to **Preston** and a doctor was called aboard, who advised he be returned immediately to Denison for care. The launch then proceeded to Baer's Ferry, where a carriage containing Mrs. Horan and Dr. Bailey, was waiting, and Mr. Horan was brought to his home. Physicians did everything possible to help Mr. Horan, but in vain, for he died Sunday morning at 8 o'clock.

Thomas Horan cast his lot with Denison a number of years before his death, as early as 1888. As a businessman he attracted immediate attention, being full of energy, but at the same time, very quiet in his methods.

Mr. Horan virtually controlled the harness business in Denison for a number of years. He had the stock and capital and when a rival attempted and did get into the same business, he was sure to land into Tom's net, who would either buy him out or freeze him out. Horan's business career was a splendid financial success. He acquired money very quickly. He was at Jacksboro, Wichita Falls and other points and came here with considerable money. He was a rustler of energetic western methods. Denison was a good field for the exercise of his business talents. For a number of years, he was a very hard-working man, giving his entire time and attention to his business.

Some people think that Mr. Tom Horan may still be hard at work in his old business establishment on Main Street in Denison. SOMEONE can be heard moving about the building to the accompaniment of the jingling of well-crafted harnesses and the creak of the finest solid oak or bois d'arc wagons and carriages ever made and seen in Denison.

The Annie P. will not come up the river until fall. She is tied up on account of quarantine regulations.

August 27, 1905

Below: 1899 and after – Horan's Harness and Buggies at 416 W. Main Street in Denison, Texas

416 W. Main today, the same two buildings used by T. E. Horan in 1899:

T. E. HORAN, INTERIOR OF RETAIL STORE.

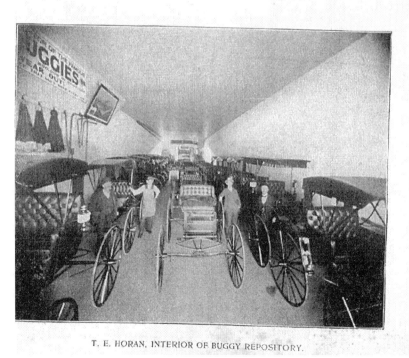

T. E. HORAN, INTERIOR OF BUGGY REPOSITORY.

Mr. Horan was also an active member of the Denison City government. In the two years before his death, business cares had rested very lightly upon his shoulders. He was an extensive traveler, going all over the United States and Canada accompanied by his wife. He was a loyal and loving husband, his wife sharing all his trips. For the last several years he had also made many camping and hunting trips to the Choctaw woods.

T. E. Horan was born in New York City, moved to Nashville, Tennessee, and then Texas about twenty-five years previous. He was married in Jacksboro to Miss Anna Gallagher. They had a son who died in infancy. Tom was fifty-five years old at his death. His funeral was one of the largest ever witnessed in Denison to that time, with a wide representation of the citizenry. Mr. Horan was a member of the Elks, the Vorwaerts, Odd Fellows, Woodmen of the World and Knights of Pythias.

His body was buried at Fairview Cemetery, but does some part of him still remain at his beloved business?

The original Annie Peruna steamboat came to Denison in April 1905 and was not exactly a great success, to put it mildly. The Annie Peruna Jr. was built in Denison later the same year (1905) and used on the river for a while. Bert Ford, one of Denison's early gasoline motor mechanics, and Lon McAleer, owners of a Sugar Bottom coal and wood yard, were builders of the boat. It became quite a spectacle not only in Denison, but also in Preston Bend.

The Annie P. & Her Performance Before ALL of Preston Bend Residents

Sunday Gazetteer, September 14, 1905 – The infamous Annie P. had not been heard from in a few months (ahem.... because she was quarantined... but don't tell anyone), but the old gal was soon on the river cutting up wild capers, as usual. On Sunday, September 7, the Annie P. was at Baer's Ferry, piloted by Commodore McAleer and Chief Engineer Bert Ford. The boat made an inauspicious beginning as it soon grounded on two or three sandbars in the river, which necessitated the Commodore and his crew to enter the water to pull her off the sand into the open stream. After finally proceeding a short distance, they turned loose the old blunderbuss, which startled the whole country. Worshippers at churches adjourned, and led by the preachers, proceeded to the river to see what in the devil was the matter. In fact, **the whole population of the Preston Bend district** gathered at the river, not for a baptism, but a spectacle, many suspecting there had been a massive earthquake.

After startling the natives of Preston Bend by shooting off some huge shells, Commodore McAleer turned the prow of his craft back east in the direction Baer's ferry. Brumbaugh and Ed Moulton then put in an appearance. Giving old man Baer a knowing wink, they invited him to go with them to inspect some shells that had been left up in the woods. Baer seemed to understand what was wanted and returned in a few moments, smacking his lips and saying that those "shells" were all right. Commodore McAleer was then invited ashore and told that he had better go up and take a look at the Brumbaugh-Moulton shells. The shells seemed to produce an exhilarating effect on the Commodore, as he appeared smacking his lips and seemed to be in the best of humor. What the aforesaid shells CONTAINED, was not officially disclosed, but they must have been loaded with HIGH EXPLOSIVES. The Commodore then boarded the Annie P., with his crew, himself and his ship all FULLY LOADED - though with two different kinds of explosives, if you know what I mean.

Charley Clymer and family and a number of others, who had read and heard so much of the checkered career of Annie P., were anxious to see how she behaved on the water. They did not have to wait long. The circus opened in a very few moments.

Commodore McAleer, standing at the wheel as proud as if standing on the quarter-deck of a battleship, started down the river with a full head of steam – or gasoline. Annie P., for a moment or so, behaved splendidly. Commodore McAleer fairly swelled with pride. All at once the old girl seemed to bump and quiver in every timber and then was witnessed one of the most remarkable sights ever seen on Red River. She began to spin like a top, performing circle after circle. Commodore McAleer rang the bell furiously and shouted his orders to the chief engineer to shut off and stop the engine. Since the chief engineer was entertaining a party of ladies in his cabin, he was oblivious to the ringing of the bell and the voice of the Commodore. The spectators on shore laid down and laughed. It looked as if Annie P. was wound up like a clock and would have to run down before she would stop. Great confusion prevailed on board.

Commodore McAleer was sweating, blowing and swearing; deckhands were rushing fore and aft; still, Annie continued to go around and around. The mystery was soon explained, Commodore McAleer had jammed the rudder against the stern wheel. The spectators on shore were now worked up to a high state of excitement and yelled to the Commodore: "Keep her a-going, old boy," "She is doing fine." "Ain't the old gal a good one," and other similar remarks.

But the climax was yet to come. One of the invited guests on board was a Katy machinist named Strahorn. All at once Commodore McAleer and the boat's crew were seen to grab Strahorn by the legs and going to the boat's side, thrust his head in the direction of the water. The first impression among the spectators on shore was that Commodore McAleer intended to drown Strahorn; that he was the Jonah and must be thrown overboard. However, they were helping Strahorn adjust the rudder. The Annie Peruna was soon righted, and the Commodore turned in toward the shore, cast anchor and then went into the woods to take a few more shots of the Brumbaugh-Moulton "liquid" shells again.

Preston Tragedies

One of the earliest tragedies was shared by many parts of the Southeastern area of North America. The Caddo tribe occupied the Red River Valley before the white exploration. Caddo Indians enter written history in the chronicles of the Hernando de Soto expedition, which describe encounters during the Spanish passage through southwest Arkansas. When the Spaniards crossed to Caddo country on June 20, 1542, they entered a nation unique in language, social structure, tradition, and way of life.

Caddo people were farmers, hunters, traders, salt miners, craftsmen of beautiful pottery who buried their dead in mounds and cemeteries with solemn rituals and a belief that the dead traveled to a world beyond this one. They lived in conical shaped grass houses. Caddo language was unlike any spoken by other groups the Spaniards met as they explored northeast Arkansas and the Southern states east of the Mississippi River and into the Red River Valley. Caddo village below from Pinterest.

DeSoto brought with him hoards of hogs from Europe to feed his men as they traveled. These hogs were not at all native to America. Hogs carry MANY diseases that are transmittable to humans, like cholera, and especially are deadly to people like the Native Americans who have no acquired immunity to them. Inevitably, some of these hogs escaped and reproduced, becoming wild, exposing the Indians to their diseases.

In their book, "The Hernando de Soto Expedition," Ann Romenofsky and Patricia Galloway suggest that millions of Native people died because they lacked previous exposure to swine borne diseases, This previous exposure was critical in building their immune systems against the deadly diseases. These diseases include brucellosis, anthrax, leptospirosis, tuberculosis, trichinosis, cysticercosis and various strains of flu.

"And considering the fact that many swine diseases can be transmitted to deer and even turkeys, the two most important food animals used by southeastern Indians, the likelihood that this occurred becomes even greater, " the authors write.

University of Arkansas archaeologist George Sabo III cites 16th- and 17th-century eyewitness descriptions comparing southeastern Native American population numbers.

"The deSoto chroniclers describe Eastern Arkansas and the Mississippi River valley as a place of large extensive Indian communities and numerous, populous villages. They describe groves of nut trees and crop fields extending from one village to the next. The chronicles are expressive of a well-populated landscape." But Sabo says that when the French traveled down the Mississippi River about 130 years after de Soto, they described Eastern Arkansas in far different terms. "They describe the land as being sparsely populated with only a few Indian villages. It's fairly certain the de Soto expedition had an impact on the Indian demographic," Sabo said.

It is likely, this was also the fate of the Caddo people of the Preston Bend area and the Red River Valley as a whole. Quite a calamity indeed. We don't really know HOW it happened that most of them and their society disappeared, but it did. A small contingent of their people settled in what is now Caddo, Oklahoma where they now have their seat of government.

There are burial mounds detected in a straight north/south line from "Treasure Island" now in the middle of Lake Texoma, in the Georgetown community in a rural area, and in the Collinsville area. These may have been made by the Caddo people.

Though they are gone from this area, their mound works stand as lasting memorials to their people and their culture.

Death by Vaccination of Edmund Russell Noble

Preston Loses One of Its Best Citizens

Denison Press Apr 27, 1901 - Edmund Russell Noble, 22, who has been connected with a local daily paper for the past three years, died after an illness of about ten days. Death was caused by vaccination. The first symptom was lockjaw, from which he never rallied. He was unconscious for several days before death. Russell represented the paper in the Indian Territory and was much liked. He was a reporter and a fine newspaperman. About a year ago he was married to a young lady of Paris, Texas. Funeral services were conducted from Coffee's Chapel, with interment in Preston cemetery.

The Sunday Gazetteer April 28, 1901 - **Edmund Russell Noble** had been associated with the Denison Daily Herald for the past three years. The death of this most estimable young man will produce profound sorrow throughout the community, but no more here than in the Indian Territory and the surrounding country, where he was so well known.

Russell Noble represented the Herald in the Territory for a long period and our neighbors became very much attached to him. He was transferred from that field to the reportorial staff and had been a reporter for several months. He was one of the best and purest types of the newspaper fraternity that has ever been connected with the Denison press. He was a gentle and most lovable young man, without a particle of guile in his character. Everybody was attached to him; to know him was to love and respect him. There is only one expression concerning his death, "Too bad, too bad." Edmund Russell Noble was the embodiment of all those noble qualities which characterize the higher and better order of young men. He was always agreeable, always courteous. He was energetic and contributed greatly to the popularity of the Herald at home and abroad. He was a great rustler for business for his paper, but very few people ever turned him away when he solicited. His motto was "The interest of the Herald." About a year ago he led to the altar a most beautiful and cultured young woman in Paris, Texas. At the time of death, he was only 22 years and 5 months old. He came to Denison from Preston Bend, and there at Preston cemetery, he will sleep forever. Funeral services were conducted at Coffey's Chapel.

FREAK ACCIDENT ON THE FARM

Sherman Daily Democrat Feb 3, 1915 - John L. Baird, living five miles north of Pottsboro, died Saturday night from injuries received Friday evening after his day's work was done. Having unhitched his team from the plow, he had allowed the reins to remain around his waist, as was usual for farmers to do, but it seems the team became frightened at some calves. When found, Mr. Baird was unconscious and holding his watch in his hand. The supposition is that he was noting the time on his watch and was caught off his guard at the time the mules became frightened. It appeared they dragged him about forty yards, striking and uprooting a tree stump, and here he became freed from the team, which then ran to the house. When the mules were seen standing unattended, still hitched, a search was made for him.

Burial services were held under the auspices of the Masonic fraternity at Coffee Chapel cemetery one mile west of Preston on Feb. 3, where he has a wife and several children buried. Bro. Baird was about 60 years old, was a long-time member of the Methodist Church and had lived in the Preston Bend community for over 20 years, before moving to the Progress neighborhood. He leaves a widow and a number of children. This community of Preston Bend recognized the worth of this good man, and join with the people of the nearby Progress community in offering condolence to his surviving heartbroken wife and children.

Bad Automobile Wreck on Preston Bend Road

Dallas Morning News Aug 10, 1907- The first serious accident to a Denison-owned automobile occurred on August 9th about 7 o'clock, when the big red touring car of Dr. H. W. James plunged over an eight-foot embankment on the Preston Bend road, three miles northwest of Denison. In the car were Dr. and Mrs. W. H. James, Mr. and Mrs. J. T. Suggs and little son, and Elmer E. Davis. The machine became unmanageable while going down a hill, and at the foot of the incline, it left the roadway, plunged down the embankment and turned completely over. Mrs. Suggs and Mrs. James were thrown from the car and escaped with a few slight bruises. Mr. Suggs, who had his son in his arms, jumped and he and his son escaped with minor injuries. Mr. Davis and Dr. James were caught under the machine and were the most seriously injured of the party. Mr. Davis was hurt about the back and ribs and is confined to his bed today. He is unable to use his lower limbs, but the attending physicians do not believe his injuries will prove permanent or serious. Dr. James sustained a broken rib and was otherwise shaken up and bruised. The machine suffered very little damage. Dr. James showed a wonderful presence of mind in shutting off the engine while pinioned under the car, thus preventing the possibility of an explosion of gasoline.

A Bad Day at Preston

Sherman Daily Democrat, May 6, 1915 - Two people had bad experiences on the same day in Preston, and it wasn't even a Friday the 13th. E. P. Jackson was painfully, but not seriously injured by falling from the upper story of his barn. Charlie Spivey was also injured on the same day while trying to raise the cable at the ferry one mile north of Preston. He and Earnest Meadows immediately left for Denison where he sought treatment for his wounds.

Bad Whiskey (and Lots of it) Makes for a Bad Night on the Road at Preston

A farmer by the name of Douglass, residing in the Preston Bend country, came to Denison on Saturday where he got "tanked up" on bad whiskey. It is unknown if he patronized the new saloon on Preston Road outside Denison which had the nearby residents in an uproar. While he was en route home late on Saturday night he fell from his wagon due to his severe inebriation and was found Sunday morning by the side of the road, still in an insensible condition. The man's team had continued on a half-mile or more where it became tangled in the harness and stopped in the road. The fellow regained consciousness later in the day and finally finished his trip back home, if a day late and a team and wagon short. Information from stories from The Sunday Gazetteer (Denison, Tex.), July 31 & Oct 23, 1892.

Death From Typhoid Fever at Preston Bend –
Two Members of Family Die One Day Apart, Same Disease

The Sunday Gazetteer. (Denison, Tex.), October 20, 1901 – The entire community came together in sympathy with Mr. and Mrs. Claypool, who were mourning the death of two children which occurred a day apart. Bacon A. Claypool, aged 24 years, died at Shawnee, Indian Territory on the 15th of October, and Josephine, a child of two years, passed away at the home of her father at Preston Bend on the 14th. Both members of the family died from typhoid fever. The son's remains were shipped to Denison for interment in Fairview Cemetery. He was well-known in Denison and held in high esteem – a fine example with his industrious habits of life. In his humble sphere of duty, whatever he did, he did well. Josephine was brought from Preston Bend and laid to rest beside her brother. Rev. W. B. Carnes conducted the funeral services.

The Mundane and the 'Shocking' at Preston

By Uncle Rip - Denison Herald June 23, 1925 - **Fish Catches Fisherman** - Clyde Carrender, having caught some fish, among which was a large catfish, lariated them in Red River and forgetting they were there, jumped in to take a swim. He struck his naked foot against the fin of the catfish, which entered the sole, pierced the foot clear through and broke off, leaving the fin in the foot. Mr. Carrender was taken to Denison for surgical treatment.

Auto Accidents in Preston - There is an average of about three accidents a year on the big hill just south of Preston. Until this steep grade is reduced, they will likely continue, and possibly increase, as the tourist travel is increasing now on this highway No. 91. If on July 28 the road bonds for Grayson County are voted, the grade on this hill will be reduced 5 percent, to the government requirements, eliminating the short curves, with a concrete bridge across the creek above high water. The water in 1908 saw the water from Red River entirely over the highest position of the present bridge and no crossing for about ten days.

A related question, we now have experts over the county to examine automobile lights. Why not let it be their duty to test the brakes and horns also? It is possible the poor condition of the last two are the case of 50 percent of auto accidents, especially on Preston's steep hills and sharp curves.

Morally Shocking Conversation of the Day: The following conversation took place in Denison, probably at a certain bank on a corner on Main Street: A pretty young lady presented a check to the bank official requesting it be cashed. The teller remarked: "The check is O.K. but miss, have you anything in your possession by which you may be identified?" She thought for a moment and replied: "I have a mole on my left knee."

Literally Shocking: Our good friend from Preston, R. L. Jackson, was seen out on crutches Sunday as a result of his shocking experience on Saturday. He had the bad luck to be run over by an automobile and then was shocked by a live electrical wire in Downtown Denison. It is very hard to kill a good man though, and he was only consigned to crutches. This writer (Uncle Rip Fawcett) and Rob Jackson have been running this range together a long time, and if he has a bone in his body that has NOT been broken, it is in his cranium, which is brim full of gray matter and in excellent health. (See more on this story in the next article)

The Mundane: Rev. Charles A. Spraggins drove from Denton, a distance of seventy-seven miles to Preston on Sunday by 11 o'clock and preached a fine sermon. There was dinner o the ground. He being a presiding elder for this, the Gainesville district, convened the third quarterly conference with Walter

Brennan, secretary, and possible fifteen officers and lay members present. After adjournment, Rev. Mr. Spraggins left for Whitesboro, where he preached at night and then held their third quarterly conference, expecting to drive in his home at Denton about 11 o'clock that night. Consider that man's dedication! **Yet, we find some persons who cannot get to Sunday school at their local church on time, try as hard as they can.**

Mr. Davis, who recently purchased the gin here, is doing a good deal of work on the house and machinery. It looks like we are going to have real service here this year. We predict that if we have a normal cotton crop, this gin will get a thousand bales of cotton. Rev. and Mrs. Lloyd Lemmon, Mr. and Mrs. Y. P. Fawcett and daughter, Miss Genevieve, of Shreveport, after a week's visit with relatives, left last Friday for Houston and Galveston overland. Mrs. John Stowe and little son Jackie of Sherman were visiting relatives here at Preston last week. Miss Fay Stroman of Kingston is here visiting her aunt, Mrs. Al Caddell.

More about the shocking story of R. L. Jackson being shocked...

SHOCKED!

Denison Herald June 22, 1925 - Robert Jackson of Preston Bend received a shock and minor bruises about the arms and legs Saturday afternoon when a supporting crosswire holding the trolley wire of the Texas Electric Railway at the corner of Burnet Avenue and Main Street in Denison broke, allowing the cable to fall over the street.

Jackson received a severe electrical shock and minor bruises according to his attending physician, Doctor James Rutledge. The wire was repaired later and no further damage was done.

Mr. Jackson is still confined to his home at Preston. He has not quite recovered from the shock. His family and friends were also extremely shocked about this unfortunate accident.

Below: 1940s postcard showing the overhead wires on Denison's Main Street powering the electric rail cars.

Trash Fire Becomes Funeral Pyre at Preston

People are fascinated by fire. They like to look at it, it seems to be a spectator sport, even when the family burns a brush pile or household rubbish. But be careful, fire is fascinating because it is a force of nature. As with most forces of nature – they can grow out of control and they can kill.

Children feel safe in their own backyard with their family around them. On one particular day in Preston, this was not the case. Elvadin Holmes, age 6, daughter of Mrs. Lilly Holmes was standing in the yard of her family home while trash was being burned. Her clothing became ignited, and could not be extinguished until she was charred from head to foot. She died in a local hospital.

217

Funeral services were conducted at 11 am Saturday at Preston by the Rev. L. R. Lamb, pastor of the Calvary Baptist Church of Denison, burial following at Preston Cemetery. Surviving besides the mothers were a brother, Leonard Austin of California, and a sister, Melvagin Holmes of Preston. - Dallas Morning News Nov 25, 1934.

PROMINENT CITIZEN A. M. BRYANT KILLED

A Team Runs Away, Crushing Him Between a Tree and the Wagon

Dallas Morning News - 24 October 1889 - A.M. Bryant, an ex-judge of Grayson County, also one of the members of the body that reconstructed the constitution of 1869, was killed this evening at his home by a runaway team. He was standing on the double tree of his wagon when the team became frightened and started on a run. After running 100 yards they ran astride of a tree and he was caught between the wagon bed and tree and crushed to death. He lived about five minutes.

The Great Depression Hits Preston Bend

Denison Press Oct 20, 1934   **RELIEF BUREAU GIVES EMPLOYMENT TO FIFTY MEN**

A relief bureau project employing approximately fifty men daily will begin at Preston Bend as soon as approval of the project can be made at Austin, J. W. Reaves, head of the bureau's work program, said Saturday.

The workmen at Preston Bend will be employed cutting wood to be distributed to relief clients. Civic organizations are supplying gasoline and oil for trucks to haul the wood and to transport workmen. Trucks owned by relief clients will be used.

218

The Denison Press   August 9, 1934

YOUTH KILLED BY AUTO AS HE SLEEPS. DRIVER FAILS TO SEE HIM THERE

Instantly killed as he slept, was the fate of the young son of Skinner Crabtree of Preston Bend. The tragedy occurred near Woodville, Oklahoma, when he was backed over by an automobile. This car was said to have belonged to A. L. Abrons of Sherman. The boy was 11 years old. He had laid down behind an automobile which was parked near an open-air Full Gospel revival, one mile south of Woodville, being conducted by Rev. L. L. Newby of the Full Gospel Church of Denison, and evidently had fallen asleep. (Too bad the preacher did not keep the poor lad awake!)

With the meeting over and the congregation leaving, Mr. Abrons is said to have backed his car out and as he did, felt the back wheels run over some firm object. His curiosity aroused and not hearing any sound, Mr. Abrons investigated and found that he had run over the little boy. According to witnesses, the child made no outcry, leading to the belief that he was asleep at the time of the accident.

The child's parents were not at the scene of the tragedy but were later found and told of the accident. The child was rushed to Denison immediately and taken to the Long-Snead clinic where he was pronounced dead by an attending physician. His back was crushed, and it is thought that death came instantly.

Mr. Abrons reported the accident to the police station soon afterward, but no charges were filed. The remains were moved to Madill, OK.

The Denison Press   December 26, 1935

CRASH TAKES TWO LIVES ON HIGHWAY HERE

TILDEN AND OSCAR KEELER LAID TO REST AT GEORGETOWN.

Two caskets were lowered side by side to their final resting places in the Georgetown cemetery Thursday afternoon as the melancholy finis of a Christmas Eve tragedy that claimed the lives of 58 year old Tilden Keeler, a Preston Bend farmer, and his 14 year old son, Oscar, when their wagon was dashed into splinters by an automobile on Highway No. 91 while they were en route to a Christmas tree party at the Preston Bend Baptist Church. The accident happened about 6:30 p.m.

Sylvester Shires, 1330 West Chestnut Street, suffered a severe gash on his head when his automobile plowed through the farm wagon. Sam H. Whitley, Preston Bend farmer who was riding on the wagon with Mr. Keeler and his son, escaped without serious injury when he was hurled several feet out on the right of way by the impact. The loss of a wagon wheel a few minutes before the tragedy probably saved the lives of Mrs. Keeler, Mrs. Whitley, and Wanda Spruill, granddaughter of Mr. and Mrs. Keeler, who had walked ahead to the church a short distance away, while the men repaired the wagon to follow them later. The entire party had left the Keeler home two- and one-half miles northwest of Preston Bend for the Christmas party as passengers in the ill-fated vehicle.

Within a few yards of the church, the wagon was traveling east along a lateral road and the automobile was moving south on the highway. The crash occurred with such force that the two victims were hurled amid fragments of the wagon to instant death about seventy-five feet beyond the intersection.

His body badly broken by the explosive impact, the youth was picked up from the middle of the highway and the lifeless form of the father was lying on the east edge of the concrete slab. The badly battered Ford V8 coupe automobile came to a stop along with the entangled wreckage of the wagon chassis on the west side of the highway.

James Shaw of Denison was the first person to reach the tragic scene and summoned Short-Murray's ambulance from Denison by telephoning from Jackson's Store at Preston Bend. Still dazed from the injury suffered when his head was thrust through the windshield, and then the top of the car, Mr. Shires himself was the first to notify Deputy Sheriffs Bart Shipp and Wesley Barnhill of the accident.

Mr. Sam Whitley explained that the two men and boy were continuing to the church after remounting the wagon wheel and that he was riding in the rear watching the wheel to signal Mr. Keeler should it come off again.

Upon seeing the lights of the approaching car as the wagon started across the highway, Mr. Whitley warned Mr. Keeler, "I don't think you are going to be able to make it." The crash followed instantly. Mr. Whitley said his being hurled from splintered wagon was like being catapulted from a springboard.

The team of horses escaped injury as the wagon was swept from behind them and were found grazing a short distance away. The old automobile chassis used in improvising the wagon was left in twisted debris seventy-five feet down the highway, with one wheel being hurled at least 150 feet from the point of collision. Fragments ripped from the front of the automobile also were mingled with the splinters of wood scattered about the death scene. After a preliminary investigation of the accident, Officers Shipp and Barnhill said they believe the tragedy to have been unavoidable. Mr. Shipp indicated that a court investigation may be held to officially dispose of the matter.

The elder Mr. Keeler was born in Williamson County, Texas, Jan. 23, 1877, the son of Mr. and Mrs. Joe Keeler, and was married in Williamson County to Miss May Preece, May 4, 1898. Mr. Keeler came to Grayson County in 1918 from Mills County, Texas and lived in the Georgetown community nine years before moving to West Texas and later to Oklahoma. After years away from Grayson County, he and his family returned to the Preston Bend district 15 years before his death. The son, Oscar Keeler was born at Preston Bend fourteen years ago and was a student in the Preston Bend school. The youth assisted his father in operation of the farm.

Surviving the victims are the widow and mother, Mrs. May Keeler; three daughters and sisters, Mrs. Besse Clements and Miss Willie Keeler, Preston Bend, and Mrs. Myrtle Travis, Pottsboro; three sons and brothers, Sam Keeler, Pottsboro, and Bill and Joe Keeler, Gracemont, Okla.; Mr. Keeler's mother-in-law, Mrs. Fannie Preece, Leander, Texas, and the granddaughter of Mr. Keeler, Wanda Spruill.

Double funeral services were held Thursday afternoon at 2 o'clock at the Georgetown cemetery with Rev. S. M. Black, pastor of Waples Memorial Methodist Church officiating. Short-Murray, funeral directors, were in charge.

Child Dies in Shooting at Preston

Paris News December 10, 1933 - Okla Christine Crabtree, 5 years old, was fatally injured Thursday afternoon at the family home at Preston Bend when a .410 shotgun in the hands of the child's uncle went off. The shot went into the left side and penetrated the stomach. The child died at a Denison hospital.

Preston Bend
Youth Killed
In Gun Mishap

The Denison Press, December 11, 1940 - Bullet wounds inflicted by an accidental discharge of a gun in the hands of a neighborhood companion proved fatal Tuesday afternoon to Nolan Cruson, 12 years old son of Mr. Jesse Cleveland "Jack" Cruson and Mrs. Viola Cruson living on South Preston Road of the Preston Bend community.

The youth died a few hours later at a local hospital. Nolan and his companion were running towards a barn in the rear of the Cruson home to inspect furs brought in by Mr. Cruson and his eldest son, Jack, who had returned from hunting in the woods nearby. The gun caught in a fence gate as the youths passed through and accidentally discharged, the bullet hitting Nolan in the back and piercing to his heart.

He was picked up by his father and rushed to the hospital, where he died a short time later.

Young Cruson was saving the furs to be sold later in order that he might have money to purchase Christmas gifts.

Nolan was born at Preston Bend on October 27, 1928, and was attending the Eureka school in 7th grade. He was buried at Layne cemetery in Denison.

Nolan's older siblings were Jack Dean Cruson, and Ava Jean Cruson, his younger siblings were Dwayne Doyle Cruson, Betty Lou Cruson, Billie Ruth Cruson, Wanda Bee Cruson, and Clora Lee Cruson.

Resident of Preston Bend Loses Her First Love in the Civil War, Stays True to Him Throughout Her Century-Long Life

Louisa Pocahontas Harris, Former Resident of Preston

June 13, 1837 – August 20, 1939

d/o Matthew Handy Harris & Millie Cochran

On June 11, 1936, there was an article in the Denison Herald about a former Preston Bend woman who was at that time almost as old as Texas' freedom. Miss Lou Harris was getting ready to celebrate her 99th birthday while Texas observed 100 years of freedom. Miss Harris had lived in Texas since 1845, having settled in Cherry Mound before the Civil War.

At that time Miss Harris was said to be the oldest woman in Grayson County, followed closely by Mrs. Helen Alexandria Morrison Cummins of Denison, also formerly of Preston Bend and Georgetown, north of Pottsboro, who had celebrated her 95th birthday. Mrs. Cummins was a bride in Texas one year after the close of the Civil War.

Every year she was honored at a reunion in August at the home at Cherry Mound where she had lived for many years. She was known as "Miss Lou" and called "Aunt Nie," although no one knew why. Having lived through four wars -- the Mexican War, Civil War, Spanish-American War, and World War I -- Miss Lou scoffed at people in the 1930s who languished under what she called "the so-called Depression." She called the times "prosperity" in comparison with the privation that followed the War Between the States in the 1860s. "People do not know what poverty and want are nowadays," she told the newspaper writer.

Miss Lou was described as a venerable lady who always had been a favorite with children. No doubt, the pet name "Aunt Nie" came from some of those youngsters. While being interviewed, she held an infant on her lap. A very small woman weighing only about 88 pounds, she wasn't strong enough to lift the husky baby but delighted in having him handed to her. A niece said that during her childhood her wounds were always healed by the kisses of Aunt Nie.

Miss Lou, like many women of her day, remained true to the love of her early youth, a young Confederate soldier who marched off to war with the thought of coming home and being married. Unfortunately, he didn't return from the war. His photo was among her cherished relics. "It was all very long ago," she said when asked about him. Miss Lou decided that she didn't want a 99th birthday party because she said it was too much trouble for those giving it. As a young woman, she played the violin and accordion and just two years before her 99th birthday she had entertained a group by playing the accordion. She was a member of the Trinity Methodist Church congregation and was a regular attendee at worship service until she was about 97.

Miss Lou was born in Illinois in 1837, one year after the battle of San Jacinto. She went to Arkansas with her parents in 1843, and two years later **in about 1845, the family settled at Preston Bend.** She and her mother later moved to Warren Flats that was near Cherry Mound. In 1928 she moved to Denison to live with a great-niece Mrs. Carrie Gilliam until she died. She was making her home with Mrs. Clint Price at the time of the interview. **She was educated in the rural schools of Preston. A brother, Mat Harris, fought for the Confederacy in the Civil War.**

FIRE AT PRESTON

Denison Daily Herald February 21, 1906 - The home of R. P. Elrod, near Preston, was totally destroyed by fire at about 9 p.m., the family barely escaping in their night clothes. Mr. Elrod was carrying a lamp, which exploded, setting fire to the furnishings. As the flames spread so rapidly, nothing could be done in removing household goods. Erwin, a young son of Mr. Elrod, attempted to re-enter the building and had his hair singed. Miss Della Warren, a niece of the Elrods, who is visiting them also had a narrow escape in entering the burning building. The house was a two-story frame structure, valued at $4,000 and insured for $2,000. The contents were valued at $2,500 and insured for $900.

Missing Child Feared Drowned & Accidental Shooting

Denison Herald December 17, 1924 - Parties from Platter, Oklahoma were here at Preston Sunday searching for a demented boy named Woods who is the same boy taken in charge earlier by Sheriff Everhart and cared for until his friends read in the Denison Herald of his whereabouts. Those searching for him traced him to the bank of the Red River and saw his tracks at the water's edge. This was the last known location for him Sunday. It is feared that he drowned. He left his home Friday.

Little Miss Tassy Tillery, age 13, daughter of John Tillery, living on the Caddell farm in Preston, in handling a pistol, accidentally discharged it. The ball just broke the skin on the end of her nose. Vina Timberlake, age 12, daughter of O. Timberlake, fell from a pecan tree breaking her left arm and shoulder.

Our school teachers are attending the Teachers Institute this week.

So far, no bad news has come from this school trip.

5. Just Plain Weird!

AUNT CASE WAS 127 YEARS OLD!

The Denison Daily News October 12, 1879 -- Mr. Hynes, who has just returned from a trip west, spent an evening with a woman of color named Aunt Case, who is 127 years of age.

Aunt Case has an authentic record of her age during the first 100 years, it being recorded in a family Bible which belonged to her old master. Aunt Case has a daughter living with her who is 85 years of age. They live in the lonely Washita Valley.

"Jimmy the Rooster" AT PRESTON BEND

The Daily Hesperian (Gainesville, Tex.), Jan 31, 1897 - Constable Lee French went to Preston Bend and got a man said to be crazy, who was running at large in that community. He brought him to Denison and placed him in jail. The man was about 25 years of age, short, stooped and had a prominent chin. He would not talk and the only thing he had ever said was "Jimmy." The inmates of the jail called him "Jimmy the Rooster" which always evoked a meaningless smile for "Jimmy". The man, together with two others, was taken to the Sherman jail.

BABY'S DAY OUT

Denison Daily Herald June 17, 1908

R. L. McWillie picked up a little girl that had been lost on West Main Street yesterday afternoon. After a diligent search of several hours he finally located the parents, who were here from Preston Bend on a visit The father and mother said that they with the little girl had entered a restaurant on Main Street for dinner and while there the youngster strayed out to the sidewalk and disappeared. When Mr. WcWillie discovered the tot she was eating some candy and looking in at the show windows. He took his charge into the moving picture shows where she seemed to enjoy everything and did not for a moment seem to miss her parents.

Calamity for .... the Squirrels, Poultry, Fish....

Of Preston Bend .... Tasty for Humans.

Sulphur Springs Gazette (Sulphur Springs, Tx), Dec. 17, 1909

Wagon Load of Squirrels.

Sherman, Tex., Dec. 10.—Leslie Hunter of the Preston Bend country brought a wagon load of squirrels which he had killed in that section to Sherman this morning. They found a ready sale. Mr. Hunter has brought to the Sherman market this year fish, peanuts, pecans, all kinds of poultry and squirrels.

CRIME AND CALAMITY AT PRESTON BEND BY NATALIE CLOUNTZ BAUMAN

Evidence of Calamity of Long Ago Unearthed at Preston Bend – Mastodon Fossils Found

Several people motored out to the farm of W. W. Steele at Preston Bend for the purpose of exhuming and recovering the remains of what appeared to be a mastodon. The party consisted of Prof. F. B. Hughes, W. B. Munson, Chas. H. Jones, W. J. Leeper, J. T. Munson, John Leeper, and others. Mr. Steele had already found and shown part of the remains of the mastodon skeleton to W. B. Munson, who afterward organized the expedition. Arriving at the farm, the work began, and while they recovered what appeared to be the lower jaw, a portion of one of the tusks, and parts of the teeth, they were disappointed in not finding the balance of the skeleton.

Prof. Hughes brought back what relics were obtained, which were amply sufficient to show that they were the remains of a mastodon. The specimens were to be preserved for the High School museum. - Honey Grove Signal, October 9, 1914 & Denison Herald.

Christmas is Coming – It's Hog Killing Time – But Get Out the Mad Stone – The Death Angel Approaches Preston Bend

In 1904, everyone at Preston Bend knows it will soon be Christmas time because the white cotton fields are now bare, and the farmers busy taking the bales to market. Captain J. B. Williams, Dr. C. A. Gibson and Mrs. Helvey have all purchased new buggies and life seems good.

There was ice in the water bucket this morning. The cool weather is a signal that it is hog killing time, in order to get those Christmas hams prepared. It isn't the same without that Christmas dinner.

But also with the chill winds, came the cold advent of the Death Angel to Preston Bend. Forty days earlier, the O'Dell family's youngest son Fred was bitten by a rabid dog. He went to Sherman to have the "mad stone" applied and thought all the poison had been drawn out, but the wound finally proved fatal this week. Funeral services were held at the M. E. Church.

Others were hoping to outrun the Angel of Death. William Blake had pneumonia. William Jackson was confined to his bed with typhoid fever. E. N Moyer had been confined to his room for several days with lung trouble. S. A. Wilson decided to move to Kingston I. T. and will make that his home. C. H. Campbell will leave for Madill tomorrow. Several are going to the Indian Territory.

Let us hope for their sake the Death Angel does not also move his residence north to the Territory as well.

Rabies and the Mad Stone

BITTEN BY A MAD RACCOON

Denison Daily News June 18, 1875 - Mr. G. W. Dismukes, of Little Mineral, informs us that a little girl was bitten by what is supposed to have been a rabid coon, a few days ago. The child is a daughter of Mrs. Denson, residing above the mouth of the Washita, in the Nation. She was playing just outside the gate, when the coon came out from the underbrush and attacked her, biting her on the leg, causing a severe wound. The girl was taken to Colin McKinney's near McKinney, and the mad stone applied. The stone adhered firmly for thirty-six hours when it fell off and would stick no longer. Mr. McKinney is confident the stone extracted all the virus. This is the first instance that ever came to our knowledge of a coon going mad.

Sherman Daily Register - August 29, 1887 - **MAD WOLF** - People living on the Red River, a few miles east of Preston, report that a wolf, evidently suffering from the effects of hydrophobia, was seen in there, and he made several savage onslaughts on dogs and other domestic animals, but so far had not bitten any of them. People were trying to destroy the wolf before it could do so.

MAD DOG BITES FAMILY

Rabies. John Combs, wife and three children have gone to Austin to take the Pasteur treatment for hydrophobia. Mr. Combs and the three children were bitten by their own dog about ten days ago.

The dog's head was sent to Austin for examination and the authorities telegraphed back that the dog had had rabies. We feel very uneasy about our neighbors and the hope the treatment may be successful.

I've known of two deaths here of persons from a mad dog bite and am in favor of taxing the dogs. Let every man have one dog free, but $50 for every dog over and let this tax help to defray the expenses of those unfortunates that are bitten.

But here am I, just a little farmer, tackling a job that the State Press of the Dallas News acknowledges is too large for them. So I'll place myself with the other simple ones that go where angels fear to tread.

But this won't keep me from writing to Mr. Reeves, telling him down here we think dogs should be taxed.

(Mr. Reeves' ancestor George R. Reeves died from rabies due to the bite of a rabid dog, so maybe he will pay attention.)

Mrs. Sallie Fawcett gave a dinner to a few friends Sunday, among whom were Mrs. Belle Williams, formerly of Preston, but now living in Denison. Tom Caddell of Denison was in Preston Saturday on business. Miss V. Meadows, who attended high school in Denison, visited her father and mother here Saturday. Mrs. Mary Bell and son, J. D., came in Friday and left for home. Sherman is now their temporary home. Uncle RIP

UNCLE RIP TELLS PRIZE SOLDIER STORY - Also says **Preston is the "Garden of Eden"** and Her People Will Be Right Here After the Prizes on "Better Seed Day"

Sherman Daily Democrat, Feb 11, 1919 - Always wanting to see Preston in the spotlight, we have therefore distributed a few copies of the program and cash premiums sent us by the Sherman Chamber of Commerce, explaining "Better Seed Day" Wednesday the 12th, and feel sure we will have quite a number from here and we will be surprised if this bunch doesn't capture some of the first premiums, for this particular location is known far and wide as "The Garden of Eden." Let me commend a young married couple through your columns: Will Langstand and Miss Monroe married about a year since, and in a few months the husband was called to the army and on leaving, he handed his girl wife who was about 18, $300 and told her that would last her until he could become settled in the army, at which time he'd send her more. The wife placed the three hundred dollars in the bank and after a while, the husband sent her a check for $50, and this she placed in the bank also and living with her father, picked cotton and thereby gained another $50. Then one day recently, Will walked in and handed his wife his honorable discharge and the girl wife, in turn, handed him her bank deposit book with $400. They soon purchased a pair of mules and a good farming outfit, rented a farm and moved into it, all within a week after the return of this soldier boy. And to complete their happiness, there arrived

232

on the 7th a little daughter. Just think, if all the young couples managed as this one has, then the divorce courts would be without grist. "So may it be." Our pike has been improved by the road grader having been drawn over it. We presume it was done by order of our commissioner. "Honor to whom honor is due." We don't think our good roads have gone to the bow-wows as some seem to think. Fill up the little chug holes with gravel and then with wind and sunshine the grader and time, they will be about as good as new.

Jackson Home courtesy of Frontier Village Museum, photos donated by Roy Jackson.

LARGE VARMINT AT PRESTON

Denison Daily Herald March 31, 1905 - Some kind of a wild "varmint" has caused considerable excitement in the vicinity of Preston, on Red River, and the country around is being scoured by hunters. As the report states, C. S. Varney, who lives about two miles southeast of Preston, was aroused Wednesday night by a terrible fight between the beast and his dogs. He rushed out with his pistol and saw a large animal as it was disappearing into the dark woods. He returned to the house, but about daybreak, he heard shots at the home of his near neighbor, W. A. Jackson, and looking out, saw a large strange looking animal headed toward his house. He seized his shotgun and ran outside, but the animal fled in another direction. Jackson came on over to Varney's and a consultation was held. Jackson said he shot at the animal twice and thinks he hit it, but the shot seemed to have been too small to have much effect on the large animal. As in the case of Mr. Varney, he was attracted by the barking and yelping of his dogs. Later in the morning, the varmint was seen by a man on the Caddell farm in the bend of the river. Those who saw the strange brute in daylight describe it as being a rather long, big bodied, yellow animal with a dark looking back and large shoulders. (An old bigfoot? The hair of the old ones' turns white like ours does. If it's dirty, it would look yellowish.)

Citizens However, Somewhat Chilled by Alleged Invulnerability

September 3, 1905, Dallas Morning News - Nearly a year ago, the people living along the riverfront near Preston were set agog by the appearance in the woods of a strange being in human form. When discovered by a party of hunters, he was on his all-fours pawing and neighing like a horse, their attention being first attracted by what they took to be the whinny of a startled horse in the undergrowth. When advanced upon, the strange being ran off on his hands and feet, but the pursuers gained upon him so rapidly, he sprang to his feet and quickly covering the short distance to the river, plunged headlong from a rather high bank into the water and swam to the Indian Territory side. When he reached that bank, he stood up, shook himself like a horse just out of the bath and with what might really be called a horse laugh, ran off into the woods.

Some months later he was seen under much the same conditions, but this time, west of Woodville, on the Indian side of the river.

Only a few weeks ago, a "man" crawled across the road in plain view of several people not far from where the horse-man was first seen, but disappeared, the pursuit being somewhat tardy.

Since Sunday last, the people living near Colbert I. T. ten miles east of Preston, Grayson County, Texas, have been hunting for a strangely acting "man" or whatever, who crawled about like a snake until pursued, when he would jump to his feet and outrun the fastest horses ridden after him. Men can't outrun horses, can they?

Others who pursued him on foot, say they shot at him at close range, but the bullets, if they struck their target, seemed to have no effect. As late as last evening, children claim to have seen the crawling man again near the Varney place, six miles from Colbert, I.T. A phone message from Colbert confirms previous reports sent out from Durant about the state of excitement and the gathering of people there have received something of a chill because some of the parties who were present when the close range shots were fired say that although the peculiar being was in the open and very close, he disappeared with the smoke of the powder. At the Varney place, he crawled into the henhouse. It is stated that out in the field, a dead chicken, bitten in the neck, with all the blood having been drained, was found.

After this alarming news, the people of the Varney neighborhood, with somewhat reduced enthusiasm, prepared for another big roundup tonight. Hopefully, no blood will be drained from anything or anyone tonight.

Appearance of Wild Man Again

September 6, 1905 - Dallas Morning News - East Durant was thrown into a state of excitement last night by the sudden appearance and disappearance of the supposed wild man who has been terrorizing the people six miles east of Colbert and at Preston Bend.

A woman by the name of Manus, residing east of the city at the edge of corporate limits, was attacked after night by some unknown fiend just as she stepped out the back door. Grabbing her around the throat, he choked her almost to insensibility. Being a large woman, she succeeded after several minutes' time in getting loose from the man and ran into the house and notified her husband, who grabbed his gun and ran out into the yard and fired several shots into the brush into which the man had flown. Marshals Wilcox, Anderson, Parker, Scott, Anderson and Yarborough, being notified of the assault, went with the bloodhounds of James B. Davis to the scene and made a search for the supposed wild man, but no trace of him was found. The dogs failed to locate a trail and the chase was given up. The wild man disappeared as with a gust of wind. A view of the grounds shows no tracks; the affair seems to be wrapped in mystery.

Be the wild man story a hoax or whatnot, it is arousing the people and excitement runs high, especially near Colbert, and the women and children will not leave their homes after nightfall.

Peculiar incident where Mr. Porter from Preston Bend met all six of his brothers at a restaurant by accident.

Houston Post July 21, 1900

A PECULIAR OCCURRENCE.

Seven Brothers Met at a Restaurant by Accident.

Denison, Texas, July 20.—At noon the restaurant of J. A. Standales was the scene of a rather remarkable incident. When dinner was announced a Mr. Potter came in and took a seat at the dining table; he was from Preston Bend; in a moment or so a brother from the Indian Territory came in and without knowledge of his brother's presence took a seat at the same table. The brothers had not finished their greeting when in came another brother from near Sherman. He in a few moments was followed by another brother from near Pottsboro and this continued until seven brothers were seated around a single table. The meeting was purely accidental. They are all from Tennessee, no two reside in the same community and neither one knew of the other's presence in the city until the meeting at the restaurant. The names of the brothers are C. W., B. S., A. T., J. A., S. F., C. J., N. H. and N. W. Potter and their ages range from 34 to 53.

Preston Bend UFO Denison Daily News Mar 25, 1880

A gentleman who arrived in the city from Preston Bend stated that while proceeding leisurely along on horseback, he was startled by a loud noise in the air. On looking up, he saw to the east a huge globe of fire, attended by what looked like a fiery cloud. He described it as a most wonderful and startling phenomenon. The occurrence took place at 10 a.m.

Dallas Morning News Feb 26, 1905

HUNTERS BADLY WANTED.

Orchard Men at Sherman Ready to Welcome Any One Who Can Kill Rabbits.

SPECIAL TO THE NEWS.

Sherman, Tex., Feb. 25.—The rabbit pest has assumed an alarming phase in this section. Orchardists have suffered throughout North Texas an aggregate loss that reaches into the thousands of dollars. Truck gardeners are alarmed to more than a passing extent at the prospect of inroads upon their crops. Farmers and others having valuable vegetation open to attack by these industrious little animals are soliciting the visit of hunters, and while the slaughter has been very great, to no appreciable extent has the menace been reduced.

The greatest damage has been to orchards where not only the young trees but some of them as large as five inches in diameter have been so gnawed and bitten as to render them useless. On the Helvey estate, near Preston Bend, Grayson County, an orchard ten years of age has been practically devastated.

One of the most successful preventives from inroads of rabbits and boring insects used by orchardists in the past has been a tree paint, in which tar has been a principal ingredient. Trees upon which a liberal coating had been placed have suffered just the same as the untreated trees this winter. To the fact that the number of rabbits is unprecedentedly large must be added the weather conditions. The snow and ice have made the roots of the grasses and small shrubs inaccessible.

Today The News representative called the attention of John S. Kerr, secretary of the State Nurserymen's Association, to the complaint coming from the orchards of North Texas, Oklahoma and Indian Territory and especially this immediate section, and his information on the subject was in substance corroborative of the situation stated above; he said in addition that damage of this nature was heard of all over Texas.

He is now gathering data and will be able in a few days to address an open letter of advice to orchardists upon this very interesting, though annoying, dilemma.

6. THE SPIRIT of CRIME -
.... MOONSHINING

Sunday Gazetteer. (Denison, Tex.), September 3, 1905

An enterprising fellow, who claimed to be from the North, was caught in the act of boot-legging whiskey in the courthouse, the very heart of the precinct of justice, at Sherman, one day last week. He was doing a lively business disposing of pint bottles at 75 cents each, when taken in by Sheriff Russell.

MOONSHINING ON THE RED RIVER
AROUND PRESTON BEND

Texas Rangers, Moonshiners and Still captured

Moonshine in America began with George Washington, and has continued since then....... Denison Sunday Gazetteer October 29, 1893 - Moonshine is whiskey produced in stills that

239

are not under the control and inspection of the federal government. Such distilleries are recognized as outlaw concerns and the people who operate them do so at their peril, as the government tax revenue collectors, together with their deputies and assistant deputy marshals, are very diligent in looking after that department. These stills and moonshine operations often lead to other crimes like family violence and murder. Many states have mountains and remote river valleys that make hiding stills very easy. It is not quite so easy in Texas. One resident of Fannin county came to the conclusion that a jungle down in the Red River bottoms would be a good place to operate a moonshine business and with that end in view, he selected a location on an island, or properly speaking, a cut-off in the bend of the river, some twenty miles east of Denison, and here he established his sour mash vats, boiler, distiller and "worm." The name of the young man owning the outfit was Stewart, and his knowledge of distilling whiskey was no greater than his knowledge of Uncle Sam's Texas officers, as his first attempt to make a "doubler" was an absolute failure.

Stewart was the young man who shot and killed another man by the name of Martin a short time since, for which offense he was confined in the Fannin County jail. It was known far and near that the still had been erected and the matter soon found its way to the ears of Captain George L. Patrick, deputy collector for this district. In company with Mr. Jim Birch, of Denison, the captain visited the cut-off and very little time was consumed in unearthing the distillery. It had not been used for some time; in fact, everything presented a very crude appearance and it is doubtful if a "run" was ever successfully made there. The outfit was loaded on a wagon and conveyed to Ravenna, where it was stored subject to the government. It was quite probable the killing of Martin grew out of trouble between the men over the illegal distillery operation.

What is Moonshine?

What's the difference between beer, wine, and moonshine whiskey? Beer and wine is just fermented fruit or grain and is fairly low in alcohol content by percentage. Moonshine whiskey or brandy uses that beer, wine or grain mash and then distills it, capturing the alcohol steam that condenses down off the bowling liquid making a clear liquid that is almost pure alcohol if done well. The moonshiner must monitor distillation temperatures carefully and pour the first and the last of the production off because it can produce poison methanol. They then add water to it to "proof it down" or make it about 1/2 alcohol so it is smoother and more drinkable. But moonshine is MUCH stronger than beer or wine, homemade or not.

Alex Kirkpatrick was a well-known Locust man who lived alone in a cabin on the Red River for decades living off the land. He was accomplished in many fields and could have lived in any manner he wished, but he turned his back on "civilized" life in favor living in the woods. He said he would live the same way if he had it to do over. "I've been happy," he said, "and I've always had what I wanted – plenty of food, a place to sleep, and a little money for tobacco and things a fellow needs. I never had any whiskey trouble, because I used to make my own. It's easy to do once you get the hang of it." A fisherman going through town stopped to ask Kirkpatrick directions once, and later he offered him some money. "I don't need your money, mister," said Kirkpatrick, "I've got everything I need." A wise man named Jesus said something similar once: "Beware! Be satisfied with what you have. Guard against every kind of greed. Life is not measured by how much you own." Maybe Kirkpatrick, as accomplished as he was and as many walks of life that he had experienced, was more like another wise man named Solomon. Perhaps he had seen and done it all, had seen that it was all in vain and could not provide happiness;

but opted for the simpler things in life – those closer to nature and closer to God.

However, speaking of making whiskey, Preston Bend, Georgetown, and Locust were excellent places for that to occur because of the abundance of fresh water springs. Mr. Kirkpatrick made use of them to distill moonshine for personal use, others were not were more entrepreneurial in spirit.

Moonshining has been an American tradition, like it or not, that started before George Washington (who was said to be a large-scale moonshiner/ whiskey maker). Nothing has stopped it – not prohibition, the lawmen, nor the revenuers of the I.R.S. As long as there has been grain or fruit, sugar, water, and fire – there have been moonshiners. In the old days before propane burners, the moonshiners had to use wood fires. In order to avoid detection, most of them found remote places and used woods that produced less smoke. Our local remote heavily wooded communities were perfect! There were miles of dense, deserted woods, the perfect place to hide a still. It was said that the community of Locust was so named because of the abundance of locust trees there, which are known to moonshiners as a "low smoke" wood to use for their fires, also to avoid detection.

The old moonshiners usually used mules at a whiskey still not only as motive power but as alarms. If you have ever seen a mule turn its head toward a sound and turn its ears forward, that's what's known as the pricking of the ears. Moonshiner's often kept one or two mules tethered near their still and keep an eye on them. They were used as silent sentries because of their acute hearing. Donkeys were sometimes used but they are more vocal, and so are less desirable, since moonshiners DO NOT want to call attention to themselves. If a mule heard a sound it would prick its ears toward the sound. The moonshiner now knew where the intruder was coming from. He would grab his rifle, move away

CRIME AND CALAMITY AT PRESTON BEND BY NATALIE CLOUNTZ BAUMAN

from the still and hide. If the intruder was a law enforcement officer a retreat was made by the moonshiner. If it was just someone who unknowingly had wandered into the area, a shot or two fired from the brush usually caused a rather hasty retreat by the intruder.

Preston Bend was a perfect place for large tracts of remote woods, and fresh water. There were stores in Preston and in Woodville (just across the Red River from Preston) which were known to provide supplies for moonshiners and/or a cut of the whiskey. They would leave sugar and sacks of ground grain, normally considered as animal feed, beside an old stump, or hidden in an old barrel in the woods at a place on the River bottom near a spring known only to the parties involved. The money for the goods would be left behind.

Some merchants or grocers rationalized this by saying they were selling legal products and they couldn't rightfully refuse to sell to anyone even though they suspected that the purchaser was using them to make an illegal product like moonshine.

Russ Thompson once worked in law enforcement and often rode a black horse. He once rode up to where a known moonshiner lived. There was a baby boy in the yard, dressed in nothing but a diaper, but nobody else acknowledged his call. Russ asked the baby, "Where's your daddy?" The baby pointed down the hill and said, "He's down at the still." The father later swore "He's down at the still" was the first words ever uttered by the baby, so often were those words spoken in his vicinity.

BOOTLEGGER KILLED - Sherman Courier August 18, 1917 - Ty Tippett, an alleged bootlegger, was killed after midnight Thursday night at the Henderson Ferry, north of Pottsboro and west of Preston Bend. He was crossing the river into Oklahoma when fired on by officers. A man said to be named Watkins escaped.

There was a large quantity of liquor in the automobile in which Tippett was riding. He was well known to peace officers on both side of the Red River. It was said he was married and lived at Madill, where the body was taken by the officers.

"Plain Clothes" Officer Charles Worbes, Beaten

Sherman Daily Democrat - May 29, 1917 - Charles Worbes of Preston Bend, who has been working for Sheriff Tom Roberts for some time in the capacity of a plain-clothes man, was knocked down and badly beaten and kicked on the southwest corner of the courthouse square, near the Hall annex. Officers immediately took in custody Red Odom and placed him in jail. So far, he has only been charged with aggravated assault.

Deputy Sheriff Frank Reece stated that Worbes is the principal witness against Charles Odom, father of Red Odom, in several cases of alleged violation of the **local option law (liquor).**

It was stated by the officers that Worbes was employed by Sheriff Tom Roberts some time ago on the recommendation of some of the best citizens of Grayson County. He belongs to one of the best families in the county and bears a most excellent personal reputation. The officers also state that he has worked faithfully and successfully since his appointment by Sheriff Tom Roberts. When he was picked up by Joe Rigby and others who went to him as soon as they could get there after he was felled with a bottle, he was dazed and bleeding, and could not remember his name. He was taken to a physician's office and his wounds dressed by Dr. Andrew Swafford. He had a large gash on the back of his head, which Deputy Sheriff Frank Kidd states was made by a heavy glass bottle, and there were ugly gashes over and under his right eye, nose and on his right hand. These, the officer's stated, were made when Worbes was kicked after being knocked down.

Kicking a man when he is down - now that's pretty low down.

RED ODOM – Well Known at the Jail - Bootlegging

Sherman Daily Democrat June 2 & 29, 1917

Among the Courts

Red Odom's Bond Set.

Red (Jess) Odom, charged with assault to murder in connection with the attack made on Clayton Holland, youth of the Pottsboro community, in this city recently, had an examining trial before Judge R. A. McCrary and his bond was set at $1,500. So far Odom has failed to make bond.

Judge McCrary yesterday assessed a fine of $1 and costs on a young man of Whitesboro charged with running an automobile without a license, and also fined a drunk $1 and costs.

Arrested on Indictment.

Red Odom, who recently attacked Clayton Holland, a youth of the Pottsboro community and a witness in a bootlegging case against Odom's father, has been arrested on grand jury indictment charging aggravated assault and lodged in the county jail.

The Sherman Courier September 18, 1917

Given Heavy Penalty.

Red Odom was tried in the county court yesterday on a charge of aggravated assault, alleged to have been committed on Clayton Holland, who was working under instructions from Sheriff Roberts last summer. Holland was a witness in a case against the father of Odom. Holland was struck with a bottle and severely injured but recovered. The bottle was broken to fragments. A jury fixed the penalty at a fine of $500 and a year in jail, the severest penalty for a similar offense for some years, if not the severest assessed here. There are several cases against Odom the charges being bootlegging. Holland was assaulted near the southwest corner of the square one day about noon.

Dean Act "Waters Down" the Booze Too Much for Some People's Liking -Whitewright Sun Oct. 24, 1919

Dean Prohibition Act Becomes Effective

Austin, Texas, Oct. 20.—The Dean prohibition act of the Thirty-Sixth Legislature which puts into effect constitutional prohibition in Texas becomes effective tomorrow. It is the most drastic prohibition legislation ever enacted in this state and not only prohibits the manufacture, sale, barter or exchange of intoxicating liquors but makes it a felony for a person to have in his possession a formula for making intoxicants.

Under the Dean act alcohol in excess of one per cent is prohibited in beverages. In other words, all beverages that contain over one per cent of alcohol are intoxicating.

So...Hello Moonshine.

A River of Moonshine Flows North and South Across Red River at Preston Bend: Whisky Seized Near Preston Bend on Red River

Whitewright Sun, Dec 27, 1918 – W. W. Mahoney and J. H. Blalock from Monroe, LA were arrested for bootlegging by Sheriff Boyd Craig and Deputy Sheriff Bart Shipp. The officers also seized 100 quarts of whiskey which the men were trying to carry across the river into Oklahoma in an automobile. The men laid their own trap in getting arrested by inquiring of Deputy Sheriff Bart Shipp the way to Woodville, OK across from Preston Bend. His suspicions became aroused and an investigation of the back end of the car revealed the 100 quarts of whiskey.

Many other liquor seizures took place the same week at Pottsboro and Denison.

246

Sherman Daily Democrat December 31, 1912

For Local Option Violation.

H. H. Delay, city marshal of Kingston, Okla., came to Sherman this morning, bringing with him Sim Potts, a white man whom he arrested for Sheriff Lee Simmons on a grand jury indictment charging him with violating the local option law. Potts was arrested on Red river, in the Preston Bend country, and was placed in the county jail on his arrival here.

Naked Bootleggers Caught Red-Handed and Red-Faced on the Red River

Whitewright Sun, Sep 23, 1921 – One alleged bootlegger was captured and one of two who escaped were wounded by a pistol shot when Deputy Sheriff T. G. Bell of at Preston Bend surprised the gang as they climbed out on the Texas bank of the Red River in the evening after swimming across with eight gallons of corn whiskey. When the three men clambered out on the Texas bank in the moonlight, naked, Deputy Sheriff Bell stepped forward and ordered them to throw up their hands. Upon doing this, being naked, there was absolutely nowhere for concealment, and in the extended hand of one of the men was a pistol.

The officer stepped forward to disarm the man, and as he did so the man tossed the gun into the river. Two of the other men used this diversion to jump into the Red River to swim back across to Oklahoma. Bell fired at the men who were swimming and caught the third man before he could jump into the river.

Preston Bend's Frank Miller Lives Short but Intoxicating Life

Denison Herald - Oct 27, 1921 - Frank Miller was arrested by Sheriff Boyd Craig in Denison. He was then lodged in the county jail on a charge of transporting intoxicating liquor. It was alleged that Miller was the man who transacted a corn whiskey deal on the Sherman-Denison Eighty Foot Road with J. J. Johnson who was arrested a few hours after the transaction which was witnessed by Deputy Bart Shipp. Miller claimed it was his brother and not him, who sold the gallon and a half of corn whiskey to J. J. Johnson, but Mr. Shipp declared that he saw the whole deal and was sure that the man arrested was the right person.

Denison Herald, 08-26-1923 - Frank Miller was arrested by Deputy Sheriff Miles in connection with some liquor law violations in Oklahoma. He was held under a $500 bond by Judge W. D. Parker until Sheriff Conn of Bryan County could secure the necessary requisition for his return to Durant to stand trial. It was brought out in the trial that to be convicted of possessing a still, wash, worm, or mash ready for distilling, constituted a felony, carrying with it imprisonment of one to five years. This was the charge preferred against Mr. Miller. A still was confiscated on the farm of Bennie Post in the river bottoms just across the line in Oklahoma and Miller was said to be connected with the deal.

Whitewright Sun - April 8, 1926 - Frank Miller, about 20 years old, was killed April 7, 1926, at a gas filling station just across the Red River from Preston Bend. Miller was shot by an older man and died instantly. Miller was said to have owned an interest in the filling station where he was killed. The man who killed him was found guilty by a jury in Durant, Ok and was sentenced to four years in the state prison according to the Whitewright Sun on May 27, 1926.

Miller was the son of William Miller, who lived on the Ray farm south of Kentuckytown for several years before moving to Oklahoma. The body of Miller was brought to the home of J. H. Alexander, uncle of Miller, to await burial at Cannon Cemetery.

ANOTHER WHISKEY STILL RAIDED AT PRESTON BEND

Dallas Morning News - June 6, 1923 - The Sheriff's department raided an illicit liquor still in the county near the Preston Bend road. They seized fifty-one gallons of finished intoxicants along with manufacturing equipment. The raid was made on a small truck farm operated by two Italians, a short distance west of the city limits of Denison on the Preston Bend road.

A typical scene in any Texas county during prohibition. It shows captured stills used to make moonshine whiskey, and equipment to make poisonous high-powered home-brew.

Jess and Rosa McClure

Jess McClure's Whiskey Still is Busted – Rebuilt and Busted Again

Then Turns From Whiskey to Water

There was one family who were THE family for moonshining in the Georgetown and Preston Bend areas. The following family owned a still site that was cited in the newspaper as the biggest source of illicit spirits in Grayson County!

Jess McClure and his family moved to a large farm Grayson County on the Red River bottom about 1918. The federal government coincidentally about the same time enacted the Eighteenth Amendment to the Constitution which established the prohibition of alcoholic beverages in the United States by declaring the production, transport, and sale of alcohol (though not the consumption or private possession) illegal.

The Amendment was the first to set a time delay before it would take effect following ratification, and for its ratification by the states. Its ratification was certified on January 16, 1919, with the amendment taking effect on January 16, 1920.

For the following 13 years, Prohibition was officially in effect. The amendment was repealed in 1933 by ratification of the Twenty-first Amendment, the only instance in United States history that a constitutional amendment was repealed in its entirety.

But by 1921, things were getting a little "dry" around northwestern Grayson County. Jess McClure and others had the perfect land on which to remedy this situation. It was secluded in the Red River bottom, complete with fresh water springs and streams. So, he did his part to fill a void - not only did he lubricate a dry situation by being a successful water well driller in the area – he was also a moonshiner, which alleviated the other "dry" situation where alcohol was concerned.

Jess McClure made a nice living as a moonshiner in the early days during prohibition and in his latter days, he turned drilling water wells. Jesus turned water into wine, Jess turned water into whiskey and then back to water again. Amazing.

The Denison Herald on November 6, 1921, reported that Deputy Sheriffs Lee Cantwell and George Brinkley from the Sherman office, together with officers Grover Bell and Sam Franks of Whitesboro, captured a large whiskey still and arrested two men in a raid made on Jess McClure's farm late Friday afternoon. The two men arrested were Jess McClure, white, and C. L. D. Moore, a negro. The party left Sherman at 3 o'clock Friday afternoon and arrived at the McClure farm about 5 o'clock.

The officers swept down upon the still, which was in the shed adjoining the house so suddenly that neither of the men arrested had time to resist or attempt to destroy any of the liquor. Three gallons of first-class corn whiskey, together with about 250 gallons of mash and a 20-gallon copper still were taken in the raid.

The capture of the McClure still made number thirty-eight that had been uncovered by the sheriff's force since the Eighteenth Amendment went into effect.

Mr. McClure, it was stated, owned a two or three-hundred-acre farm in the Red River bottom, and had lived in this county with his family for the past three years. The negro, Moore, is said to be from East Texas. Both men were lodged in the county jail.

Sherman Daily Democrat January 15, 1922

OFFICERS HELD UP AND PISTOLS TAKEN FROM THEM

WERE MADE TO "PUT 'EM UP" INSTANTER

WAS IN PRESTON BEND

But Guardians of the Law Stage Come Back and Get Their Men.

Deputy Sheriffs Bart Shipp and George Brinkley and Deputy Constables Sam Franks and Tim McCormick Friday night raided the farm of Jess McClure, west of Preston, in the northern Georgetown community, and destroyed a fifty gallon whiskey still and arrested McClure and one other man, after they had earlier been disarmed by McClure and held at bay with a double barrel shotgun while McClure and others destroyed and hid the finished whiskey on hand.

Another chapter in the story of law enforcement in Grayson County was written Saturday when the remaining members of McClure's alleged band were safely confined in the county jail, and to the level-headed actions of the officers participating in the raid, and more particularly the persuasive powers of Deputy Sheriff George Brinkley must go the credit for the final outcome of Friday night's experience, which, for a while at least, was potent with tragedy for the officers attempting to enforce the law. For, according to the humor which McClure showed while holding the officers at bay, after having one of his associates take their guns from them, it is remarkable that no bloodshed marked the efforts of the officers upon the occasion.

Deputy Sheriff George Brinkley told the story in the Sheriff's office Saturday afternoon. The four officers had reached McClure's place, which is situated off the Georgetown Road, leading west from Preston Bend, about one mile into the timbered hills skirting Red River. Three of the officers were proceeing through the timbers, Deputy Sheriff Bart Shipp having remained at the car to repair a puncture in a tire. Out of the darkness of the wood, the men suddenly heard the command to throw up their hands and found themselves looking into the twin barrels of a shotgun held in the hands of a determined appearing individual, who was recognized as McClure.

The officers readily complied. McClure's next action was to have a confederate, who appeared out of the darkness from behind him, take the guns from each of the officers. While the officers were thus held, according to their story, McClure's helpers began systematic work nearby, which they later learned was directed toward doing away with the stock of whiskey which the gang had distilled in a location not far away. At least one of the three men was not idle, however, and while McClure's band was engaged in "destroying the evidence," Deputy Sheriff George Brinkley started talking with McClure, pointing out the risk he was running, and the consequences which would certainly follow if he put into execution his threat to put all of the officers out of his way for good.

McClure then asked the officers if they would return to Sherman and say they had found nothing, Mr. Brinkley said. Upon their refusal to promise this and upon the gang's completion of their jobs of concealing or destroying the whiskey, McClure lowered his gun and invited the officers to come over and inspect his plant. Still disarmed, the officers complied and found a mammoth still outfit set up in the open, but complete in every detail.

Deputy Sheriff Brinkley having succeeded in convincing McClure of the folly of his actions, and McClure's band having succeeded in disposing of the stock of whiskey on hand, McClure asked the officers if they could identify their guns. When they said they could, he permitted the officers to secure their guns.

According to Mr. Brinkley, McClure evidently believed himself safe from any actions of the officers, after the manufactured whiskey was done away with, and the still stopped running. He made some resistance to arrest, and it is stated that one of the officers struck him with a gun when a member of the band attempted to come to his rescue. This member promptly dropped a club he held, however, after Brinkley pointed his gun at him.

Mr. Brinkley and his party started a systematic cleaning up and breaking up of the plant before starting back to Sherman, using an ax on the still. The plant was put totally out of commission. McClure was placed in the car and brought back to Sherman. Later, officers again visited the place and arrested Sam Blythe, McClure's son-in-law, and Luther Lamb of Oklahoma, McClure's nephew. Two of McClure's sons were also implicated in the illicit business, the officers stated, but had not been arrested Saturday afternoon.

McClure was arrested about a year earlier at his farm by county officers, and a smaller still was destroyed. He told the officers that distilling was a matter of "meat and bread" with him, but according to the officers, his home was well provisioned with hog meat and other food.

McClure's efforts to conceal the finished whiskey included the burning of a small shed containing part of the plant, the officers stated. He showed them this while attempting to persuade them to return to Sherman and report they had found nothing. The destruction of this plant destroys one of the largest moonshine distilleries in the county, the officers believe, and will do away with one of the chief sources of illicit whiskey in the county.

At least for the time being........

Jesse McClure Acquitted of Whiskey Manufacturing Charge

Sherman Daily Democrat, September 6, 1922 - A verdict of acquittal was tendered in the case of the State Vs. Jesse McClure, farmer from the northwest part of the county, charged manufacturing intoxicating liquor for sale. McClure, a well to do farmer, has won acquittals twice from Grayson County juries on liquor violation charges.

One case, several months ago followed a raid on McClure's large farm in which the officers making the raid had their guns taken from them by two of McClure's sons, who surprised them in a wood, and who held them while fire consumed a shed. It is claimed the remnants of a liquor still was later found in this shed.

It appears the incriminating evidence went up in smoke before the case against Mr. McClure could be proved. The liquor he allegedly produced had long since been consumed. No trace of it could be found.

Sherman Daily Democrat   February 5, 1922

GRAND JURY RETURNS MORE INDICTMENTS

Duff Hood of Sherman was indicted on a charge of transporting intoxicating liquor.

Jesse McClure, Jesse McClure, Jr., Luther Lamb and Sam Blythe, members of the party which, it is alleged by officers, held up several deputy sheriffs searching for stills on McClure's farm near Preston Bend a few weeks ago, and later submitting to arrest for moonshining activities, were billed for manufacturing whisky. The elder McClure was billed on two counts.

Around 1934, Jess McClure lived in Durant, Oklahoma for two years managing the golf course there.

CAR FROM UNDER CONTROL OF DRIVER; PLUNGES HEADLONG INTO NEARBY PHONE POLE
C. E. Parham Dies In Hospital Soon After the Crash

Denison Press - June 28, 1934 - C. E. Parham, local railway postal clerk, died shortly after receiving injuries sustained in an accident when the car he was driving plunged off the road on West Crawford street road and hit a telephone pole. Parham and his life-long friend Jess McClure were heading home from the Katy Railroad Golf course. McClure at this time was in charge of the Durant Golf course and was in Denison on business and had joined his friend for a game of golf before returning to Durant. McClure was not injured in the crash which proved fatal for his friend Parham, but he was overcome with grief at the loss of his friend.

Mr. Parham was born in the vicinity of Pottsboro April 12, 1888. He entered the railway mail service January 29, 1912, and resigned on April 17, 1914, to accept the position of Postmaster of Pottsboro. On December 15, 1920, he re-entered the Railway mail service at which he was engaged at the time of his death.

Jess McClure was also a prominent water well driller in the rural areas around Pottsboro.

Denison Press, October 19, 1936 - Jess L. McClure's 42nd wedding anniversary announcement in the newspaper confirms that he had been a water well driller and contractor for 35 years up to that date (since 1901 to 1936). At least, that was his legitimate business. "Ask for Mr. Jess." He was the best water well driller in the area. After he retired, Alexander L. Moser Jr. took over in the 1950s along with Faulkner Drilling, which still operate today.

**McCLURES CELEBRATE
FORTY-SECOND WEDDING
ANNIVERSARY SATURDAY**

Mr. and Mrs. J. L. McCulre, 714 East Crawford street celebrated their forty-second wedding anniversary Saturday when a large number of friends dropped in and tendered congratulations and gifts. The celebrants were married Oct. 17th, 1894 at Howe and with the

Mr. McClure has been a water-well contractor for 35 years Eight of their eleven children are living. They are H. B. McClure, Mrs. Harvey Thomas, Mrs. Wayne Watson and Mrs. Bertha Lusk of Denison; Mrs. Dan Christman of Sherman; John McClure of Ardmore Okla.; Mrs. Sam Blythe of San Antonio and J. J. McClure of Durant. There are 22 grandchildren.

Not All Moonshine Was Safe

Wikipedia has a good summary of the "safety" of moonshine: Poorly produced moonshine can be contaminated, mainly from materials used in the construction of the still. Stills employing automotive radiators as condensers are particularly dangerous; in some cases, glycol, products from antifreeze, can appear as well. Radiators used as condensers also may contain lead at the connections to the plumbing. These methods often resulted in blindness or lead poisoning for those consuming tainted liquor. This was an issue during Prohibition when many died from ingesting unhealthy substances. Consumption of lead-tainted moonshine is an important risk factor for saturnine gout, which is a very painful but treatable medical condition that damages the kidneys and joints.

Although methanol is not produced in toxic amounts by fermentation of sugars from grain starches, contamination is still possible by unscrupulous distillers using cheap methanol to increase the apparent strength of the product.

Moonshine can be made both more palatable and less damaging by discarding the "foreshot"—the first few ounces of alcohol that drip from the condenser. Because methanol vaporizes at a lower temperature than ethanol it is commonly believed that the foreshot contains most of the methanol, if any, from the mash.

258

Research shows that this is not the case and that methanol will be present until the very end of the distillation run.

But the foreshot does typically contain small amounts of other undesirable compounds such as acetone and various aldehydes. Many unscrupulous or sloppy moonshiners might not have poured out this early part of the "run" of moonshine, or may not have been worried about what contaminants were in the equipment he used to manufacture the liquor.

Poison Moonshine from the McClure Family Kills Carl Nix

In 1924 and 1925, Carl Nix, Jess McClure and his son Burt are all at Georgetown going about their lives. In a few months, their lives will become connected in a way which leads to young Carl Nix being buried in the Georgetown Cemetery and with young Burt McClure in prison for a year for selling him the instrument of his death.

Denison Herald - September 23, 1924 – Misses Clara and Josie Summerhill of Denison and Dreyfus Cato of Denison and Carl Nix attended church at Georgetown Sunday night. Jess McClure of Georgetown was in South Ray community Saturday gathering up his milk cows, which he had out for their feed, taking them in for the winter.

A few months later, 21-year-old Carl Nix died on Friday the 13th, 1925 because of drinking contaminated moonshine. He was buried in the Georgetown Cemetery.

Denison Herald February 16th, 1925 - Son of Jess McClure, Burt McClure was charged with the murder of Carl Nix, having sold intoxicating liquor in connection with the poisoning death of Nix. Nix died near Preston after having drunk poison liquor alleged to have been sold by McClure. George Boggs was arrested and charged with driving while intoxicated. It was said that he was with Nix shortly before his death. The crime was investigated by Sheriff Everheart.

Nowhere does the term "crime and calamity" apply more aptly than with the case of Carl Nix. Nix was a 21-year-old farmer who resided six miles east of Denison. He had attended a dance near Preston. After securing liquor, it is said he was put to bed and was dead when found the next morning.

You might say, "He reaped what he sowed." But surely death by poisoning was much too harsh a sentence for this youthful indiscretion of attending a dance and imbibing of some illegal moonshine. If everyone who had ever made a mistake in their younger days suffered the ultimate penalty, the earth would have devoid of humans long ago. We need but look to his gravestone which still eloquently speaks that he was a beloved son, who was sorely missed.

People began to realize that "but for the grace of God go I" and decided to bring those responsible for his poisoning to justice for his death - the manufacturers and sellers of the poison moonshine at Preston Bend.

Denison Herald - February 20, & April 1, 1925 - George Goode, 31, Robert Curtiss, 18, and Everette Goode, 28, testified at the trial they were with Nix when the sale took place. George Goode said from the stand he arrived at a dance held that night at Cleve Miller's place, near Preston, between 8 and 9 o'clock Friday night on February 13th and that he mentioned buying some whiskey.

He made arrangements to buy it before leaving the dance about 10 o'clock. George Goode left the Miller place in a car driven by Carl Nix, accompanied by Everette Goode, George Boggs, Robert Curtiss, and Bert McClure. The group drove to the McClure place, where they stopped and Burt McClure left the car and returned shortly with a half-gallon jar of corn whiskey. Goode stated that McClure handed the jar to Goode and received a $5 bill in payment. Robert Curtiss and Everett Goode also corroborated his statements on the stand in court. Curtiss stated he did not believe any of the men possessed or drank any liquor that night other than that which was purchased from McClure. After purchasing the moonshine, Nix returned to the dance.

County Attorney Blames Apathy & Acceptance of Moonshining for Carl Nix's Death

Denison Herald -May 18th, 1925 - "Moonshiners of Grayson County are backed by men who sit in Denison and Sherman banks," Roy Finley, County Attorney, charged in a fiery speech at the First Baptist Church of Denison Sunday night while speaking on the subject "Grayson "Grayson County's Moonshiners." "The day of the simple bootlegger has passed. The day of the moonshiner is at hand," Mr. Finley said. "I have thought it appropriate for this occasion that I report to you, as your public servant, some of the conditions that exist in Grayson County and at the same time sound a warning to you concerning your boys and girls," Mr. Finley continued. "I can understand how a law-abiding, church-going man might take the life of his fellow-man in defense of his home or his honor, but I have never been able to understand how anyone can deliberately make and sell whiskey, a poison that robs men and women of their reason and intellect and of their life. "I have come to make a report to you and plead for your co-operation in waging war on the moonshiners of Grayson County. It is a fact that more than ten thousand gallons of moonshine whiskey was made in this county last year." Mr. Finley said that one man, whose name he mentioned, (probably Jess McClure) had made more than four thousand gallons of whiskey in the last year. Throughout his speech, he called the names of those whom he charged were responsible for the moonshine industry in Grayson County. He mentioned rural, Denison and Sherman people, several of whom have already been convicted in the courts for the manufacture of intoxicating liquor. "This man who made more than four thousand gallons of whisky last year had a bigger business organization than most of your businessmen," the speaker said. "His organization was as tight as any business house. He had a production department, a sales department and distributing agents. He had his camp guarded by men armed with rifles, with orders to shoot down the officers of the law without hesitation. "The day of the simple bootlegger is passed. The day of the moonshiner is at hand. They are backed by men who sit in Sherman and Denison banks. And in my opinion, these men who give financial aid to bootleggers are as guilty in the sight of God and man as those who manufacture the damnable stuff.

"But, more than that, these bootleggers have friends in the churches. They came to me and asked, through my church connection, for leniency. The day the church gets rid of such members, the better for the church. "I never thought the moonshine industry would become established in Grayson County." Mr. Finley told of the death of **Carl Nix,** who died several months ago, allegedly from drinking **poisonous whiskey,** and declared: "**The lifeless body of Carl Nix as it rests in Georgetown cemetery stands as an eternal monument to the moonshiners of Grayson County. Nix was as splendid a specimen of physical manhood as I ever saw and responsibility for his death rests upon Grayson County moonshiners.**"

Mr. Finley told of the unsanitary methods employed at the distilleries, saying that the boilers and utensils were never washed, that court testimony showed that in at least one instance a moonshiner had picked dead rats out of a barrel of mash, and declared that the men employed to tend the stills did not use even the slightest sanitary precautions. "Every restriction around the old saloon, if there was any, has been swept aside by these moonshiners. They violate every law of God and man. They are selling this rotten stuff to your boys and to your girls. We have six girls in the jail at Sherman now who have come down the road of ruin because of bootleg whiskey. These moonshiners have even sold whiskey to little chaps too small to testify in court—too small to know the meaning of a court oath."

In conclusion, Mr. Finley made a plea for good citizens to serve on juries, saying "If you men refuse to serve on juries, despite the efforts of the sheriffs and officials, your home will not be safe, nor can we protect the ones you love."

Mash Barrels Found at Preston Bend

Denison Herald, March 25, 1924

About three gallons of alleged "choc" was confiscated in two raids conducted by Deputy Sheriffs Miles and West late Monday afternoon. The liquor was found at two places and two arrests were made. The violators pleaded guilty to charges preferred against them and paid fines of $17.70 each in justice court.

Approximately one hundred gallons of mash were confiscated by Sheriff Floyd Everheart and Deputies Brinkley and Dishner Monday afternoon when a raid was conducted on a creek near Preston Bend. The creek was located on the Bxxleln farm, although a considerable distance from the house. The mash was found buried in the sand near the creek. No arrests have yet been made.

THE LAST PLACE THEY WILL _EVER_ LOOK -

LIQUOR STILL FOUND IN WATER TANK

The Whitewright Sun, 29 Mar 1923 - March 24.—After spending two hours in a fruitless search of the house and all outbuildings for a moonshine still believed to be on the place, Sheriff Floyd Everheart and Deputies Bart Shipp and W. L. Evans were about to leave the farm of Jim Fox, two miles northwest of Gunter when the officers spied the last remaining place on the farm that they had not searched. This was a water tank, mounted on a platform 20 feet in the air. Deputy Sheriff Shipp climbed out of the Sheriff's car, climbed up the ladder of the water tank and peered over. As a result of this final look, the Sheriff's force was soon removing from the water tank a copper still of 20 gallons capacity and the remainder of a complete outfit, together with two barrels of mash which were sitting in the tank.

The officers arrested Fox and at Gunter filed a complaint charging possession of equipment for manufacturing intoxicating liquor. He was allowed $1,000 bond. According to the officers, the still was operated on a stove found in a woodshed. It was removed from its hiding place in the water tank, together with what mash was needed, at night.

Its disclosure in the water tank marked a new hiding place for stills in the experience of the Grayson County officers. Officers state that Fox owns a farm of 127 acres on which he was living. He has 15 children. Officers have suspected the existence of a still in the neighborhood for some time but never looked in the water tank until now.

It's always in the last place you look – of course! (Why would you keep looking once you found it?)

NOW, THIS IS _REALLY_ THE LAST PLACE YOU WOULD EVER LOOK FOR A STILL –

WHISKEY STILL IN _CHURCH,_ BUT SCANDAL IS LACKING

Sherman, Texas, Nov. 5.— Here is a shocker for you. A small whiskey still was located in the First Baptist Church of Sherman Sunday! The still was in charge of H. A. Ivy and was viewed by a large number of persons. Prof. Ivy used the still, which was a regular moonshine outfit formerly in operation in Grayson County and confiscated by Deputy Sheriffs, in a prohibition lecture at the church Sunday afternoon. He pointed out the danger to persons drinking bootleg liquor. So as it turns out, it was as nefarious as it first appeared!

Pictured below, at Glen Eden in the early 1930s are Mrs. S. D. Steedman, Mrs. H. L. Grace and Mrs. M. W. Morrison, picture from Frontier Village Museum.

Thank you for reading my book, I hope it has been interesting and informative for you. I hope you will want to read more about this wonderful area! I have many books about the history of the people and area I love.

They include:

Gone With the Water … The Saga of Preston Bend and Glen Eden

Crime and Calamity in Preston Bend – When the West Was Wild Vol 3

When the West Was Wild in Denison Texas (Wild West series Vol 2)

Quantrill's Raiders In North Texas & Jesse James Gang in Grayson County Texas

The Many Faces of Texoma's Red River

Pottsboro Texas and Lake Texoma, Then and Now Volume One

Pottsboro Texas and Lake Texoma, Then and Now Volume Two

When the West Was Wild in Pottsboro Texas (Wild West series Vol 1)

School Days Around the Pottsboro Area & NW Grayson County

Ghost Towns of Texoma, Vol 1 – Preston Bend

Ghost Towns of Texoma, Vol 2 – Hagerman

Ghost Towns of Texoma, Vol 3 – Martin Springs

Ghost Towns of Texoma, Vol 4 – Georgetown, Fink

Ghost Towns of Texoma, Vol 5 - Locust, Willow Springs

Reflections on the Beauty of Lake Texoma

Texoma Tales Volume 1 – NW Grayson County's People & their Stories

The Old Country Store

True Ghost Stories of Grayson County Texas…and Other Strange and Scary Tales Volumes 1, 2 & 3

I am, God willing, intending to write many more history related books, since we have such a rich heritage here, and I am sure I will only scratch the surface. People ask me why I don't think I will run out of material. I respond, there have been a LOT of people in this area and they ALL have a story.

I have given several local history related speeches and costumed living history presentations.

I have produced an inspirational art book called "Reflections on the Beauty of Lake Texoma".

All my books are available on:

Amazon.com, my author name is Natalie Clountz Bauman,

On etsy.com from the store PottsboroTexasBooks

You can order books directly from the author,

and you can get the books in Denison on Main Street at The Book Rack and The Main Street Antique Mall;

in Sherman at Touch of Class Antique Mall and Orchid House Antiques and at

Patsy's Café in Pottsboro.

They can also be found at the Frontier Village Museum at Loy Park in Denison and at my personal event appearances.

Thank you for considering my books. I hope you find them interesting and informative. God bless you!

Made in the USA
Columbia, SC
07 January 2022

52927395R00146